Comprehensive Family Therapy

An Integration of Systemic and Psychodynamic Treatment Models

By

Diana Adile Kirschner, Ph.D.

and

Sam Kirschner, Ph.D.

BRUNNER/MAZEL, *Publishers* · New York

Library of Congress Cataloging-in-Publication Data

Kirschner, Diana Adile, 1948–
    Comprehensive family therapy.

    Bibliography: p.
    Includes index.
    1. Family psychotherapy. I. Kirschner, Sam, 1948–
II. Title. III. Title: Systemic and psychodynamic
treatment models. IV. Title: Psychodynamic treatment
models.
RC488.5.K57   1985   616.89′156   85-18607
ISBN 0-87630-403-X

Published by
BRUNNER/MAZEL, INC.
19 Union Square
New York, New York 10003

MANUFACTURED IN THE UNITED STATES OF AMERICA

This book is dedicated to our children,
Connie and Jason

Foreword

Comprehensive Family Therapy represents an important integration of psychodynamic concepts and structural/systemic treatment approaches. The book is intellectually challenging as it introduces new concepts and synthesizes old ones in interesting new ways. The Kirschners clearly delineate their theoretical base and the "how to" of their approach.

Detailed and colorful vignettes of successful cases enliven the text. In these vignettes, the authors use a wide variety of techniques, including metaphor, hypnosis, regressive techniques, advice-giving, confrontation, and role reversal. They blend these together quite smoothly, so that their choices contribute to the flow of therapy rather than impeding it or making it seem like a "bag of tricks" approach.

The Kirschners describe a solid model of optimal family functioning synthesized from extant literature. This model shapes the ultimate goals of their therapy, such that they have high expectations for the outcome of each case. Thus, the work is not only comprehensive but goes into considerable depth.

Comprehensive Family Therapy represents a significant advance in the search for a more effective means of helping the family and its members. As such, it is an important step forward in the continuing evolution of individual and family therapy.

Florence W. Kaslow, Ph.D.,
Director,
Florida Couples and Family Institute,
West Palm Beach, Florida

Contents

Foreword by Florence W. Kaslow, Ph.D.   *vii*

Preface   *xi*

Introduction   *xv*

1. The Family Holon   1

2. Optimal Family Process   21

3. Role of the Therapist   47

4. Techniques   63

5. The Initial Interview   85

6. The Child as the Presenting Problem   124

7. Marital Therapy   147

8. Marital Case Examples   176

9. Treatment of the Single Adult   188

10. Treatment of Alternative Family Constellations   214

Afterword   *249*

References   *253*

Index   *257*

Preface

Comprehensive Family Therapy, or CFT, was developed by Arthur Stein, Ph.D., who began working with families in 1959 (Stein, 1980). This book represents our interpretation and refinement of his ideas and approach.

Dr. Stein served as Chief Psychologist at the Child Growth and Development Research Center at the Children's Hospital in Buffalo, New York, from 1959 until 1962. Although he had a psychoanalytic background, Dr. Stein began to see families while working with the children in this setting. Initially, his work focused on improving child-rearing in these families. Over time, Dr. Stein concluded that such a focus was piecemeal and of limited effectiveness. He realized that other factors in family life directly impinged on the childrearing that took place. Accordingly, Dr. Stein began to include marital therapy and to work on the spouses' careers as part of family treatment. Thus, CFT evolved to the point that it involved the entire family dynamic.

In 1962, Dr. Stein moved to Long Island, New York, and established a private practice in which he developed and refined his approach. CFT was introduced to the mental health profession in 1964, when it was taught at the Bleuler Psychotherapy Center in New York City. Subsequently, Dr. Stein presented his work through the American Institute for Psychotherapy and Psychoanalysis.

In 1979, the Institute for Comprehensive Family Therapy was founded by the junior author, Dr. Sam Kirschner, and Rita Mulligan DeMaria, M.S. The senior author, Dr. Diana Kirschner, served as a founding faculty member. Dr. Stein served as consultant from March 1980 until February 1982. The Institute, located in Spring House, Pennsylvania, is dedicated to the development and refinement of the theory and practice of CFT. Through its clinical division, the Gwynedd Family Psychotherapy Center, the Institute offers CFT treatment for individuals, couples, and families. The Institute also offers on- and off-site workshops, lectures, and training to mental health professionals; conducts research on the effectiveness of CFT; and provides courses on family life for the general public. Through its programs, the Institute seeks to further the study of the person and of family life, to develop the psychotherapeutic art, and, in so doing, to contribute to the knowledge and well-being of mankind.

ACKNOWLEDGMENTS

We are grateful to Dr. Arthur Stein, who created CFT through his theoretical brilliance and clinical artistry.

We are also grateful to Rita Mulligan DeMaria, M.S., who currently serves as the Associate Director of the Institute, and to the founding faculty of the Institute, who include Dr. Jack Gregory, Dr. Judi Smolanoff, Audrey Brua Herbert, A.C.S.W., Grace Strauss, A.C.S.W., and Dr. Jerry Kleiman. They have helped us to further develop the work, and have provided us with a great deal of encouragement and inspiration. Thanks also goes to our students, especially Dr. Michael Bopp, Dr. Molly Layton, Linda Glaser, M.S.W., and Linda Wantman, M.Ed., for helping us to refine our understanding of the approach, and supporting our writing efforts. Institute Board members, Ray Adolf and Jay Glickman, were also very encouraging of our writing efforts.

Dr. M. Duncan Stanton also deserves thanks for some helpful suggestions on an earlier draft of Chapter 1. Our publisher, Bernie Mazel, and our editor, Ann Alhadeff, were also tremendously encouraging and helpful. We would also like to thank our research assistant, Beth Coltoff, M.A., for her invaluable assistance, and Marilyn Luber for additional help in literature research; Sandy Adolf, Anne Skoogfors, and Jacqueline Starace, M.A., for help with the artwork; Connie Kirschner, Dorothy Lawson, JoAnn Mensinger, Mary Frances Sowers, and Constance S. Tambourine, who patiently and diligently typed our manuscripts; and Gloria Lutz, our housekeeper.

Various agencies have been extremely helpful in terms of supporting or collaborating on projects with the Institute that have furthered the work. These include the Edna McConnell Clark Foundation in New York City, the Montgomery County, PA, Office of Children and Youth, under the directorship of Bill Wrubel, and the Montgomery County, PA, Department of Juvenile Probation, under the directorship of Anthony Guarna.

In addition, the senior author, Diana, would like to thank her parents, Biagio and Concetta Adile, as well as her sisters, Camille Dull, Dr. Rosalie Van Tichelt, Nancy Delisi, and Clare Lorentz, for their support and helpfulness. The junior author, Sam, would like to thank his parents, Israel and Sonia Kirschner, for their education and encouragement.

Finally, thanks to all our clients, who have taught us so very much.

Introduction

Billy Jones, age 17, robbed the local convenience store at gunpoint.* After his arrest, he was placed in a secured psychiatric facility for treatment.

The psychiatric report suggested that Billy manifested immature ego development along with a severe impulse disorder. The treatment plan recommended individual therapy with medication to help control the acting out. However, the presiding judge at Billy's trial selected him to participate in a clinical research project on family therapy with juvenile offenders. The project was conducted at the Montgomery County, PA, Juvenile Probation Department.

At the initial consultation,** the therapist, Sam Kirschner, met with Billy, his 15-year-old sister Pat, his parents, and his probation officer. The therapist examined every major aspect of the family's psychosocial dynamic, noting how each aspect impinged upon Billy's problems. He found a severe marital schism in this family, such that the parents were not even sleeping in the same room. Billy's symptomatology played a part in drawing them together. However, the fabric of the marriage was so torn that the parents could not function together as a unified parental team. Billy filled Mother's needs for a close, empathic relationship, while remaining in an antagonistic stance toward Father. His sister functioned as an affectionate ally and companion for Father, while being distant toward Mother.

---

*The cases described in this book are those of clients who have given us permission to discuss their treatment. Names, occupations, and other data, which may expose the clients' identities, have been disguised.

**An annotated transcript of the initial interview can be found in Chapter 5.

During the consultation, whenever his mother cried, Billy became severely agitated. Not only was he enmeshed with her, but he also seemed to be primarily identified with his mother. Both of them expressed a sense of inadequacy and purposelessness in life. On an intrapsychic level, Billy did not have a sense of himself as a competent young man and experienced much self-hate. Being punished by the authorities represented a way for him to discharge some of his self-destructive feelings. It seems likely that all of these factors served to maintain Billy's immaturity and acting-out behavior.

And what other key factors have generated such severe marital and rearing difficulties? Not only did Billy's mother manifest intrapsychic disturbances, but his father did as well. As he stated in subsequent interviews, Billy's father viewed himself with self-hate, a complete failure as a husband, father, and provider. Thus, both executives and role models in the family system manifested low self-esteem and intrapsychic dysfunction. In subsequent interviews, Billy's parents presented material concerning their families of origin, which suggested, not surprisingly, that they themselves were not parented properly. Mrs. Jones, during the first interview, summarized the situation when she turned to the therapist and said: "We need a new everything, Dr. Kirschner. We need a new everything. We really do."

The case of Billy has been described in both psychodynamic and systemic terms. At this point in time, contemporary family therapists might feel uncomfortable about reading descriptions of intrapsychic phenomena alongside a triadic analysis of this case. Others who were trained psychodynamically might welcome the addition of intrapsychic material to our study of the Jones family. Whether comfortable or not, contemporary family therapists are faced with the dilemma of either rejecting psychodynamic thinking or somehow integrating it into a systems orientation. Individual therapists are faced with the same type of dilemma.

FRAGMENTATION OF THERAPEUTIC APPROACHES

In clinical practice, most family therapists, in their zeal to adopt a systemic position, neglect the individual family member as a unit of treatment. Individual therapists, on the other hand, neglect the family system or subsystems as units of treatment. However, both claim adequate case outcome.

The two-faced Greek god Janus best describes the two faces of the field of psychotherapy. One face is turned inward, examining intrapsychic processes in the individual. The other is turned outward, investigating the network of family relationships. The question at hand is, psyche or system? Does the contemporary practitioner choose content or context as the focus of treatment?

Not only are the unit of treatment and the psyche/system issue problematic in everyday practice, but the goals of treatment are as well. The so-called medical model was attacked by many pioneers of family therapy (Ackerman, 1958; Haley, 1962; Satir, 1964). Yet, more and more, the focus of family therapy has narrowed to symptom amelioration (Haley, 1976; Minuchin, 1974; Selvini Palazzoli, Boscolo, Cecchin, & Prata, 1978). The growth-oriented therapy called for by Ackerman (1958) and having as its goal healthy family functioning has apparently been forgotten. In its zeal to establish the family as the epistemological basis for conceptualization and treatment, the field of family therapy has "thrown out the baby with the bath water." Potentially useful ideas about the individual, self-actualization, and even family actualization have been discouraged and downplayed.

TREND TOWARD INTEGRATION

There is evidence, however, of a trend in family therapy away from the divisive milieu of the past 15 years – a trend toward integration of disparate theories. This pattern is common in philosophy and science where thesis and antithesis are inevitably followed by synthesis. Attempted syntheses in family therapy have been offered by Pinsof (1983), Gurman (1981), Friedman (1980), and Wachtel (1977).

There are important advantages inherent in an integrative approach to family therapy. We know that no one approach can totally account for the complexity of individual behavior and family functioning. Thus there is very little likelihood that one general theory will explain the etiology and maintenance of psychopathology, or psychological health and well-being in individuals and families. A synthesis of psychodynamic, behavioral, and systemic theories within one coherent framework would appear to offer the clinician greater flexibility in understanding the empirical data of a case.

Treatment itself can be enhanced. With richness and depth of individual thought, family therapy gains vitality and meaning. On the other hand, with systems thinking, individual therapy becomes an active, exciting, and effective mode of treatment. Furthermore, an integrative approach offers a wide variety of treatment strategies drawn from different schools of therapy. Such flexibility allows the clinician to switch techniques when resistance is encountered or when a new type of problem/situation arises. For example, when the clinician moves from problems of children to marital or individual issues, flexibility in strategy within the clinical orientation is critical for successful practice.

An integrative approach can also be applied to a broader segment of the population and to a greater diversity of problems than can any one particular school of thought. As Lebow (1984) has pointed out, when a clinician is limited in his or her approach, absurd situations can arise — for example, when "clients who enter treatment desiring to further explore the meaning of their lives are offered paradoxical interventions" (p. 130). Or conversely, an acting-out child can be seen for years of nonproductive play therapy. Effective, short-term work that can produce lasting change must be part of an integrative approach in order for it to have wide applicability.

A system that allows for thesis and antithesis to coexist can be open to a variety of advances in theory and technique. Where research suggests that particular interventions work with particular issues, those techniques can be incorporated into the framework of treatment. For example, structural techniques have been shown to be effective with drug abuse (Stanton & Todd, 1982), while behavioral techniques have been used successfully in sex therapy (Kaplan, 1974) and marital therapy (Jacobson & Margolin, 1979; Stuart, 1980). While structural and behavioral family therapy schools may clash theoretically, specific concepts and techniques can be integrated into a coherent synthesis. Similarly, ideas from individual psychology, such as the role of transference in the healing process, insight in treating marital couples (Sager, 1976), familial loyalties and guilt (Boszormenyi-Nagy, 1973), and the role of object relations theory in family dynamics (Dicks, 1967; Framo, 1970), have proven to be valuable contributions to family theory and therapy.

Thus an integrative approach would have at its foundation a dialectical metatheory that could describe the whole of family life. It would include a description of the dialectical process in which individual psychologies define the family system, which in itself redefines intrapsychic process. This interface between system and psyche would be depicted in terms of not only the etiology and maintenance of psychopathology but also psychological health and well-being. Treatment would therefore focus on both interpersonal relationships and intrapsychic functioning. Goals would include both symptom relief and client growth. With such broad foci, the clinical approach would have to be flexible enough to incorporate psychoanalytic, behavioral, and strategic/structural techniques, yet stable and coherent enough to maintain a sense of continuity and client trust.

A dialectical metatheory signifies two basic notions: 1) the sense of a pattern of existential change, i.e., the interaction between a changing individual in a changing context; and 2) the process of change, which in the case of the family generates a rationale for the treatment approach. Basseches (1980) and Bopp & Weeks (1984) have described the dialectic as a developmental transformation with four major elements: form, relationships, movement, and transformation.

COMPREHENSIVE FAMILY THERAPY

Comprehensive Family Therapy, or CFT, developed by Arthur Stein, attempts to provide such a dialectical metatheory. Both the pattern and process of change in individual/family life are described within a dialectical framework. This ecological description of human development is paired with a derived treatment approach. Each of the four elements in the dialectic is delineated in the CFT model of the family: forms and their relationships, movements, and ultimate transformation.

In CFT, these elements are described in terms of the family holon. The term holon (from the Greek "holos" [whole]) was first proposed by Koestler (1980). The holon is a Janus-faced entity that "manifests both the independent properties of wholes and the dependent properties of parts" (p. 447). In the family holon, there are two major components: the intrapsychic phenomena of individual family members and the systemic transactions through which family members interact. Thus one face of the holon is turned inward and represents the individual's internalized system, while the other face is turned outward and represents the larger, familial context of which the individual is a part.

In the clinical practice of CFT, the practitioner's goal is to remediate presenting dysfunction and elevate the holon toward optimal psychosocial functioning. To accomplish this, the practitioner utilizes a wide variety of interventions that are organized by a reparental strategy. The reparental strategy permits the therapist to elevate family interactions, while at the same time giving him or her deeper access to the inner world of each individual family member.

ABOUT THIS BOOK

This book is an introduction to CFT. It should be noted that while the ideas presented were originally developed by Arthur Stein, he has not been involved with us for the past few years, and our thinking may have diverged from his. Thus, he may disagree with some of the material that is presented.

Chapter 1 delineates the dialectic of the family holon in terms of its forms, relationships, movement, and transformation. Intrapsychic and systemic components and their exchanges are presented. Chapter 2 depicts the hypothetical end state of family transformation: optimal family process. This is an important model for use in clinical diagnosis and goal setting with clients. Chapter 3 describes the role of the CFT therapist – a reparental agent who augments the intrapsychic and systemic growth trends that are already present in the client family. Specific techniques are presented in Chapter 4. Then, in Chapter 5, there is a brief description of the foci in the initial interview followed by an annotated transcript of an initial interview. Chapter 6 describes treatment when a child is the presenting problem and illustrates the work through several case examples. Marital therapy, which forms the heart of CFT work with intact or blended families, is covered in Chapter 7. Three marital case examples follow in Chapter 8. Chapter 9 describes the CFT treatment of the single adult and Chapter 10 closes with the treatment of alternative family constellations.

A NOTE OF CAUTION

CFT is a powerful therapeutic approach. When used in a cautious, measured, and conservative manner by mature clinicians under supervision, CFT can be extremely helpful to clients. Conversely, when used in an irresponsible or less skilled manner, CFT can potentially have a destructive effect on clients. Please bear this in mind before attempting to implement the approach.

CHAPTER 1

The Family Holon

> To see a world in a grain of sand,
> And a heaven in a wildflower,
> Hold infinity in the palm of your hand,
> And eternity in an hour.
>
> —William Blake (1946, p. 150)

The family is a complex living organism with behavioral and intra-psychic subsystem components all in dynamic exchange. Like Blake's "world in a grain of sand," each subsystem component provides a mirror image for the other embedded within. Furthermore, behavioral transactions and intrapsychic subsystem components influence, shape, and transform each other in a dialectical process. The family, therefore, is viewed as a social holon with tendencies toward self-assertion and self-absorption (intrapsychic phenomena) and an orientation toward the other (behavioral transactions). The intrapsychic and transactional components have their own rules and properties and yet each defines the context for the other. The laws of circularity, together with other principles of cybernetics that describe living systems, provide a background for each individual family member's intrapsychic life. The linear, developmental, historical stages of individual growth provide the context and backdrop for the interplay between family members in the behavioral transactions. Thus the linear and historical coexist with the circular and ahistorical within the family holon.*

---

*Note the striking similarity between this model and the model of physics proposed by Capra (1975) and others. Newtonian laws of mechanics coexist alongside Einstein's theories of relativity—the linear deterministic model and the circular relativistic one standing in bold relief to each other.

1

In the family holon, behavioral change in any family member or transaction has fluid repercussions of different strengths on all other individuals and transactions in the family. Disharmony in any transaction or in the intrapsychic functioning of any family member can detract from the psychosocial equilibrium of members in other areas of family life. Conversely, success and fulfillment for any member in any transaction can enhance functioning in other parts of the family system.

Over the life cycle, the entire family holon tends to follow a growth pattern that, by and large, moves in the direction of healthy family process. Professional intervention, when needed, is maximally effective when concerned with assisting the family as a whole organism to move in this direction. Individual psychopathology, as well as interrelated dysfunctions in family transactions, can then be dealt with as needed in order to move the entire configuration toward more effective functioning. Furthermore, by capitalizing on the natural growth processes inherent in the holon, the practitioner can organize parts of the family system into growth-promoting milieus. In this manner, therapeutic leverage is amplified so that families can actualize their native potential more quickly.

In this chapter, the dialectic of the family holon is delineated in terms of forms and relationships. Pathological forms and their relationships are then highlighted. Movement and transformation in the holon are also discussed, with a special focus on the positive, health-seeking trends.

The family, along with all living systems, is governed by two basic principles: homeostasis and morphogenesis. Homeostasis represents the system's tendency to return to a state of quiescence or stability. Morphogenesis (from the Greek words "morph" [structure] and "genesis" [creating]) represents the system's tendency to expand in the direction of instability and novelty. In the family holon, both are necessary for the maintenance of successful family life. Homeostasis leads to cohesiveness and family unity, i.e., form and relationships. Morphogenesis leads to adaptation to new conditions along the family life cycle, i.e., movement and transformation.

As Olson (1983) has pointed out, healthy families tend to operate in a balance between cohesiveness and adaptation. Without homeostasis, family life would be characterized by a constant state of uncertainty, chaos, and instability. Without morphogenesis, systems become stuck, predictable, and unable to expand to assimilate new information. Since the family is the basic social unit of civilization, the very survival of the species depends upon the dialectical interplay between homeostasis and morphogenesis.

Homeostasis and morphogenesis occur not only at macroscopic levels, as in the family, but also at microbiologic levels. Recent theoretical papers in biochemistry have argued that complex biological systems may be separated into deterministic and random components. Mandell and Salk (1984) noted that nucleic acid codes for many proteins are composed of "smaller regions of fixed sequences and even larger ones with random arrangements" (p. 305). Whether we study the micro- or macrostratum of reality, the findings usually point to an interplay between fixed and random sequences of interaction.

FORMS AND RELATIONSHIPS IN THE HOLON

In CFT, the forms of the family holon include the behavioral transactions among nuclear family members and the intrapsychic phenomena of each individual member. Homeostasis provides for internal consistency between these forms. The intrapsychic structures generate behaviors in the family transactions that help to create external realities verifying the correctness of internal models. That is, there is an innate tendency for the individual to find and generate experiences that maintain his or her internal constructs of reality. For example, if the world is experienced as essentially nurturing, then the person is likely to create a caretaking interpersonal environment that verifies this internal paradigm.

The Behavioral Transactions

The behavioral transactions are organized conceptually into three interlocking subsystems: the marital, rearing, and independent transactions (Stein, 1980).

The marital transaction

At the hub of the family dynamic is the marital transaction, which is defined as the pattern of behavioral interactions between husband and wife. These patterns consist of repetitive sequences of behaviors that control and shape intimacy, sexuality, giving, taking, affect and expressiveness, anger, power, and competence.

Early on, the couple also establishes healthy romantic and sexual patterns of behavior. Each spouse must help the other develop appropriate sex-role behaviors so that the couple will work as a united team in preparing for having and raising children. Power and control issues that arise must be dealt with in order to ensure the marriage's stability and unity. The resolution of individuation, sex-role allocation, love, and power issues then become ongoing processes in the marital transaction throughout the family life cycle. The couple's interaction in these areas determines the psychosocial functioning of the entire family.

At the beginning of a marriage, the mates transfer powerful attachment needs from their parents to each other. In a regressive burst, termed falling in love, mates idealize their partners in a manner resembling that of a young child with a parent. This process sets the stage for each spouse to accept the other's suggestions and ideas about him- or herself and the nature of reality, much as a child does with a parent. The new bond replaces the old parental relationship and thus promotes individuation from the family of origin, one of the first tasks of marriage.

Attachment needs between the spouses predominate. The need for dyadic attachment in humans is a primary one, perhaps because of the long period of dependency children require in order to mature. Fear of loss is a fundamental principle that tends to cement in marital behaviors and congruent intrapsychic structures. This makes each spouse powerful in his or her ability to shape the other to play out the roles in the marital transaction. Of course, the marital transaction also shapes each spouse intrapsychically.

The spouses' roles vis-à-vis each other are homeostatically maintained (Haley, 1976; Sager, 1976). By selectively reinforcing specific marital behaviors, the spouses are able to choreograph each other to repeat predictable sequences of interactions. These homeostatic cycles eventually tend to include other family members, such as the children. For example, when marital tensions are high, marital cycles will often include children's acting out as part of the repetitive sequence. Marital roles are to a large extent reenactments of parts of the original marital and rearing relationships that the mates observed and experienced in their own families of origin. The spouses function, with powerful effect, both subjectively and objectively as figures who are similar to their original parental figures.

As Sager (1976) has indicated, the spouses develop some of their role functions in a complementary manner. Each programs the other to play out aspects of personality that are undeveloped in the self. These aspects are disowned and projected onto the other. Marital dyads include the husband with sane behavior and the crazy wife, the victim and the abuser, the parent and child, the talkative husband and the shy or observant wife, and many other interlocking and complementary roles. These roles are usually homeostatically maintained. If maintained in a highly rigid fashion, they may "lock in" intrapsychic structures and thus be personally limiting to the spouse. As Bowen (1961) has suggested, although spouses function with complementary levels of overadequacy and inadequacy, they usually manifest equivalent degrees of immaturity and self/other differentiation.

Couples establish roles with each other that help to define their relationships with others. As Minuchin (1974) has pointed out, the spouses must circumscribe a boundary around the marital subsystem to separate it from the family of origin and, later, the children. In no area is this boundary more critical than in the couple's intimate interactions. The following case example illustrates this well.

A young couple, Bob and Sarah, had been married for five years when they presented for treatment. The marriage had already lost the spark and magic of the courtship period. Bob was still very much involved with his mother, whom Sarah perceived as her enemy. She resented Bob's involvement with his mother and described him as a weak "momma's boy." Bob, on the other hand, criticized Sarah for never being happy or satisfied and said he doubted he could do anything to change the situation.

This couple's marital transaction was replete with repetitive and emotionally unfulfilling sequences. One typical pattern would begin with Sarah saying that she wanted more self-disclosure and romance rather than "straight sex." Her inner model of men, however, did not allow for self-disclosure. When Bob made attempts to accommodate Sarah by telling her how he felt at work, she would view his behavior as a prelude to sex, as per her inner model. She would resent Bob and he would then withdraw. This provoked Sarah's anger and tears. Bob would then move to comfort her and to reconcile their conflict. The couple had never experienced a satisfactory closure to this homeostatic sequence of interactions, and they were considering separation. The couple's son, Robert, age four, filled the void left by this marital interaction. He spent a great deal of time in an infantilized relationship with his mother, at great sacrifice to his own independence.

Spouses must also decide who will initiate sexual activity, and what forms of sexual relating are acceptable to both husband and wife. Repetitious sequences of behavior govern these activities as well. For example, a husband may cough or twitch to signal that his wife is getting too sexually excited, whereupon she may become angry and withdraw. The husband then apologizes and comforts her. The lovemaking that ensues is more toned down and thus acceptable.

The marital transaction exerts great impact on the spouses' development of personal power. The couple may vie for control over the finances, the rearing transaction, frequency of sexual activity, and so forth. Homeostatic sequences of behaviors often maintain the mates' ongoing power positions. For example, Stan and Mary maintained a relationship in which Mary had no idea of the family's finances. Stan was in control, choosing new purchases for the home and family. Mary would at times suggest a buy, but in an awkward and childish manner. Stan would reply that "things were fine" if he wanted the item, or that they were "strapped" if he was against buying it. Mary would then withdraw in anger. Stan, in turn, would mutter that he "should never discuss finances with such an emotional dingbat." This sequence reflected how decision making was choreographed by the couple such that Stan was empowered by Mary to be in charge of the finances.

Marital interactions also shape the spouses' power and competence in independent functioning. Most top business corporations today recognize this dynamic in choosing senior executives, and appraise husband and wife as a team by either interviewing both directly or questioning a candidate about his or her marital status. A spouse's conscious or unconscious ambitions are played out partly through his or her partner. Even Shakespeare's Macbeth became king at the urging of his ambitious wife. Conversely, marital battles may undermine a spouse's progression in the work arena.

For example, in one repetitive marital sequence, a husband would come home after a difficult day at work, looking for some peace and quiet. Typically, he would spend the evening in front of the TV. His wife, feeling neglected, would react by berating him and calling him a loser. He would then scream at her something about her never helping him with the important things in life, like "what pays the bills." This sequence is one which will maintain the husband's current adequacy at work but will not promote it. His success or failure is part and parcel of his marital battles.

The rearing transaction

The rearing transaction includes the entire network of interactions between parents and children, between the parents themselves regarding the children, and between the siblings. The power hierarchy, patterns of enmeshment, distantiation, and conflict, and the provision of nurturance, discipline, and guidance are important components of the rearing transaction.

Like the marriage, the rearing transactions are also organized in repetitive sequences. Rearing patterns might involve distantiation on the part of both parents, role reversals, or homoaffiliative alliances between parents and child(ren). Static coalitions between a specific parent and child against another parent are common examples of how homeostasis is achieved in the rearing transaction.

For example, in the White's rearing transaction, Mother was over-protective of and symbiotic with 10-year-old Peter, while Father was distant and uninvolved. Mother vented her anger and frustration on eight-year-old Wendy, the "bad one," who was aligned somewhat with Father. At the dinner table, Mother served Peter his favorite foods and allowed him to read a book during the meal, while she scolded Wendy for not using her fork. Father read his mail at the dinner table while occasionally urging mother to "quit bugging" Wendy.

The marital transaction governs the rearing transaction. Enmeshment, coalitions, and the like are viewed as emanating from dysfunctional marital transactions. Even the siblings' relationships between themselves in the rearing transaction reflect the emotional tone of the marriage.

Independent transactions

The independent transactions include each member's interactions with his or her environment in the areas of vocational or school performance, religious activities, social relationships, and hobbies. Homemaking is considered an independent transaction.

The independent transactions in part represent each family member's contributions to both the nuclear family and society. As part of the family holon, these interactions manifest the tendency toward constructive self-assertion in each family member. For example, the wife may be a homemaker who regulates the domestic roles of the household and who organizes and develops the couple's social life. The husband may have a profession or trade through which he supports the family financially, and he may also engage in some hobby or sport. The children go to school, have peer relationships, and engage in organized activities, such as scouting. All of the family members experience varying degrees of personal power or impotence, competency or inadequacy, success or failure, and creativity or stagnation, based on their performances in these areas.

Achievement and performance in school, work, homemaking, and social activities are also homeostatically maintained in large measure by the marital and/or the rearing transaction. Spouses' expectations for each other's independent functioning influence achievement, while parental demands and encouragement in the rearing transaction regulate children's performance in their independent transactions. There is a tendency in the family to promote the types of behaviors that result in the status quo of success, power, and creativity.

Relationships Among the Behavioral Transactions

CFT theory posits that the marriage is critical in family life. The marriage affects the spouses' independent transactions, underlies parental teamwork, and shapes each mate's interactions with the children. The rearing transaction, in turn, governs the independent transactions of the children. Rearing and independent transactions feed back to affect the marital transaction, although to a lesser degree. Thus the three subsystems form a multiloop feedback system regulated by the marital transaction.

The marital transaction has great impact on the mates' intrapsychic functioning, and it is the mates who are the executives and role models in the family. The marital relationship and the spouses' psyches are, in fact, the most powerful forces in the family holon in their effect both on each other and on the other transactions between family members.

The Family Holon and Society

Since the family is a microcosm of the larger society, the marital, rearing, and independent transactions are also shaped by society's tendencies toward stability or change in values, mores, and standards for marriage, childrearing, work, or play. In our society, for example, greater demands have been placed on families to break out of stereotypical role functioning. Women are entering the work force in greater numbers, with concomitant expectation that men will expand their roles to include homemaking. Independent transactions in families, then, are being reshaped and enlarged in the direction of psychological androgyny and role plasticity.

Intrapsychic Phenomena: The Self-system

Intrapsychic phenomena comprise the other major form at work in the family holon. In CFT, the intrapsychic phenomena make up the individual's "self-system." All three of the major familial transactions are shaped by and in turn shape the spouses' self-systems. The self-systems of each spouse are considered to be the most influential in the overall family process.

The spouses' intrapsychic functioning has a tremendous impact on the children. The mates project or assign parts of their own or their parents' personalities onto their children and treat them accordingly. Hypnotic-like programming of the child's identity and role results in the development of the anticipated intrapsychic structures and concomitant behaviors. The child is shaped to be a character in the parents' intrapsychic script.

The self-system is composed of intrapsychic structures that were initially formed by transactions in the family of origin. These structures are organized in a linear deterministic fashion, with one stage of development being the basis and context for the next stage. This model, like Freud's and Piaget's, is, of course, useful in demarcating plateaus and milestones of development, so that normal maturational processes can be differentiated from immature or dysfunctional patterns.

The self-system is organized conceptually into three levels: the foundation of the ego, sexual identification, and the triangulation level. Self-system structures usually have deep unconscious or preconscious roots in the psyche. They are usually available, at least partially, at the conscious level of awareness as well.

Foundation of the ego

At the core of the self-system is the foundation of the ego (Guntrip, 1969), which is formed in infancy through the relationship with the mothering one(s). Satisfactory experiences at the foundation level are critical for future personal and interpersonal success. The infant must experience both acceptance and limit setting in relation to the mothering one. The symbiotic relationship with the mother confirms the infant's sense of belonging and lovableness. Her limit setting or refusal to meet the child's needs at times helps to define for him a separate sense of self.

The foundation of the ego is formed through the introjection of aspects of the mothering one and the essential characteristics of the infant-mother dynamic, which oscillates between symbiosis and separation/individuation (Mahler, Pine, & Bergman, 1975). When the mothering one creates a "good enough" environment, the infant experiences fulfillment of physiological and safety needs, and a sense of the mother/world as attentive, prizing, mirroring, filling, adoring, and soothing. The infant forms a core feeling of the good self and experiences self-love.

The introjection process profoundly shapes the ego's development, such that internalizing a good enough environment creates the basis for relatively conflict-free movement to later phases of maturation (Fairbairn, 1952; Winnicott, 1965). The good environment internalized gives the toddler enough selfhood to explore and learn about the world. On the other hand, times of autonomous exploration, or times when Mother is frustrating or limit setting with the child, help the latter to differentiate between himself or herself and Mother, thus setting the stage for the recognition of a separate self. Anxiety at such times leads to a regressive movement – a rapprochement – to the secure environment of symbiosis with mother.

Over time, the child comes to know the mother in a more realistic way, as a separate, but steadily available object rather than as a set of stimuli that are all good or all bad. By lessening the absolute dichotomous perception of his or her mother/world, the infant learns to develop tolerance of frustration and the resultant ambivalence.

In a healthy outcome of this complex growth process, the child begins to perceive interpersonal relationships as containing inherent contradiction between the needs of self and those of the other, and that satisfaction lies in the ongoing balance between the two. As health predominates, there is a steady internalized object available to assuage normal fears and anxieties encountered in the world, and also a sense that such a mothering object will be available in the interpersonal environment. The self becomes differentiated from Mother, the primary other, and yet still perceives her as available for soothing regressive contact when needed.

If, on the other hand, mothering was experienced as smothering, haphazard, unresponsive, or dangerous, the individual may become schizoid, i.e., not truly emotionally reactive to the self or other, or he or she may enter an anaclitic depression. Significant others may then be experienced as engulfing or abandoning, or so frustrating that they may be destroyed by the individual's anger and need. When the foundation is formed through such adverse inputs, and subsequent experiences are not reparative, the infant becomes an adult who is unable to trust or form real relationships. In general, the earliest paradigm of relating – that of mother and child (of either sex) – becomes the model of intimate interaction, which in some form will be reenacted when the child grows up and is married.

Sexual identification

As the infant becomes a toddler and steps out into the world and away from the mothering one, he or she experiences either a sameness or an otherness in relation to her. Chodorow (1978) has suggested that the mother conveys to the child at an early stage that he is either of the same or of a different gender than she. The child, in turn, is developing a greater self-other dichotomy. With increased self-reflection, he or she begins to have a sufficiently differentiated picture of self to feel like a boy or girl. This image is also shaped by the child's observing physical and anatomical differences between him- or herself and mother and between self and father (Freud, 1923/1975b). The child also learns about his or her sexual identity through the parents' cultural expectations for the two sexes. These expectations form the nucleus of the sexual identity of the child, which is the second level of the evolving self-system.

The child seeks to imitate behaviors modeled by both parents. In addition, each parent provides programs, which are hypnotic-like suggestions, both direct and indirect, regarding their definition of the child's self and their expectations concerning his or her cognitive, emotional, and behavioral functioning in the world. Within these programs the child is usually oriented toward an identification with the same-sex parent.

Longings for the same-sex parent are characteristic at this level. These homoaffiliative needs, if fulfilled, shape appropriate gender-related role behavior. An image of this parent forms an integral part of the child's identity. If homoaffiliative needs are unmet or partially unmet, the child will seek the same-sex parent at the triangulation level and later in life in the form of a surrogate parent or mentor.

The opposite-sex parent also becomes a role model who is internalized by the child. The father becomes the prototype of the child's own masculine potentials while the mother becomes the prototype of the feminine potentials. Various characteristics of each parent are incorporated into the blueprint that becomes the child's template for future behavior as a marital partner (Dicks, 1967).

For example, Joanne's basic sexual identification was with her mother, a depressed, ineffectual woman who prided herself on appearances. Her father, a railroad engineer with no sons, spent time with Joanne as a substitute son. He called her "Chip" and played basketball with her. As an adult, Joanne became a woman who was neat and fastidious. Her speech and gait were similar to her mother's. She was unassertive in the world and never worked outside the home. In her marriage, Joanne developed a buddylike relationship with her husband and played out what she called her "tomboy" side with him. In CFT we deduced from these phenomena that her basic sexual identity was feminine and weak, while her masculine side was played out maritally.

The triangulation level

Up to this point we have described the emerging self in terms of sameness or otherness with regard to significant parental figures. The child first differentiates himself or herself from the mothering one and later develops a dyadic relationship with each parent. We might say, then, that he or she experiences first a unit of one (the self) and then a unit of two (the relationship with either parent).

The next phase of development includes those experiences that are generated in the triangle of relationships with mother and father. At this time, the child develops certain self-system structures as a result of his or her involvement in a triangle of relationships, in which there are competitive struggles for attention, loyalty, and alliance. These experiences form the basis of the triangulation, or oedipal level, of the self-system. The child learns parentally sanctioned behaviors with members of the same or opposite sex and is also programmed regarding sexual and marital behavior.

In this phase, the child is jealous of the parents' affection and seeks to separate them. If the spouses are able to tolerate the child's jealousies and yet maintain appropriate generational boundaries, the child will further develop an internal tolerance of his or her own ambivalences toward the parents. The child realizes that he or she cannot drive a wedge between them and becomes reconciled to the reality that he or she cannot steal one parent away from the other.

For the male child, this level represents experiences in which his hatred and fear of the father force him into greater autonomy from the father. On the other hand, his desire to be like the father, whom the mother loves, helps the boy to internalize the father as a role model.

For the female child, the triangulation level contains experiences in which her hatred and envy of the mother also lead her to be more separate and autonomous. On the other hand, her desire to be able to be like the mother, who represents her future identity as a role model, is further fueled by her internalizing and identifying with father's love for this woman. Thus, for both sexes, identification with the same-sex parent is coupled with cross-identifications with the opposite-sex parent (Dicks, 1967).

By about three years of age, the child has a clearly scripted role to play in the family drama. The inherent tensions in the triangle between child and parents can lead to dyadic enmeshments, illicit coalitions, scapegoating behavior, or oedipal wins and losses. Dyadic enmeshments between a parent and a child generate interactional models in which the child perceives marriage as an adult-child bond, rather than as an adult-adult arrangement. In one type of enmeshment, the child is allowed to "win" the opposite-sex parent. Rather than relating to the spouse, the parent attends to, confides in, and/or is affectionate toward the opposite-sex child. In highly dysfunctional families, the spouse actually has sex with the child. The other parent colludes by withdrawing from the marital transaction and organizing the child to fill in as a substitute partner. The child feels superior to the same-sex parent and develops grandiose feelings. However, he or she also experiences guilt over the win and is fearful of rejection by the same-sex parent. In incestuous families, the child may develop a revulsion toward the opposite sex.

Illicit coalitions between a parent and child versus another parent generate triangulation models in which a parent and child are joined together around a common enemy, the other parent, whom they ridicule or verbally attack. For example, in the Smith family, Scott was always very close with father and distant from mother, who tended to be sharply critical of him. Father programmed Scott to believe that women were "awful bitches," creating an adversarial standoff between Scott and his mother. The dysfunctional mother-son relationship was part of the parents' war with each other. We might deduce that the script Scott would follow at the triangulation level includes a homoaffiliative alliance strengthened by mutual hatred of women.

Another dysfunctional model is one in which the parents bond together around a misbehaving child. In this scenario, the scapegoated child joins spouses together who otherwise might split up. For the child, this represents a tremendous responsibility and burden. The scapegoated child will grow up with a triangulation model in which marital cohesiveness is fostered primarily through shared negativity toward a third party.

In the oedipal loss, the child is vehemently rejected by the opposite-sex parent. This situation is unlike a successful oedipal resolution, in which the opposite-sex parent rejects the child as a lover or primary life partner. However, that parent does love, nurture, and prize the child, and facilitates a close and positive identification between that child and the same-sex parent. In an oedipal loss triangulation, the opposite-sex parent abandons the family, makes no contact with the child, or physically or verbally abuses the child. The child feels unloved, unappreciated, or threatened by the opposite sex. This may create an inner model in which the opposite sex is viewed as less attractive than the same sex.

In general, abandonment or ongoing physical or verbal abuse is supported by the same-sex parent, who covertly organizes the opposite-sex parent to scapegoat the child. Usually this process helps reduce marital tension and detours marital hatred through the rearing transaction.

Relationships within the self-system

These three models — the self in relation to self, the self in relation to significant other, and the self in relation to two significant others — coexist in the self-system. Like the behavioral transactions, the three levels of the self-system are interactive and shape each other. Successful and fulfilling developments at any one level promote similar movement at any other level, and vice versa. Earlier developmental stages are, of course, much more powerful in their effects on later stages. Earliest experiences at the foundation level profoundly color the subsequent interactions that imprint the sexual identification and triangulation models. And, of course, sexual identification affects the way in which formative triangulation interactions take place.

There is a similarity between this model of self-system development and the way in which explanatory models of psychopathology and the unit of psychotherapeutic treatment have evolved in this century. First, single unit models like psychoanalysis were developed. Later, dyadic explanations of behavior were formulated by interpersonal theorists, such as Sullivan (1953), and were practiced in child guidance clinics, where mothers were seen with their children. Finally, the locus of pathology and health was broadened to include the triangle, or unit of three. Family treatment evolved. These models are all useful in understanding the developing child, the adult, and the family.

Pathological Forms and Their Relationships

At the heart of all psychopathology lie failures in relationships with significant others (Fairbairn, 1952; Framo, 1970). When parental figures provide inadequate or negative models and/or behavioral inputs to their children, pathogenic self-system structures develop in the children. These structures solidify themselves throughout the maturational process of the life cycle by an ongoing replication of the historical, marital, rearing, or independent transactional dysfunctions.

From a systemic viewpoint, contemporary replication of pathologic or inadequate family-of-origin transactions that occurs maritally is the most potent agent in the solidification of these pathological self-system structures. As previously mentioned, each mate has chosen a partner who is similar to his or her parents. Together they repeatedly reenact and/or reexperience in rigid homeostatic fashion the original failures they each had in relation to their own parental figures (Boszormenyi-Nagy, 1973; Bowen, 1978; Dicks, 1967; Jackson, 1957). This has a powerful impact on each spouse. Transactions characterized by hatred and abuse, negative verbal and nonverbal programming, and/or lack of nurturance or limit setting solidify basic terrors and self-destructive or inadequate sexual identities, and exacerbate repulsions, guilts, and fears in regard to the opposite sex.

This dialectical process between marital dysfunction and pathogenic spousal self-system structures is considered to be the major factor in the development or maintenance of psychopathology in the family, whether it is manifest in a child, a spouse, or a behavioral transaction. It adversely affects the mates' functioning as marital partners, as individuals in the outside world, and as parents.

For example, a middle-aged couple presented for treatment, complaining that the marital transaction was devoid of romantic involvement and honest communication. The therapist found the site of the dysfunction in both the marital transaction, which was quite distantiated, and the spousal self-system structures. The dearth of intimate interaction held at bay the wife's foundation terror of engulfment, which she expressed during therapy sessions as a fear of "suffocation." On the other hand, the couple maintained enough contact to assuage the spouses' fears of abandonment. This was manifest in a cyclical process of interaction, in which, as the couple tried to relate intimately, they would approach a level at which the woman felt uncomfortable and "small." Then they would fight and distance themselves to the point at which the man's abandonment terror flared. He would then pursue contact with his wife, and the cycle would begin again.

At the level of sexual identification, the woman felt confused about her own masculinity and femininity, while the man experienced himself as rather boyish and inadequate. Their distance protected them from experiencing unpleasant anxieties connected with these self-definitions. Both spouses had triangulation models in which a spouse met relational needs through contact with the children. For this childless couple, show dogs took the place of children. Both spent great amounts of time grooming and showing dogs. Thus, the marital transaction and the spousal self-system structures formed a dialectical interaction which maintained and reinforced the presenting problem.

Within the self-system, triangulation models and programs that are negative include: those that are incompletely developed; those that are characterized by repulsion, hostility, fear, and anxiety in regard to normal aspects of mating and sexuality; those involving dyadic enmeshments or coalitions with a child vis-à-vis a mate; and those prescribing the use of a child as the scapegoat for marital tension or as an object to fulfill sexual needs. These types of inner models tend to generate dysfunctional marital and rearing transactions.

Pathogenic sexual identifications are those made with parental models who are anxious, depressed, psychotic, self-destructive, immature, and/or confused about their own identities. Confused or incomplete identifications can also develop when there has been psychological or physical absence of a parent, or cross-sex programming. Cross-sex identification, which occurs when a child's basic identification is with the opposite-sex parent, generates residual self-hate, in that one's gender is viewed as less valued or inferior.

Sexual dysfunction and lack of romance or marital vitality are often generated by these problematic identifications and/or unmet homoaffiliative needs, i.e., longing for the same-sex parent. These issues may also generate failure in independent transactions.

At the foundation of the ego are negative introjects reflecting the basic terrors of engulfment, annihilation, and/or abandonment. In CFT, fears of loss and separation are viewed as the core anxieties in every person (Bowlby, 1973). When profound needs for attachment and belongingness go unfulfilled throughout the early bonding period with the mothering one, schizoid or depressive phenomena may develop (Klein, 1975a). These core phenomena usually underlie and shape individual psychopathology and contribute heavily to marital dysfunction.

If the mothering one permitted little autonomous exploration of the world, the individual has difficulty differentiating self from other and develops engulfment fears in the face of intimacy. If she provided little nurturance, the individual develops a sense of inner emptiness and depression, along with abandonment terrors. If she was hostile or threatening, the child will develop fears of annihilation in connection with intimacy.

Mother may not have been in synch with the child's cues in the rapprochement dance. In an ambivalent fashion, she may have drawn the child close when he or she sought to explore; but, when the child moved in, she may have prevented intimate, loving contact with her. The child then becomes an adult with terrors of both engulfment and abandonment. If Mother's behaviors are too disparate and erratic, the child may also learn to split experiences of relating to significant others who come to represent the "good" or "bad" mothers.

These self-system gaps and/or pathologies lead to the choice of a marital partner who is inadequate or pathogenic, and also to the creation of transactions that entrench the self-system deficits. Another case example will serve to further illustrate this process. A married woman sought treatment for what she characterized as an intrapsychic problem, depression. At the foundation level, she experienced a profound abandonment, based on the death of her mother, which occurred when she was three years old. At the sexual identification level, she experienced herself with some confusion, as both feminine, like her mother, and yet much like her primary role model, her father. Her father experienced himself as rather incompetent in the world. Based on her experiences with her father, who never remarried, her triangulation model involved a relationship between a child and a parent, in which the child was related to only sporadically, and at times with angry outbursts about how stupid she was.

The therapist found all of these dynamics reflected in this woman's marital transaction with her husband. In fact, in repetitive exchanges of behavior, which they created and shaped together, she received little attention or approval from her husband. She tended to play the incompetent role with him, and he frequently and impatiently labeled her slow and dumb. Occasionally their exchanges resulted in a burst of physically abusive behavior from him. When not working, the husband went out with his preferred companions, his golfing buddies. Inner pathogenic realities mirror and shape powerful marital transactions and vice versa.

Symptomatology in children (when organicity is ruled out) can almost always be traced to a dysfunctional rearing transaction, which in turn is usually generated by a malfunction in the marital transaction/spousal self-system dialectic. When a child presents with problems in his or her independent transactions, the locus of the difficulty may be present in the child's relationships with teachers or peers. While individual diagnoses of the child may be useful under certain circumstances (e.g., in ruling out organicity), in general, a diagnostic evaluation of the rearing transaction, which is the larger context for children's transactions, will prove more fruitful in shedding light on the child's independent problems. Through the parents' relationship with their child, difficulties in his or her independent life are maintained, amplified, or reduced. The parents' attitude toward school performance, peer relationships, hobbies, etc., will determine whether the child is more or less successful in these endeavors.

For example, in the Adams family, the youngest child, Tom, was a serious disciplinary problem both at school and at home. The parents were unable to team together in a consistent fashion in their disciplining of Tom. At times mother would undermine father's authority over Tom by rescinding various punishments, but at other times she would lose control and scream furiously at the boy, while father defended him. This type of parental disagreement is common in families with "problem" children. Confusion about the provision of discipline, nurturance, and guidance for a child is a symptom of dysfunction in the rearing transaction. When such confusion is cleared up, behavioral problems in children usually stop quickly. In the Adams family, the rearing confusion was settled in a few family therapy sessions, in which the parents actually signed agreements concerning how they would team to parent Tom; and Tom began to function more harmoniously at home and at school.

In a situation like Tom's, however, further treatment is necessary. This is because rearing dysfunction is itself symptomatic of a much larger and more powerful issue – a problem marriage. While a change in the rearing transaction does affect the marriage, it will not cause sufficient change in the marital transaction to prevent either recidivism in the parents' relationship with the child, or the occurrence of other family problems.

MOVEMENT AND TRANSFORMATION IN THE HOLON

Morphogenesis or change in family life proceeds in an oscillating pattern in both a positive or growth-seeking direction, as well as in a negative or pathogenic direction, with the former trend predominating.

Positive Morphogenesis in the Marital Transaction

Many theorists have posited a tendency toward positive morphogenesis or growth in marriage (Framo, 1976; Napier & Whitaker, 1978). Mates are chosen for qualities they possess that could potentially promote personal development. They usually identify with each other much as a child identifies with a parent. If role complementarity is flexible, it can serve for growth here. The mate provides a role model and a vicarious experience of success in ego-alien behavior. For example, a talkative outgoing husband may learn how to be quiet and listen through identification with his shy, observant wife.

CFT theory posits that there is also an innate tendency toward active growth promotion of the mate in the marital transactions. The shy wife may have chosen a man who not only is talkative but also has some paternal concern for her. At some point in their marriage, he might instruct, encourage, and urge her to venture out socially while he takes the silent role. Because this man has a strong parental influence and refuses to function in this role for her, the wife discovers her own conversational abilities. When a mate validates and promotes the extension of self-definition and behavioral repertoire in this way, the spouse/ marital unit grows. The individual is freer to move forward in the world. Furthermore, he or she is motivated out of thankfulness and appreciation to promote the other mate's growth and development.

Stein (1980) termed these health-seeking trends progressive abreactive regression, or PAR. The PAR process is composed of progressive and regressive growth trends, which develop in both the individual and the system. A spouse moves out to new behaviors and accomplishments, which are available at each new stage of the family life cycle. This progression oscillates with an abreactive regression, where the individual turns inward to experience fears and dysfunctional programs that need to be worked out through a regressive interaction with the other spouse that is reassuring and validating.

Transformation is generated at the heart of the family holon, in the dialectical relationship between the mates' intrapsychic structures and their marital interaction. Positive morphogenesis is fueled by innate drives to growth that are manifest in both the intrapsychic structures and the marriage. Systemic reorganization takes place in such a way that the needs of individual family members are more fully satisfied, while, at the same time, family stability, flexibility, and generativity in the marital, rearing, and independent transactions are enhanced. Such change proceeds in a circular relativistic fashion, moving through the self-system and the transactions in a definite pattern.

The telos, or end state, toward which the PAR, or self/family growth process, moves is termed optimal family process. The PAR transformation will be delineated in the optimal family model presented in the following chapter.

Negative or Pathogenic Morphogenesis

The family holon can and does move in the direction of dysfunction at times, in a kind of entropic process. The holon can be "run down" in a pathogenic process where mates foment and promote greater failure, craziness, and dysfunction for themselves and each other. A mate's progressive activities end in failure and/or self-doubt. Then the other mate is either unavailable for reassurance and validations or programs the mate to fail completely or go crazy. The family holon can then spiral down in dysfunction.

However, even entropy often results in growth and the establishment of a PAR movement. For when a spouse reaches a critical point of psychosocial dysfunction and pain, he or she will often turn in the regressive phase to a new, more adequate helpmate, i.e., a therapist or a minister to resolve the crisis. This morphogenic step can then lead to the creation of a more stable, growth-promoting configuration.

SUMMARY

In CFT the dialectic of the family holon is delineated in terms of systemic and intrapsychic forms and their relationships, movement, and transformation. Systemic forms include the marital, rearing, and independent transactions. Intrapsychic forms include the foundation of the ego, the sexual identification, and the triangulation phenomena. Marital, rearing, and independent transactions work together in a highly inter-related fashion with self-system structures to generate family process. At the heart of the holon is the marital transaction/spousal self-system dialectic. This dialectic largely determines psychosocial pathology or health in family process.

Psychosocial pathology is largely generated by transactional and in-trapsychic phenomena which reinforce and homeostatically maintain dysfunctional patterns learned in each spouse's family of origin. Fami-ly health, vitality, and stability are generated by functional patterns learned in the families of origin and by a transformative process, pro-gressive abreactive regression (PAR). In this biphasic process, family members' needs for achievement and success, as well as those for inti-macy and validating contact, are fulfilled.

CHAPTER 2

Optimal Family Process

All happy families resemble one another. Each unhappy family is unique in its grief.

— Tolstoy, *Anna Karenina* (1960, p. 1)

If the family unit is indeed a holon in transformation, toward what end state, or telos, does it move? The answer to this question could prove quite useful in clinical practice. A theoretical model of optimal family process, as Olson, Sprenkle and Russell (1979) have indicated, could be used as an aid in clinical diagnosis, in understanding potentially helpful inner resources available to client families, and most importantly, in the targeting of treatment goals.

Goal setting in clinical practice is important in terms of its effects on the client family. In treatment, the therapist's subjective constructs and/or conscious goals for clients shape the therapeutic process (Abroms, 1978; Bandura, 1971; Truax & Carkhuff, 1967). Since the practitioner has a strong covert and manifest influence on the clients (Frank, 1974; Haley, 1963), his or her goals may prohibit the client family from developing beyond professional intent, at least during the existence of the therapeutic relationship. Thus, the therapist's concept of healthy functioning may form a ceiling barrier to the family's growth and movement. The growth agent's use of fully conceptualized and operationalized models of optimal functioning helps to prevent such limitations.

Yet theory and research that delve into the nature of healthy family functioning have been sparse. The field of family therapy, like that of its sister field, individual therapy, has focused much of its attention on psychopathology and dysfunction. This is somewhat ironic in that many of the family therapy pioneers severely criticized the pathology-focused medical model, which they saw as the basis of individual work. Perhaps

21

issues of ideal family functioning have been avoided as uncomfortably value-laden (Abroms, 1978) or controversial, touching as they do on philosophy and religion, all of which share with psychology speculation on the fundamental nature of human experience.

Since the realm of optimal family process is vague and incompletely charted, practitioners have of necessity relied on intuition and personal experience as the main guides for termination goals in clinical practice. As a result, contemporary family therapists are more effective in the opening and middle phases of treatment, when the focus is on more explicit goals revolving around the amelioration of presenting problems.

Higher level behavioral objectives, when targeted by clinicians, have been described in ambiguous or piecemeal terms. No major family theorist has attempted to present a comprehensive theory describing fully vitalized family structure and process. Stein developed the CFT model of optimal family process in an attempt to fill this void.

This chapter starts with a brief review of the literature pertaining to healthy family process. It then presents the CFT model, which is used extensively as an aid in diagnosis and goal setting in CFT. Optimal marital, rearing, and independent transactions, as well as self-system structures, are described, with special focus on the critical PAR growth process. The chapter closes with sketches of optimal single-parent and reconstituted families, and a description of the clinical use of the CFT model.

A BRIEF REVIEW OF THE LITERATURE

Family Therapy Goals

Satir's (1964) goals were delimited to the realm of communication. Goals revolved around the development of honest, meaningful communication between family members that was congruent with feelings. Bowen (1978) has also worked for the personal growth of each family member, but his focus has primarily concerned individuation from the "undifferentiated family-ego mass."

Ackerman (1958) has presented the most comprehensive set of treatment goals, including consolidation of the marital relationship, individual development, and successful individuation for the children. In an interview with Foley (1974), Ackerman described these goals primarily in terms of role differentiation and function. The three important targets for Lidz (1963) were a strong marital coalition, complementary heterosexual identities, and hierarchical arrangement of generational subsystems. Minuchin (1974), echoing Ackerman and Lidz, targeted as his goals clear generational boundaries with adequate-functioning spouse, parental, and sibling subsystems.

The more psychoanalytically oriented family therapists have yet another set of goals. For example, Framo (1965) and Boszormenyi-Nagy (1965) worked toward a restructuralization of deep psychopathologies and improvement in object relations.

Each of the described goals involves necessary aspects of successful family functioning. Upon termination, the family process should manifest symptom-free behavior, clear generational boundaries, complementary roles, overt rules, effective communication, and personal individuation. It is apparent, however, that each major contributor has concentrated on a different aspect of family process to the exclusion of other equally important elements. In each case, the selected aspect has then been viewed as a generalized indicator of the entire family configuration. None of the seminal contributors to family theory has integrated the various behavioral and intrapsychic dynamics of healthy family functioning into their goals for treatment.

What is needed at this juncture is a theoretical synthesis of the systemic and intrapsychic dynamics of the healthy family. A clearer picture of the fully vitalized family will help professionals to have a clearer standard by which to judge the progress of their clients, and upon which they may postulate goals.

Healthy Family Dynamics

In the body of literature concerned with the dynamic properties of family systems, many prominent family theoreticians, including Jackson (1957), Bateson (1961), Jackson and Weakland (1961), Minuchin (1974), and Selvini Palazzoli et al. (1978), have subscribed to a conceptual model of family process that is based on principles of homeostasis and psychopathology. Another group of theorists (Brodey, 1967; Buckley, 1967; Sonne, 1967) criticized this emphasis on negative feedback cybernetics and called for a new perception of social systems that was growth-oriented and self-evolving.

Buckley (1967) was the first theoretician to use the term morphogenic to describe social systems that used positive feedback processes as vehicles to develop and innovate. In these systems, deviation from the status quo does not necessarily trigger mechanisms to restore the previous equilibrium, but instead might set in motion an interactive process that is deviation-amplifying. Following Buckley, other theorists (Olson et al., 1979; Wertheim, 1975) have suggested that the most functional families maintain a balance between homeostasis and morphogenesis.

Three other studies have pointed to the centrality of the marital transaction in healthy family functioning. Westley and Epstein (1970) looked at the organization of the families of emotionally healthy and emotionally disturbed college students. The crucial difference between these two types of families was in the relationship between husband and wife. Couples who were emotionally close, fulfilling each other's needs and encouraging positive self-images, were able to fulfill their children's needs. Also, since each parent had a clear understanding of him- or herself, each saw their child as distinct from him- or herself, and allowed the child to grow into an autonomous, emotionally healthy individual.

Lewis, Beavers, Gossett, & Phillips (1976), in their study of healthy families, found that healthy families had strong marital coalitions of shared power. They had a great respect for and encouragement of individuation, and a capacity to accept separation and loss realistically. Their family myths were consistent with reality, as judged by outside observers, and they were able to adapt to change. Additionally, the feeling tone in these families was warm and expressive.

Kleiman (1981), in his study of families of healthy and normal adolescents, also found more effective parental coalitions and firmer generational boundaries in the healthier group. The most important factor associated with healthy psychosocial functioning in adolescents was a positive marital interaction, characterized by intimacy, trust, and mutual enjoyment.

Two additional studies focused solely on healthy couples. Cuber and Harroff (1965) found that "vital" couples in the group of significant Americans they studied had a great deal of sharing and togetherness, which appeared to promote progressively greater success and validation in the world for each spouse. Ammons and Stinnett (1980) also described a characteristic balance between mutuality and individuation in the "vital" relationships they studied.

The similarity of the findings in these studies indicates that healthy families have a common structure and process. The studies point to the importance of a healthy marital relationship in optimal family process, and suggest that these marital partners form a strong parental coalition that maintains generational boundaries. The studies indicate that these spouses create an atmosphere of intimacy and trust in which they enjoy each other and foster positive self-images. At the same time, they have a respect for individuality, are in contact with reality, and are able to adapt to change. Taken together, these characteristics suggest an admixture of homeostatic and morphogenic processes.

THE CFT MODEL OF OPTIMAL FAMILY PROCESS

The CFT model, developed by Stein, also hypothesizes that a healthy marital interaction is the key to optimal family process. It attempts to further delineate the nature of this interaction and its impact on the psychosocial functioning of family members.

Optimal Marital Transactions: Progressive Abreactive Regression

CFT theory posits that in all marriages there is a natural drive to create a healing relationship – one that not only replicates, but also transcends transactional gestalts that the spouses experienced in their families of origin. This drive toward growth generates certain marital dynamics.

Each spouse moves progressively forward in life, fulfilling tasks in the marital, rearing, and independent transactions in an increasingly productive manner. The progressive trend is an expression of our innate need for self-assertion through doing, a moving beyond boundaries and limitations to face new challenges.

This movement forward evokes and elicits conflicting anxieties and self-doubt. As new situations arise, dysfunctional maps and frightening programs emerge and become conscious, along with basic terrors and the fear of the unknown. In order for the progressive thrust to completely actualize itself, these internal impediments, or ceiling barriers, must be diminished or removed.

How are these issues transformed? Further, how are they transformed so that if the individual is set free on his or her path to self-actualization, the entire family holon will not be fragmented or dissolved? Fragmentation of the family holon leads to disruption of childrearing and threatens species survival. Progressive morphogenesis must be accomplished in such a manner that family cohesiveness and unity are maintained. The key here lies in the complementary dialectical trend toward regression and attachment.

The eruption of anxiety and internal conflict is usually also related to the breaking of contemporary role contracts in the marriage. Fear of loss of the mate arises on a conscious or unconscious level. The individual is compelled to regressively seek proximity and contact with the mate. Thus, the adult returns physically and regresses psychologically in the face of new challenges, in order to reassure the self that the primary love object will still be there. Generally, the expansion of the self is less important than the maintenance of the love relationship. As Maslow (1962) has written, belongingness is a more central and basic instinctual and species-wide need than either self-esteem or self-actualization. The individual in the progressive thrust toward self-actualization must, then, check back to see that the more primary need, belongingness, will still be fulfilled. He or she actively seeks reassurance that the movement forward is not breaching, but rather enlarging, loyalty contracts.

Mahler (1980) and others have described this type of oscillation of progressive/regressive movement in terms of rapprochement. From infancy, the individual ventures out to explore and conquer the world, only to become frightened and then retreat into the reassuring arms of Mother. This process occurs, in fact, throughout the life cycle. The emotional base is first enlarged to include Father, who generally pushes the child even further out in his individuation/mastering effort. Then, in young adulthood, the paramour or spouse replaces the parents in filling rapprochement needs. Each spouse continues to explore the world, expanding old models, maps, and programs, but now he or she regresses and seeks reassurance, security, and other inputs from his or her mate.

In order to function as a secure and knowledgeable anchor for the mate, the "mothering" one must deepen his or her emotional resonance and understanding. An atmosphere of freedom must be created so that impulses and issues can arise for examination. The parental figure can then reprogram and enlarge the other's self-definition. Successful rapprochement concludes when the parenting spouse insists that the spouse master a new progressive task. As the spouse follows through in the new progressive arena, other anxieties arise that lead to the resurgence of regressive needs.

Growth proceeds in a biphasic pattern, step by step, without family fragmentation. Both morphogenic and homeostatic processes are at work in this spiraling movement. Morphogenesis can originate either in the self-system or through novel interpersonal contact. Intrapsychic drives to self-improvement or inspirational transactions with others generate growth in the self-system as well as new behaviors. Homeostatic attachments then lead to a regressive trend, culminating in rapprochement.

The infrastructure of the healthy marriage is a healthy homeostasis that firms the contract for mutual growth. In order to maintain this positive homeostasis, each mate takes responsibility not only for his own behavior, but also, whenever appropriate, for his spouse's. Responsibility here does not imply blame, but rather a benevolent desire to do whatever is necessary to assist growth and development.

At times one spouse may be in need and the other may not fulfill his or her role as growth agent. When this occurs, either the spouse or the couple in concert works to correct this deviation from the positive homeostatic pattern. Positive morphogenesis then continues. In this way, the potential for a healing relationship is actualized in a marriage. The spouses assist each other to grow as marital partners, as parents, and as individuals.

This produces a state of mature love in which each mate trusts the other's sincerity, judgment, and intentionality. Openness, vulnerability, and receptivity to marital influence are at their height.

In mature love, constructive self-interest and self-assertion occur along with self-transcendence in the form of dedication to the other spouse. These are not simply opposing movements in the dyad's process. Rather they are part of a dialectical dance in which personal success and achievement generate a greater love and dedication to the other. Successful and productive dedication to the partner, in turn, generates more positive self-esteem, which fosters further self-interest and success in autonomous functioning.

Healthy self-interest

Healthy self-interest in a marriage is a critical ingredient for the success of the relationship. Two opposing movements constitute the process of healthy self-interest: autonomy/individuation and dependency on the other for validation. These two trends also reflect an individual's dual needs of separation and attachment.

Autonomy is heightened maritally when each spouse learns to appreciate his or her own uniqueness. The spouse explores the world and reflects on his or her individuality in relation to various situations and experiences. As this process occurs, the other spouse is engaged as a helpful listener in the self-reflection process. The mates can then understand each other's unique needs, wants, programs, visions, and goals. They come to appreciate and respect the vastness of the gulf that exists between two unique individuals. Knowledge of the self in a context that affirms differences promotes receptivity to the other and creates intimacy.

One poet, Rilke (1975), expressed his views on autonomy in marriage as follows:

> It is a question in marriage, to my feeling, not of creating a quick community of spirit by tearing down and destroying all boundaries, but rather a good marriage is that in which each appoints the other guardian of his solitude, and shows him this confidence, the greatest in his power to bestow . . . Once the realization

is accepted that even between the closest human beings infinite distances continue to exist, a wonderful living side by side can grow up, if they succeed in loving the distance between them which makes it possible for each to see the other whole and against a wide sky! (p. 28)

The affirmative context of marriage builds marital trust. Each spouse turns to the other out of his or her own self-interest in understanding and nurturance, as well as education, validation, and guidance. When rapprochement and dependency needs are met by the marital partner, self-esteem grows, as does constructive self-assertion. The spouse becomes more competent and feels thankful to his or her helpmate. As needs are fulfilled, interest in the other grows. Self-transcendence, the other trend in healthy marital relating, then begins.

Healthy self-transcendence

Two movements constitute self-transcendence: reciprocal identification and sincere altruism. Reciprocal identification is the process in which each spouse identifies with the other's feelings, needs, hopes, and goals. May (1969) has defined this form of caring as a "state composed of identification of one's self with the pain or joy of the other" (p. 289). Reciprocal identification helps build marital trust and receptivity. It also fuels a dedication to the other's growth and development.

Sincere altruism involves active devotion to the self-actualization of the other. The partner becomes fully attuned to the other's needs and, with full will and determination, works devotedly to fill those needs. The needs of the self are relegated to the background.

As the partner's self-actualization takes place under the mate's influence, a thankfulness to the other for his or her helpfulness is experienced. The altruistic growth agent experiences greater self-appreciation and self-respect. This sets the stage for a new surge of his or her own healthy self-interest.

The dialectic

When a spouse assists his or her mate and meets with success in this endeavor, the spouse experiences his or her own benevolent potency, which furthers self-esteem. This process also leads to a greater feeling of deservedness, which in turn fosters the seeking of new opportunities for personal success and fulfillment. That is, the mate's success becomes linked to one's own success as a growth agent.

Ultimately, the spouses come to understand the dialectic, and enlightened self-interest appears. Selfishness comes to mean a "win-win" relationship. Each spouse comes to realize that all the loving commitment and successful promotion he or she gives to the other validates his or her own potency and cleverness, and will be returned in kind. It becomes clear that as each one heals and promotes the other, he or she is in fact creating a more developed and effective growth agent for him- or herself.

Thus, the cycle in the healthy self-interest/self-transcendence dialectic operates in a circular fashion as shown in Figure 1.

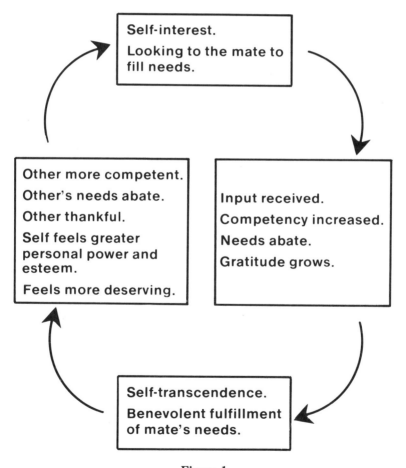

Figure 1

Progressive and regressive marital trends: A closer look

In the progressive trend, the spouses divide between them the various domestic and career responsibilities necessary to meet the demands of family life. Each then promotes the other's competence and success in his or her role functions. When there is productive role fulfillment on the part of one spouse, the other spouse is supportive and rewarding. At times, however, as a result of deficient role models, negative and inadequate programming, and/or lack of educative experiences, a spouse may perform poorly in the marital, rearing, or independent transactions. The other spouse then assists him or her to develop more competent and successful behaviors.

As reparental figures for each other, each spouse can provide inputs that were lacking in the partner's family of origin. A spouse may program the other for self-confidence and success through suggestions and directives regarding productive behaviors. Education, modeling, confrontation, validation, encouragement, and inspiration may also be provided as needed.

Through the acceptance and integration of such input, the spouses help each other to remedy deficiencies in self-system structures that have resulted in behavioral immaturities. Functional knowledge, assertiveness, competence, and positive ambition grow. Skills in conflict resolution are enhanced in both intra- and extra-marital interactions. The spouses' successful progressive development results in the enhancement of family productivity, organization, security, and adaptation to reality.

As they progress, the mates have powerful repetitive experiences in which feelings, expectations, attitudes, and behaviors arise, both negative and positive, echoing those in their earliest relationships. When the material is negative, the spouses function in a therapeutic capacity for one another. In an affirming and empathic stance, each spouse promotes the ventilation of feelings and thoughts. Each helps the other understand and discard distorted perceptions of reality that interfere with productive behavioral functioning. Regressive thoughts, feelings, and behaviors that are freeing and fulfilling are encouraged in the marriage. The mates can be vulnerable and childlike with one another. They reciprocally fill each other's needs for approval, affection, emotional empathy, special attention, and play, as well as for sensual and sexual pleasuring.

With successful rapprochement experiences, the spouses develop a more positive predisposition toward, and a greater desire for, marital intimacy. Experiencing greater love and understanding of self and other, the mates can allow more spontaneity, playfulness, self-disclosure, and emotional resonance in their interaction. Successively more regressive needs arise and are fulfilled in their relationship. As this positive regression continues, the mates approach states of empathy and psychological fusion with each other that are deeply fulfilling. These interactions catalyze the formation of positive introjects and identifications in each mate's self-system.

The progressive and regressive marital trends are mutually enhancing. In the progressive trend, as each arena of behavior is mastered, new and challenging arenas engage the spouses' interests. A spouse may change careers or master new skills, such as public speaking or writing a book. As the individual contemplates or makes a move into the new arena, his or her anxiety flares and rapprochement sessions become focused on him or her. Assisted by the spouse to gain familiarity and mastery in the new arena, the individual then presses on to complete more and more of the new behaviors successfully. The anxiety becomes transmuted into excitement and energy. Constricted focus on the self lifts, and the individual experiences an expansive sense of euphoria, a burst of self-love and appreciation, which in turn is projected onto the world. The individual can have a peak experience (Maslow, 1962) at this point, when the mastery euphoria is at its height.

Rapprochement sessions then become less focused on the individual spouse. Instead, the couple share the mastery euphoria. They experience a form of "falling in love," in which each spouse sees the other in an extremely positive light. The spouses attend to the charming and delightful qualities in each other, in a manner similar to that of infatuated or honeymooning couples. Each then experiences these qualities as the most real and profound parts of themselves.

Continuing over a lifetime, the progressive and regressive marital trends promote biphasic ego growth. Mates become increasingly more flexible and competent behaviorally as individuals and at the same time deepen their attachment to each other. Advancing mastery in behavioral functioning occurs, along with regressive abreaction, introspection, and reparative nurturance and prizing. These biphasic developments continually advance the mates' adaptability and individuality, as well as their cohesion and mutuality. Satisfying intimacy, sexual fulfillment, playfulness, and joy develop along with competence in parenting and independent transactions. Thus, there is a spiral of health in which internal schemata regarding the self and the world continually become more positive and generate more productive and growth-promoting behaviors, which in turn promote positive self-system structures.

Self-system structures in both spouses develop so that they become secure and yet rich in repertoire of interpersonal responses. The foundation of the ego becomes more centered. Sexual identity is broadened in that both the feminine, relational side and the masculine, instrumental side are promoted by the PAR process. Triangulation phenomena move in the direction of greater marital intimacy coupled with appropriate devotion to the children.

Case illustrations

Over the past five years, the faculty and candidates at the Institute for Comprehensive Family Therapy have conducted clinical research on healthy families and stepfamilies. Two studies (Kleiman, 1981; Weintraub, 1982) have compared and contrasted families and stepfamilies with "healthy" vs. "normal" adolescents. Another study (Gregory, 1983) showed a significant correlation between marital adjustment and the self-actualization of the spouses. In addition, Institute students have conducted field studies with well-functioning families.

Most of these clinical studies have utilized structured interviews with families, which have shed light on their marital, rearing, and independent transactions. A glimpse into the lives of two of the couples interviewed illustrates the PAR process.

The Ellis family. Bob and Elaine Ellis had been married for 12 years. The couple were asked about a turning point in their marriage. Their response concerned a change in the way they had related to each other as helpmates. The issue that sparked the transformation was Bob's career. Bob, who was an engineer in a large company, was afraid to ask his boss for a raise. His boss was a father figure around whom he felt inadequate and anxious. His wife, Elaine, wanted very much to assist him with this problem. She asked him about his inner process – his hopes and dreams and the dread and fear associated with them. Elaine reported that she had helped her husband to trace his associations and negative feelings to experiences he had had with his father. She then fathered Bob, encouraging him to push beyond his father and his limits and to go for his dream.

At this point, the couple reported that Bob had become quite angry and defensive. Elaine, in turn, had become angry at Bob's reaction, but later tried to be, in her words, "cool," or emotionally nonreactive to his defensiveness. When Bob continued to be defensive, Elaine switched approaches. She reduced the pressure on Bob to move forward in his work, and simply listened to the child in her husband. By allowing him to ventilate his deeper feelings, she built a sense of trust and security.

Bob was able to air his feelings of self-hate in the context of relating to a basically validating woman.

After using this approach for a few weeks, Elaine disciplined Bob so that he could make the frightening move. Elaine announced one day that she was postponing their vacation until Bob asked for the raise. Bob reported that after this interaction he went to his boss to ask for additional responsibilities and a salary increase. His employer promoted Bob and gave him the raise.

The couple reported that the sequence of interactions leading to the promotion resulted in tremendous growth. Bob said that he learned how to confront the reality of his own poor upbringing and deal with it, initially, with the help of his understanding wife and, later, on his own. He began to separate himself more from his family of origin and therefore had less anxiety about his past. This allowed him to deal more realistically with the contemporary work situation and to have more reasonable and positive expectations of himself. Bob also said that he experienced a sense of power and competency that came from the knowledge that he was handling his work situation well and was providing his family with greater economic security and social status. He also felt that after this interaction, he was more open to Elaine. Thus, in this powerful process, Bob developed his sexual identification in a more androgynous fashion—becoming simultaneously more competent instrumentally and more receptive to input from a loving mate. In addition, Bob reported that he was thankful to Elaine and eager to reciprocate by assisting in her growth.

As a result of her contribution to the growth process, Elaine reported feeling more powerful as well as closer and more affectionate to Bob. She had, of necessity, refined her feminine ability to be empathic, receptive, and in tune with her husband, in order to help construct a firm foundation of nurturance and trust in the marriage. She also had to develop her more masculine side, in order to be powerful and aggressive enough to help her husband conquer his terrors and behavioral constriction.

The Ames family. Helen Ames, age 39, had not attended college at the time she was married and had functioned as the homemaker. With the last child off to school, the Ames's discussed Helen's career goals. Brad, age 41, her husband of 15 years, encouraged her to dream for herself. Helen was interested in going back to school. Upon questioning her, Brad learned that Helen's parents downplayed both her intelligence and her abilities. Brad spent time listening to Helen as she discussed her negative experiences in high school. In the interview, Brad reported that he had taken a very fatherly stance with her. He encouraged Helen to take a college course, and he validated her keen mind. Brad was a successful doctor. He told Helen that his success was in no small part due to her, and that if she chose to, she could also do very well. Helen decided to go back to college to pursue a business degree. Brad helped out by cooking meals on those nights Helen was away.

The interviewer discussed with the Ames's how, through this type of interaction, both of them had expanded their triangulation models. The prototype for the opposite sex was enlarged. Brad perceived his partner as more courageous and intellectual. Helen saw her husband as benevolent, understanding, and supportive. The couple spoke about how this process helped to dispel residual cultural stereotypes of the weak, hysterical woman and the withdrawn, nonrelational man. And it was clear to both spouses that their marriage was the most critical factor in their lives and that it was even more important than their children.

We would hypothesize that in both families the PAR process facilitated the resolution of abandonment terrors at the foundation level. Bob Ellis and Helen Ames both reported experiencing tremendous anxieties related to moving beyond parental programs. Instead of finding themselves alone in the world, however, they found themselves in closer relationships with their spouses. The helpmate spouses, meanwhile, had to work through any abandonment fear they may have experienced in connection with their spouses' success.

Optimal Rearing Transactions

The advent of children fosters growth in the regressive and progressive marital trends. The spouses tend to recreate interactional patterns experienced in their own childhoods. These patterns reflect the self-system structures that manifest themselves in behaviors, emotional responses, and attitudes toward the children and spouse. As each mate's parental internalizations are played out behaviorally, they become more apparent to both spouses. Protective impulses toward the child motivate both parents to work in the therapeutic coalition to diminish the negative impact of these internalizations on the family. The regressive marital trend is also furthered as a result of each spouse's identification with the child. The identification process brings to the surface forgotten material from childhood, which then becomes available for intramarital discussion and understanding. Also, through identifying with their children, the mates can more easily contact their own childlike needs, which may then be fulfilled intramaritally.

Optimal marital transactions result in the evolution of optimal rearing. Dysfunctional or immature behavioral patterns are disrupted as a result of the spouses' therapeutic interaction. The parents can then function as a coordinated team in a more healthy rearing transaction to triangulate each child in a manner that furthers his or her growth.

The parents fulfill their children's needs. As Maslow (1954) has noted, these include, at the foundation, fulfillment of physiological needs for food, clothing, and shelter, as well as needs for safety, belongingness, self-esteem, and self-actualization. Healthy parents actively satisfy and fulfill all of these basic needs. Each child is made to feel cared for, safe, part of the family, and favored or special. This builds a foundation upon which the child will grow to actualize his or her potential.

Parental teamwork aimed toward the child's self-actualization starts when parents who are both emotionally invested in the child agree upon how he or she is functioning presently and how they would like the child to function. Then, within a family hierarchy that maintains generational boundaries, the parents function in executive, sex-linked roles in order to promote the fullest development of the child's potential. Although both parents provide nurturance, programs, and discipline, they usually divide between them the provision of these inputs to the child.

The same-sex parent (SSP) tends to function as the primary programmer and disciplinarian. The SSP promotes maximum ego development by setting limits as well as progressively higher level goals and standards intrinsically suited to the child's unfolding skills and talents. The SSP uses reward and discipline, education, inspiration, and modeling to help the child to attain these goals. The opposite-sex parent (OSP) functions primarily as the facilitator or mediator within the triangle. In this manner. he or she meets the rapprochement needs of the child.

If the SSP disciplines a misbehaving child in an inappropriate fashion, the OSP takes responsibility for correcting the interaction. The OSP encourages the child to ventilate all the reactive emotions arising from the dysfunctional interaction. Usually, the child is experiencing some fears and anxieties regarding loss of love in connection with the difficult interaction he or she has had with the SSP. In a manner that creates a satisfactory rapprochement, the OSP is stable and loving and points out that the SSP still loves the child. He or she reaffirms that the child is good and worthwhile as a person. While providing emotional validation for the child, the OSP nonetheless indicates the reality of the child's misbehavior.

Furthermore, the OSP explains the situation so that the child can see the SSP's point of view. Then he or she impacts on the spouse in whatever way necessary, in either the regressive or progressive modes, in order to promote more effective parental behavior. After the OSP has eased the situation, he or she persuades the child to relate anew to a now more understanding and appropriate parent.

The triadic interplay in this rearing transaction has a powerful and positive effect on the child's psychological development. The child can identify more easily with the SSP, who is authoritative and powerful, yet flexible and understanding. He or she perceives the OSP as a potent ally who is nurturant and validating, and this perception will transfer to other members of the opposite sex. The close relationship with the OSP also offers opportunities to identify with the positive characteristics of the opposite sex. The child sees the parents' close and effective teamwork, which serves to frustrate oedipal fantasies and provides an attractive model to follow.

Furthermore, over time the parents' teamwork becomes refined. Their intramarital involvement builds, which helps to dissolve the child's emotional ties to them. This type of triangulation paves the way for a child with a stable sexual identity who is primed to leave the family in order to secure a satisfying and intimate relationship like that of his or her parents.

Along with the development of the capacity to establish a healthy marriage, both male and female children are also oriented, primarily by the SSP, to achieve success and creative generativity in independent functioning. Thus, the stable yet flexible parental behaviors in the triad help shape a young adult who is in the process of actualizing affective, relational, and assertive aspects of him- or herself. The goal of the rearing transaction is the fullest development of each child's potential for successful living in every arena.

There are times in the rearing process that OSP-SSP role division is not followed. The parents switch roles whenever the need arises. When the SSP is unavailable, the OSP may set limits, and at some later point the SSP will facilitate. In this way no matter who disciplines, the child always has an outlet to whom he or she can ventilate feelings, as well as someone who can act as an appeals board.

Role division may also become more diffused when the parents function as educators of their children. In order to promote optimal development, the parents decide between themselves who will be the more active parent in taking on the responsibility of teaching the child certain specialized skills, such as reading, math, art, music, or sports. This is done so that the child is taught by the parent who likes and excels in that area and is not confused by different teaching styles and diverted from the task at hand. The more passive parent—similar in his or her position to the OSP in the triangulation model—becomes the audience for the child and his or her new skill. As there are many different areas of learning for the child to explore, each parent will have something special to impart. And the child has role models who are excited and knowledgeable about different aspects of the world.

The triangulation of the son

According to the optimal family process model, the father becomes the son's primary disciplinarian and the mother, his primary nurturer. For the son to form his own identity, he must move from the familiar identification with the mother to the less known world of the father. In the optimal rearing transaction, the father moves in and takes charge more and more as the child grows out of infancy. With a strong masculine role model impinging on him, the boy is able to develop an identity that is clearly male. But he is also able to maintain a special positive relationship with his mother. Healthy relationships with both parents allow the child to develop a core sense of self that is gender-congruent, along with the capability of identifying and communicating with the opposite sex.

In a healthy family the mother is nurturant and understanding, and consistently promotes the relationship between the son and the father. She encourages them to spend time together and engage in activities in which they share a special interest. The parents also spend much time alone together. The son is shown over and over again that he cannot be his mother's primary companion or fantasy lover because she is ultimately his father's wife and he is powerless to come between them. His only winning choice is to identify with his father. He is encouraged and challenged by both parents to go out into the world – when he is ready – to find his own woman who will be a better companion for him than his mother.

The result of this intense teamwork between the father and mother is a son who sees women as nurturant but powerful and sees men as powerful yet understanding. Thus, he sees that the two different sexes are capable of functioning in both the instrumental and affective roles and that this type of living is a part of his legacy which he will, in time, share with a wife and children. He realizes that if he wants to have the intimacy, involvement, teamwork, and romance that he sees at home, he will have to go out into the world to create his own family.

The Rogers family. Mort and Ellen Rogers discussed the rearing of their son, Tony, a bright and successful boy of 12. Mort reported that he had been the disciplinarian for Tony since the boy was three or four years old. He described how he had tended to be too harsh on Tony, as his father had been with him. The couple reported that Ellen had helped Mort to "mellow out" and get closer to Tony. The Rogers were asked to recall a typical sequence of behaviors in which this process occurred. One sequence concerned Tony's cleaning his room. Mort reported that he had thought of Tony as a dirty slob, a term derived from his own childhood. When Tony neglected his room, Mort reported, he would overreact and ground him for a month. At that point, Ellen would step in to facilitate the father-son relationship.

Ellen would listen to her son's version of the story and allow him to ventilate his angry feelings about Mort and what had just occurred. After validating his feelings, Tony's mother would point out that she nonetheless supported Mort. She would tell Tony that he needed to learn responsibility for his environment and emphasized the fact that his father was trying to teach him about this. The mother worked with Tony to take greater responsibility for his actions. But she promised her son that she would speak to his father about the matter so that he would be more understanding of Tony's behavior. Thus, Ellen nurtured him and prevented his anger and frustration from debilitating him. She also introduced the possibility of reconciliation with a more sympathetic father.

Ellen would then go to Mort and point out that he had overreacted to his son's not cleaning his room and that his punishment of not letting him go outside to play for the next month was too harsh. After this had been worked out with Mort, she returned to her son and—in one of the most important maneuvers in the rearing process—pushed him out of "her lap." She pointed out that his father was a reasonable man and insisted that they talk over together what had happened. In this way, Tony's mother set the stage for her son to experience his father as a powerful yet understanding person whom he wanted to emulate. At the same time, she prevented Tony from being illicitly overinvolved with her. Tony and his father discussed what had transpired and Tony apologized and promised to improve. Tony's father reduced the punishment to three days of grounding with an agreement that for every day Tony did not straighten up his room, he would be grounded a day.

Over the past few years, the couple reported, things had gotten much better. Mort grew more and more competent in understanding his son and in parenting him. Ellen's role as facilitator became less needed. It should be noted here that when Tony's father traveled on business or was otherwise not available, it became his mother's responsibility to assume the disciplinary role. Tony learned that both men and women can be nurturant or strong, and that he could develop both aspects of himself as well.

The triangulation of the daughter

In the rearing transaction of the female child, the parents again join together to support each other in the triangulation of their daughter. The mother changes slowly from the warm, nurturing figure of the girl's infancy to become her disciplinarian. The daughter's surprise at finding the person she loves turn into a demanding figure is mollified by her father who takes on the role of empathic nurturer and facilitator. Mother is assertive, powerful, and successful in the household, with her husband, and in the world, and more and more the daughter wants to be like her.

The Alden family. Grace and Larry Alden discussed a difficult time in their relationship with their daughter, Elsa. When Elsa reached puberty at age 14, Grace had begun to feel anxious and tense around her. Grace told Larry that at times she was experiencing feelings from her own childhood through her identification with Elsa. When Grace was 13, her mother had died. Her triangulation model, then, involved a close relationship with the father and an abandoning mother.

When Elsa reached puberty, Grace stopped having their nightly chats, and at times did not even bid her daughter good night. Elsa had become increasingly more sullen in her relationship with her mother. Grace's upset, coupled with Elsa's negativity, propelled Larry to mediate the situation. He took Elsa out to lunch and discussed the situation with her. Elsa claimed that her mother did not love her anymore. She was allowed to express her anger about her mother, while her father listened to her. After Larry had heard the whole story and listened to his daughter express her feelings about her mother, he commented on Elsa's role in this scenario. At times she had rejected her mother for "treating her like a baby." He emphasized to Elsa that her mother really did love her, and that Elsa could still get the nurturance she needed from Grace. In order to do this, Larry suggested that Elsa ask Grace for attention and advice at bedtime. Larry also promised Elsa that he would discuss the situation with Grace.

On their next date alone Larry asked Grace to further elaborate on the relationship between her and Elsa. He found that his wife felt rejected by Elsa. Grace cried about how she herself was abandoned by her own mother and that she had vowed never to do the same to her children; nonetheless, she felt trapped in the same role. Larry listened empathically and then insisted that Grace recognize she was the parent and ought not be dependent on her daughter's acceptance or rejection. He programmed her to press on and maintain contact with Elsa. Describing Elsa's emotional outpouring at lunch, he emphasized how much

Elsa still needed her. Larry offered to be her coach in this endeavor, sending her into Elsa's room each evening to make contact with her. Grace agreed. After one month of successful contact between the two, Larry took his wife out to dinner and gave her a gold charm necklace which carried the program, "Number One Mom."

When this type of rearing transaction takes place, the daughter holds her father in great esteem. He has listened to her and then spoken on her behalf to her mother. He has helped her through a difficult situation. She may begin to entertain fantasies of an oedipal win in which she runs off with him. But to prevent this, the father has performed a crucial function in the rearing transaction—he has fostered a reconnection between mother and daughter. He also has solidified contact with his wife through his therapeutic exchange with her. The daughter has resumed contact with a mother who is even more mature and powerful than before. The daughter cannot have her father, and she must find someone like him who is her own age and speaks her own language. The road is thus paved to identification with her mother and healthy marital partner choice.

Optimal rearing transactions such as those in the above illustrations have considerable growth impact on the couple as well. The wife experiences a man who treats her with respect and love, helps her work out her closely guarded anxieties, and is responsive to her daughter's needs. Her negative images of men slowly fade, and she finds herself more and more wanting to nurture and promote the development of her understanding husband. Growing with the benefit of his care, she becomes not only less selfish, but also more self-loving. She finds she is developing her receptivity by becoming vulnerable and opening herself up to her husband, which deepens her femininity. She feels more at ease in her maternal role as she sees her daughter feeling good about herself, doing well in school, making friends, and doing chores. As mothering gradually becomes less of an effort, the wife discovers the time and energy to go out into the world to develop her native abilities in another career.

Meanwhile, the husband in this transaction has become a hero. He is his daughter's protector and nurturer and has reached his wife in a way no one ever has. Both wife and daughter respect and love him, and both his marital and rearing transactions are enhanced. With all of this validation, he grows more flexible, compassionate, and understanding. He finds he can deal with personal and intimate issues without becoming overly reactive. He becomes a good listener and learns he can love his daughter best by being understanding and empathic with her. By opening these aspects of his personality, he develops the feminine in himself, thus furthering his androgynous fulfillment.

Optimal Independent Transactions

In healthy families, ideal independent transactions are targeted for all family members. The spouses work in the regressive and progressive marital trends to see family members without distortions, to validate members' self-worth, and to develop realistic objectives for each child, as well as for and with each other. They can then impact on one another, as well as on the children, utilizing positive programming, education, inspiration, and other progressive maneuvers to stimulate productive and fulfilling behaviors. Spouses experience success for themselves and the children, which engenders greater love and respect for the self and marital partner, and strengthens the growth-oriented marital contract.

As each member grows and develops, expectations and accomplishments elevate and are shaped by more exacting moral principles. Goals in these families usually involve satisfaction of needs for competency and success, generativity, power, and creativity. Stimulating friendships and participation in physical exercise are also important for family members. Healthy families can often promote rapid advancement in a member's career if the therapeutic marital coalition works well.

Success in independent transactions is measured by both achievement and movement forward to fulfill new needs. For example, a man who owned a thriving retail business for 20 years was socioeconomically quite advanced, but not at all challenged in his work. A move forward for him entailed a switch in midlife to a career as an author, which involved a setback in income, yet provided excitement and creative fulfillment. In optimized independent transactions, the individual moves forward to new forms of conquest and generativity.

Of course, life-cycle and gender-related issues limit flexibility in choosing and elevating independent transactions. When children are young, most women find themselves in the arena of homemaking. Here a woman can function as an anchoring parent who is more available to the children. The husband during this period is also somewhat limited as he must ensure that he provides for the family's economic needs. Thus, in early family life, there tends to be traditional male and female role division. When all the children reach school age, the parents usually find more freedom to pursue novel and attractive independent pursuits. The wife may develop her masculinity by starting her own business or pursuing a higher academic degree. The husband may choose to modify his schedule to include communing with nature through long-distance running or gardening. These activities themselves will, of course, grow and change over time. Later in life, the mates' independent goals may become more humanitarian or spiritual in nature.

Children's ideal independent transactions also change with maturational development. For the preschooler, educational exploration of the world and peer interaction predominate. For the prepubescent child, school performance, constructive peer relationships, sports, and creative hobbies are developed.

In adolescence, when counterproductive oppositional issues and diversionary sexual involvements loom, the child is even more tightly structured. At this stage the child is nearing the launch point and must be loved, guided, and disciplined so that he or she is communicating openly with parents, is on track scholastically, and is oriented toward some target careers. Peer interaction and dating are controlled and tracked to ensure that social pressures, which are particularly potent at this age, constitute a more positive influence. The adolescent is encouraged to participate in sports and hobbies, and to experience independence by getting a part-time job and earning money. The tight scheduling of the adolescent's time serves well to diminish oppositional behavior or sexual promiscuity. Sexual involvements are directly discouraged as they might lead to teenage parenthood or a premature marriage, either of which interfere with the development of a full and rich life plan.

Healthy Self-system

Within each individual at birth are the seeds of a healthy self-system structure. When basic physiological and safety needs are met, the self is biologically programmed to seek releasers in its environment that are required in order to bring forth the full flowering of the self-system. These releasers consist of nurturance, benevolent discipline, and positive programming supplied by maternal and paternal figures. From birth on, the human being seeks the unique combination of these inputs, which he or she must have at each successive maturational stage in order to achieve the highest level of functioning at that stage. If the inputs received are adequate for the developmental stage, the individual moves on to the next stage in the maturational progression. If the inputs received at a certain stage are not adequate, the individual will be left with certain immaturities. The person will continue to seek the appropriate growth releasers, not only in childhood, but throughout the life cycle.

Releasers facilitate the process of progressive abreactive regression so that intrapsychic health and behavioral competence are promoted. Nurturance provides for relational modes that are self-transcendent, leading to the ability to bond and identify with others. Discipline and programming catalyze the self to greater individuation – a self/other dichotomy that results in enhanced instrumental performance and mastery of the world.

As the individual develops in the two directions, he or she becomes more conscious of internal schemata and finds that each ceiling barrier to deeper relational capacity or greater productivity can be surpassed. Thus, the individual experiences him- or herself as growing and changing, and is less emotionally attached to a rigid definition of self. The foundation of the ego moves in the direction of a more whole, self-loving state and a feeling of unity with a world that is viewed as basically trustworthy and fulfilling. This may involve a more spiritual approach to living. A differentiated and internally integrated sense of self predominates, and yet there is the ability to maintain attachment to and regard for significant others, even in the face of frustration, aggression, and disappointment. In general, there is the capacity to delay gratification and to tolerate frustration.

The core sexual identification builds on the positive foundation of self as part of the larger whole. The individual experiences him- or herself as able to act on the world in a powerful and capable way, while at the same time being able to identify with the world at large. An observing ego develops which is free of transferential and parataxic distortions. The individual is able to experience the reality of him- or herself and others in a clearer, less emotionally charged manner.

The sexual identity becomes at the core congruent with one's age and gender, although it allows for flexible use of both expressive/relational and instrumental/objective capabilities. The individual can be passive and meditative or deeply receptive and empathic in relation to others. At other times, he or she can be an active and separate agent who initiates and directs activities, and impacts on others in a goal-directed manner.

There is a highly developed inner code of ethics, principles, and standards of behavior to be followed. Goals revolve around satisfaction of not only the person's own needs, but the needs of others as well. At the highest levels, there is a true altruism toward mankind, a sense of benevolent responsibility and caretaking of other people.

The mature core of the identity holds court over more childlike parts. Childlike states are utilized actively to gain needed reparental input, to stimulate fantasy, or to facilitate playfulness and primitive and gratifying states of psychological fusion with a loved one.

Triangulation models evolve toward congruency with the optimal rearing transaction model. Fulfillment and growth are seen as part and parcel of the marriage. Spouses are expected to act as a benevolent parenting team, taking each difficulty in this endeavor as a challenge for growth in the triad. Children are increasingly experienced with altruistic love and devotion.

With greater psychosexual health, individuals manifest less rigidity of musculature and facial expression. They are more fluid, spontaneous, and alive in their expression and behavior. They are usually more graceful and poised in their demeanors. More psychological energy is available for use in the person's transactions, as there is less repression of unconscious issues.

The healthy self-system possesses all the capacities required for mature love in the marital transaction. A clear sense of the self as a separate entity, coupled with self-love and esteem, leads to a healthy self-interest. On the other hand, the understanding that one is a part of the interpersonal world leads to self-transcendence and altruism. Androgynous flowering of the self provides for the development of personal power needed to successfully program and discipline the self and the mate, along with the relational skills needed for fulfilling rapprochement. Success in independent transactions is achieved. All of this, in turn, helps to generate a vitalized and effective rearing transaction, so that children grow up as relational and competent human beings.

In healthy families, PAR continues over the cycle, helping to perpetuate family life. The repetitive drama generated from negative internal schemata in the self-system plays itself out. Healthy self-system structures, conscious understanding, and willful action are pervasive. The spouses enjoy higher and higher levels of love and work. The collaboration for growth bonds the couple together as they age, and this fosters their children's independence. Continuing positive marital regression elicits more profound states of ego transcendence. Thus, the person is more prepared for the eventual loss of the spouse and the acceptance of death.

Single-Parent and Stepfamilies

Single-parent and stepfamilies manifest growth processes similar to those found in intact families. In the healthy single-parent family, the parent develops both him- or herself and the child. Finding new experiences in the realm of work and dating, he or she grows instrumentally and relationally. This fosters healthier childrearing.

The single parent takes on both the SSP and the OSP roles. This

CHAPTER 3

Role of the Therapist

We serve the patient in various functions, as an authority and a substitute for his parents, as a teacher and educator. . . .

—Sigmund Freud (1923/1975a, p. 181)

THE SEARCH FOR COMPLETION

Many schools of thought from the time of Plato in the West and the Buddhists in the East have suggested that man has an inherent drive for completion. This movement toward self-actualization or integration of opposites (yin-yang; male-female; progressive-regressive) is depicted in CFT as a transformative process that occurs via PAR. One regresses in a more fulfilling way in order to progress forward in a more competent manner, and vice versa.

Even in biology, a similar transformation occurs. In evolutionary theory, Koestler (1980) quoted Garstang, who believed that novelty in the evolutionary process occurs in the larval or embryonic stage of the ancestor and disappears before the ancestor reaches the adult stage. The novel evolutionary development then reappears and is preserved in the adult stage of the descendent. So, for example, the human adult resembles more the embryo of an ape than he or she does the adult ape. Thus, even in biology one regresses to find the seeds of progression.

The CFT approach works with the biphasic tendencies toward regression and progression which occur at the psychosocial level. The practitioner utilizes a regressive strategy along with a progressive strategy to foster growth and psychosocial completion. In this chapter, the rationale for this type of an approach is presented. This is followed by an overview of treatment and a section in which the regressive and progressive strategies are delineated. The chapter closes with a description of the three phases that occur in the progression of treatment.

THE TRANSFERENCE

As the quote at the beginning of this chapter illustrates, Freud (1923/1975a) was the first to point out that clients tend to perceive and organize the therapist as a parentlike figure. In psychoanalysis, this phenomenon has been referred to as the transference. One view of the transference is that it is a homeostatic mechanism whereby a client reexperiences and reacts to significant others in the environment in a compulsively repetitive manner. But perhaps in line with our previous discussion on the dual nature of family systems, transference phenomena have not only homeostatic but also positive morphogenic properties in their impact on an individual's functioning.

Perhaps the impetus to assume a childlike posture when in the presence of a potentially helpful authority figure is part of a thrust toward transformation of the self. Out of an innate drive to completion, the client regresses in relation to the therapist and becomes psychologically more open to him or her. Phenomena that occur in treatment support this hypothesis. At the outset of treatment, the transference to the therapist is usually positive. Every word and gesture, be it even so small as a glance at the watch, is critically important to the client. This degree of reactivity and responsiveness is characteristic of the child at a younger age, when he or she is most open to influence and psychological shaping by his or her parents. Later, if the therapist seems to be an adequate figure for the parenting tasks required, the client will, over time, further regress, in a manner that would seem to allow the therapist access to the client's self-system structures.

Thus, through transference, clients may actually be attempting to solicit from the therapist reparental nurturance, programming, or discipline that was not available to them in their families of origin. With these inputs internalized, clients can resolve conflicts and deficits at various stages of development and move forward more successfully in fulfilling life-cycle tasks in the marital, rearing, and independent transactions.

Most theoreticians have noted that clients do seek a reparental agent in the person of the therapist, and some have recommended concomitant reparental approaches in the consulting room, either for specific disorders (Levenkron, 1982; Rosen, 1975) or as a general procedure (Peck,

1978). For example, Guntrip (1969) stated: " . . . What the patient is fundamentally seeking is a relationship of a parental order which is sufficiently reliable and understanding to nullify the results of early environmental failure" (p. 287).

In line with this approach, many treatment outcome studies have indicated that the critical variable in treatment may be the therapist and not the specific treatment modality. Those therapists who are rated as empathic, warm, and congruent have more successful treatment outcomes (Truax & Carkhuff, 1967). Emotional congruence and positive regard are, of course, the bedrock of good parenting. Also, clients seem to incorporate whatever treatment schema their therapist utilizes — adopting its language and basic premises, or dreaming scenarios consistent with its beliefs (Frank, 1974).

These findings would indicate that in meeting the natural drive to growth, the therapist actually functions as a reparental agent, no matter what his or her approach. Clients, then, use the therapist to compensate for deficits or damage in their early environment.

THE THERAPIST AS REPARENTAL AGENT

CFT theory postulates that clients are seeking exactly what they need in order to grow: a parental figure who can offer "good enough" remedial inputs in a facilitating rapprochement environment. By accepting the responsibilities inherent in the reparental role, the therapist is freer to provide the milieu necessary for client growth. He or she can tailor and refine a reparental stance with each client, much as a parent learns to deal uniquely with each child. In CFT, the provision of this tailored reparental stance is considered to be the most powerful and effective means to bring about change.

With two-parent families, the therapist moves to the heart of the family holon by becoming the rapprochement figure for each spouse and working on their marital transaction. With single adults and single-parent families, he or she assumes the reparental role with the adult client. These relationships allow the therapist to amplify the regressive/progressive growth trends already latent in the client or client family.

In practice, this means that the CFT therapist assumes a great deal of responsibility for the success or failure of treatment, as well as the development of goals and criteria for termination. He or she is not merely a blank screen, or a reflective and empathic kindred soul, or a strategically oriented technician, as in some other treatment modalities. Rather, the CFT therapist becomes a real person who functions as a

benevolent authority figure. The therapist shapes his or her own feelings and reactivity to the client and uses them to impact on the client
in order to achieve specific goals. The therapist also allows him- or
herself to be identified with the client and invested in the client's growth,
much as a biological parent would.

THE THERAPIST'S VALUES AND GOALS

The CFT practitioner's role as a reparental agent does put him or her
in an unusually strong position of influence on the client family. Along
with the family, the therapist actively plans and guides clients' growth
and development. When treatment is successful, the clients usually
identify with the practitioner and incorporate many of his or her values.
Thus, in CFT, the therapist's values and goals are critical.

If the practitioner relies purely on subjective and idiosyncratic goals
for clients, he or she is left in a posture that is easily confused or upset
by countertransference issues. He or she might inadvertently create a
ceiling barrier to the family's growth and development, or, worse yet,
have a highly destructive effect on clients. If the therapist's goals are
unclear or poorly developed, he or she might unwittingly prolong states
of dependency beyond an appropriate time.

In order to minimize these dangers and also to work more efficiently
and effectively, the CFT growth agent actively utilizes the theoretical
model of healthy family functioning as a guide in clinical practice. Goal
setting is determined by a consideration of each family's unique characteristics as they might be developed in accordance with the CFT
model of optimal family process. This forms a clearly designated target
for the client family which helps to organize the progression of clinical
work. Since goals then fall in line with the natural growth tendencies
in the family holon, clinical efficiency and effectiveness are enhanced.

THE REGRESSIVE AND PROGRESSIVE STRATEGIES

Traditionally, therapists have argued against the gratification of
client demands for nurturance and direction on the grounds that this
type of stance engenders too much client dependency. Such dependency
could be debilitating to a client's sense of self-esteem and autonomy and,
thus, ultimately destructive to the client. This is, in fact, the case if there
is only gratification of needs for dependency. However, in CFT, the
parenting proceeds in two broad movements, one regressive and the
other progressive. In the regressive strategy, the therapist is backward-

looking, using the reparental stance to build positive self-system structures and to bond with clients at a deep level of object relations. In the progressive strategy, he or she is forward-looking, promoting clients' competence in the behavioral transactions (Stein, 1980).

Bonding and gratification of dependency needs are always followed by timely demands for independent functioning. Both processes occur rhythmically within the entire treatment process at a macroscopic and microscopic level. On the macroscopic level, there are two broad phases in the treatment. The therapist at first provides a relationship of relatedness that meets rapprochement needs, followed by a firm push toward a new independence. At the microscopic level, most sessions contain both regressive and progressive elements, although the ratio of one mode to the other changes dramatically over time. Thus, the parenting in CFT practice mirrors the parenting found in nature.

The process of maturation through treatment involves the development and fulfillment of dependency needs with the practitioner and the promotion of more competent behavior in the world. As clients mature, they are expected to take a high degree of responsibility for their behavior and also, although to a lesser extent, for the behavior of others in their families. In this manner, the danger of destructive dependency on the therapist is avoided.

OVERVIEW

CFT treatment, then, can be conceived of as multi-layered, with the reparental stance as the basic organizing aspect. This stance shapes the next level down – the regressive and progressive strategies. These strategies are plans that the practitioner utilizes to help the family move in the direction of more optimal functioning. The strategies guide the therapist in his or her ongoing interactions with clients. Therapeutic techniques form the third level of treatment. Specific techniques emanate out of the regressive or progressive strategy used by the practitioner. They represent the means by which the therapist carries out the therapeutic plans.

The Regressive Strategy

Regressive strategy at triangulation level

The regressive strategy is targeted toward the three levels of the self-system. The strategy is basically the same with adult clients, whether they are married or single.

At the triangulation level, clients reexperience aspects of a sexualized/asexualized or competitive transference toward the practitioner, depending on the practitioner's gender. Marital partners will often experience a form of sibling rivalry in relation to the practitioner. The therapist interprets and highlights these aspects of the triangulation model as they emerge and ties them back to family-of-origin transactions.

The practitioner tailors the remedial stance to reshape the triangulation phenomena. If, for example, the transference emerging out of an oedipal win is too seductive and sexual, he or she desexualizes his behavior and conducts sessions with less physical proximity. If, on the other hand, the client has never been properly admired and courted in a manner appropriate to normal parental heterosexual relating, he or she will be more courtly. The practitioner may, for example, take a client out to lunch or give her a rose. He or she allows normal feelings of attraction to emerge, which, of course, as in a normal family, are never sexually acted out. As Levenkron (1982) has noted, such an approach is akin to the courtship experience that occurs naturally between parents and children.

When competitive transference phenomena arise, the therapist becomes an audience of one who is identified with the client. For example, in one case, when a spouse succeeded in generating positive marital behaviors, the therapist congratulated him on his progress, but also gave himself some credit. In this example, the therapist generated a win/win relationship. He gave this client, who had grown up with a competitive father, a model of a strong parent who was not weakened by his son's success. The message given to the client is similar to that given by the healthy parent to his or her child: "I'm good, but you will be better. And the better you are, the better therapist (or parent) I am."

When marital partners exhibit strong sibling rivalry, the practitioner works to make each one feel special and favored in his or her own way, much as a healthy parent does. The therapist also builds in a healthy identification between the spouses by congratulating one on the accomplishments of the other, and by encouraging the esprit de corps of a winning team.

Regressive strategy at the sexual identification level

In both family and individual work, the practitioner works to enhance the client's internal sense of a competent, gender-congruent person. This is especially important if there is confusion or a dysfunctional program associated with a spouse's sexual identification. At first, the therapist may interpret and describe the nature of the sexual identification and its roots in the client's experience in his or her family of origin. Dysfunctional aspects of the spouse's programs are highlighted to help induce motivation for change.

The practitioner programs to foster a sexual identity that is successful and creative and yet also relational and empathic. Often he or she will give the spouse nicknames which sum up the new identity in metaphor or through identification with a cultural hero. Therapeutic interactions are organized around playing out aspects of this new image. If needed, the client may be encouraged to develop a more presentable and desirable appearance which reflects the new identity.

Through verbal and nonverbal gestures, the practitioner works with each spouse as if he or she were a competent and attractive son or daughter. Clients may be given appropriate gifts or taken shopping for clothes with emphasis on the male or female role. Homoaffiliative longings that surface are fulfilled through specialized contact with the therapist. Fathers or male clients may be approached in a somewhat more competitive and demanding way, but in the spirit of warmth and play. The therapist may arm wrestle or have a round of basketball with the client. Clients who have lacked a close relationship with their mothers are given more relational input, in which the therapist mirrors body positions and breathing, and generally is more feeling-oriented and empathic. Because the stance can be tailored in this manner, even opposite-sex therapists can put themselves in touch with the needed male or female side of their own personalities in order to mother or father the client as a healthy parent would.

Regressive strategy at the foundation level

As the regression proceeds, the deeper, unfulfilled needs of each spouse surface. If prizing, empathy, warmth, and approval were lacking in the family of origin, the therapist will provide these inputs. Intense attachments to the practitioner develop, which are important for the repair of object relations.

The practitioner creates a relationship with the client that is aimed at calming and vanquishing the basic terrors of abandonment, engulfment, and annihilation of self and/or others. It is these terrors that have kept the client from relating to significant others in a close and loving way.

By steadfastly maintaining a benevolent relatedness in the face of the client's attempts to destroy their relationship, the practitioner dispels the client's abandonment terrors. The framework of treatment is critical in this regard. The therapist does not condone acting out through broken appointments, broken agreements, or threatened termination. At times like these, the therapist will call the client by phone, reengage him or her, interpret the behavior, and maintain the therapeutic relationship.

Annihilation fears, on the other hand, are amplified as the client moves closer to the therapist, spouse or lover, or as he or she progresses beyond parental programs in his or her career. By providing a consistently benevolent and in control demeanor, the therapist helps calm the client's annihilation fears. He or she provides a safe environment in which the client also has room to move away to a degree, as needed, in order to have a sense of comfort and control. At times the practitioner may become angry or elicit the client's rage over transferential or real issues in their relationship in a manner that demonstrates to the client that his annihilation fears are groundless (see next section). Finally, in dealing with engulfment terrors, the practitioner resonates emotionally with the client by entering into his inner reality via shared metaphors and feelings. The client then learns that he is not engulfed and destroyed by fusion, but rather strengthened and enhanced by the symbiosis that occurs.

Introjection of the practitioner at this level of relatedness promotes the ability to love self and others (Balint, 1979). The client experiences a profound sense of being lovable and of being special to the therapist. The link between them helps heal the "basic fault" of the client and the feelings of being cut off from the world. As the client opens psychologically to the therapist, he or she becomes more able to reach out to significant others. Mirroring the practitioner's movements, the client becomes more relational and emotionally congruent with his or her loved ones.

Anger and negative transference

In the course of the intense emotional involvement with the practitioner, clients inevitably experience disappointments, hurts, anger, and even rage, based on both real therapeutic errors and/or perceived, transference-based events (Searles, 1965). Negative feelings toward the therapist are an extremely valuable and important part of the whole treatment process, particularly in the later stages of treatment.

The healing process depends upon the practitioner knowing and accepting the client as he really is. This is impossible to accomplish if the client remains in the role of the good child filled with nothing but warmth, admiration, and respect for the practitioner. The client's behavior is then generated by approval seeking, rather than natural impulses and inclinations. The essential self remains hidden and inwardly labeled as undeserving of approval.

Additionally, if anger and negativity remain unexpressed, the client's positive feelings and actions toward the therapist often are not arising solely out of real attachment and affection for the therapist, but also out of the client's unconscious process. The pseudo-positive feelings often mask the client's sense of guilt over angry feelings or destructive wishes toward the practitioner that have been suppressed or repressed. The client may involve himself, usually unconsciously, in making reparation for these feelings and thoughts by becoming more devoted to the therapist (Klein, 1975b).

Whether such behavior is generated by outer-directed, approval-seeking, or inner-directed, reparation-seeking behavior, the client is in fact acting in relation to the therapist, rather than being a whole and real person. Under such conditions, the practitioner will never apprehend the secret parts of the client's self, the parts arising out of foundation terrors and sexual identifications that the client labels bad, hateful, selfish, ugly, disgusting, murderous, and so forth. While the client may become quite productive behaviorally to please the practitioner, on a deep level of healing little change will occur.

Furthermore, if disagreements and conflict are avoided, the client's distorted thinking about himself, significant others, and the world remains hidden and unexplored, and hence, uncorrected. The client will also remain guarded interpersonally and will have difficulty utilizing anger in the service of assertiveness. Often the client will blank out defensively in thinking about issues that might trigger anger. Or he or she may play out the anger unconsciously in a more passive manner, i.e., by forgetting to pay the therapist's bill or by coming late to sessions.

When the client experiences and expresses anger toward the practitioner, he or she comes to understand that anger is perfectly acceptable in an intimate relationship. Such an experience affords the client the opportunity for dealing with his or her primitive fears of annihilation of self and/or others, or rejection and abandonment. These terrors usually subside after the client has rage reactions and repeatedly discovers that no one is injured or abandoned. To the client's amazement and relief, he or she finds that anger can be ventilated in a close relationship and that this experience furthers the relationship's maturational process.

The client also comes to be able to resolve any difficulties he or she has with psychological splitting of persons into all good or all bad categories. The client is helped into the real world, in which the therapist is a person with both good and bad parts, who nonetheless is available for relatedness and emotional connection in a consistent manner. This experience will, in turn, be generalized so that significant others will be experienced as consistent love objects having both positive and negative aspects. Ultimately, the client is able to tolerate ambivalence in self and others, and this tolerance is a prerequisite for the capacity to love maturely.

The client's getting in touch with his or her anger is an important enabler in the successful resolution of the dependency that occurs in the first stages of treatment. In the ending phases of treatment, the positive transference upon which the client's dependency rested must be dissolved. The illusion of the therapist's perfection, created by the client, must be realistically dismantled. This, too, parallels the process of growing up in relation to one's parents. As a child matures, he or she develops a sophisticated and critical eye toward his or her parents. The child finds his or her own base of authority and can realistically critique the parental figure. So too, the client, having incorporated what he or she needed from the practitioner, must be able to deal with him or her on a peer level. The process of becoming angry and fighting with the therapist can be viewed as a training ground for the client. Conflict and resolution help the client to find his or her own authority and power base as a separate and independent person. Thus, the elicitation of anger and negative transference is a critical aspect of the regressive strategy.

The Progressive Strategy

In the progressive strategy, the practitioner works transactionally and builds the adult clients' behavioral competence. The practitioner educates, models, programs, goal sets, rewards, and disciplines in a manner that compensates for the deficient parenting the spouses received as children. In this strategy, the therapist utilizes a vision of the potential development of each family member. Working toward that vision, he or she builds chains of new behaviors which promote more successful functioning. This aspect of treatment ultimately results in the clients' growth out of the regressive/dependent position into more autonomous functioning.

In the two-parent family, the most important goal in the progressive strategy is the development of individual competence and spousal teamwork so that the couple can successfully master their various marital, parental, and career roles. In the case of the single-parent or single adult, the therapist focuses on the behavioral transactions in which the client is involved. Children in the family are worked with directly, but they have less contact with the practitioner than the more critical adult members of the family.

Transactional aspects

The practitioner and the spouses plan for movement toward healthy functioning in the rearing, marital, and independent transactions. In the rearing transaction work, programs, directives, and tasks, as well as paradoxical interventions, are used with the family. These are aimed at changing such debilitating homeostatic patterns as severe distantiation or enmeshment, scapegoating, and illicit parent-child coalitions. The CFT growth agent bonds with the spouses, while modifying the rearing transaction through the use of structural (Minuchin, 1974), strategic (Haley, 1976), and other family therapy techniques.

As the rearing transaction becomes more normalized, the practitioner uses similar techniques to move it in the direction of the optimal rearing configuration. He or she programs actively for each parent to be nurturant, disciplining, and programming toward the children in an OSP-SSP triangulation. Parents are helped to form an effective team that can promote each child's full development.

The therapist's position in the triangle of relationships between him- or herself and the spouses is utilized to full advantage. Both spouses are usually in a transference relationship with the therapist and this allows the therapist to build in contractual agreements between the spouses that they can trust. They know that the therapist can facilitate the completion of these contracts. Each spouse can then more optimistically negotiate and trade desired positive behaviors with the other spouse. The therapist may, for example, arrange for a husband to spend time in a sports program with his son in exchange for special attention from his wife.

In working on the marriage, the practitioner reverses homeostatic roles and contracts to provide for the flexible functioning needed at higher levels of marital interaction. Reframing, giving tasks, providing paradoxical interventions, and the like open up new and enhanced ways of relating. The therapist builds up chains of positive reciprocity in the marriage (Stuart, 1980). He or she encourages marital contracts for mutual courtship behavior, and reciprocal prizing and caretaking. The practitioner uses fears of separation and loss strategically to promote greater maturity, investment, and loving behaviors in the marriage. For instance, the therapist may advise a wife to take a vacation alone in order to awaken the complacent husband to the fact of her existence as a separate being. He or she also may triangulate one spouse vis-à-vis another. In this maneuver, the therapist functions as the disciplinarian, while the mate functions as the rapprochement/mediator figure or vice versa, in order to foster learning of disciplinary or nurturing role functions with each other and with the children. The couple learns how to develop their marriage so they can fulfill each other's needs.

Progressive movement in the independent transactions emanates out of work on the spouse's sexual identification. Clients are encouraged to develop their potential for greater productivity and creativity so that they move gradually to more gratifying levels of success and fulfillment. The therapist acts as a coach and mentor in this process. He or she may suggest that clients get further education or develop new assertiveness or risk-taking behaviors. Or the therapist may direct clients to network in order to develop a business so that they can move little by little toward greater independence and generativity. Depending on his or her own areas of expertise, the therapist might help clients with homework, help to structure and organize school or work activities, give some business advice, or prescribe strategic ladder-climbing maneuvers.

As clients grow in behavioral competence, internal changes also begin to occur. This is especially so with triangulation and sexual identification models and programs. For example, as parents team more appropriately to raise children, their expectations and models for how to interact triadically become more congruent with templates for healthier parenting. At the same time, the spouses' original triangulation models begin to fade and have less impact on their behavior.

Sexual identification models also evolve in the direction of gender-congruency, health, and flexibility, as clients become more competent in the three transactions. For example, a depressed father who was reclusive was encouraged to participate in organizations and network with other men who were warm, successful, and creative. Involvement in these groups helped fulfill unmet homoaffiliative longings. The client reported that he felt like "one of the big boys" for the first time in his life.

THE RELATIONSHIP BETWEEN THE PROGRESSIVE AND REGRESSIVE STRATEGIES

The progressive and regressive strategies in CFT support and promote each other, and the practitioner shifts flexibly between them as needed (Stein, 1980). As the practitioner develops transactional behaviors in the progressive mode, each spouse experiences fresh perceptions and suggestions regarding the self and the world that contradict earlier programming. These perceptions, along with direct or indirect suggestions by the therapist, foster more productive activity. New and challenging situations arise that will increase anxiety, trigger dysfunctional programming, and reveal and amplify transferential distortions.

The resultant increased tensions induce the need and enhance motivation for further regressive work.

On the other hand, the depth of feeling and relatedness opened in the regressive work primes the client to accept and internalize hypnotic-like programming for progressive development. And the ventilation of feelings and insight gained in the regressive relationship free energies for ego functioning, so that progressively-oriented behaviors can be actualized.

The dance between progressive and regressive strategies is seen in the following example with a single parent. In the progressive strategy, the therapist encouraged her client, Joan, a 31-year-old depressed housewife, to apply to a graduate program at an Ivy League college. She was accepted and enrolled in a Master's level special education program. With this progressive movement, Joan's old parental programming arose. She began to feel stupid, incompetent, and out of place at school. Rapprochement needs escalated. She asked the practitioner if she could have contact on the phone with her on a daily basis. The practitioner agreed and met her needs in the regressive strategy in a more committed and giving manner. Joan's anxieties quickly abated with this support. She felt more trusting of the therapist, who had come through for her during a crisis. Joan began to do well at school and became more effective with her children. Success led to greater self-esteem, as well as greater openness and receptivity to the therapist.

PROGRESSION OF TREATMENT

When a family enters CFT treatment, any presenting problem is viewed as simply the tip of the iceberg, i.e., only a small manifest portion of the dysfunction in the holon. In order to remediate these problems and prevent symptom substitution or resumption, the major contributory factors to the dysfunction must be corrected. Stein (1980) developed a treatment plan where the main focus of family treatment shifts in a definite pattern as treatment progresses. The three phases of CFT focus on: 1) remediation of the presenting problem and bonding as a reparental figure; 2) work on the spousal self-system structures and the marital transaction; and 3) the development of the intramarital therapeutic coalition. There is considerable overlap at all times among these foci, and in particular, an ongoing dialectical process between work on the transactions and work on the spousal self-systems. Of course, if a couple presents with a marital problem, treatment begins with phase two. If a single adult or a single-parent family presents, treatment starts with phase one, and then moves toward a focus on the self-system of the adult and work on the independent, courtship, and/or rearing transactions.

Phase One

In phase one, the practitioner focuses on the presenting problem and bonds with each spouse or adult client as a parental authority figure. In initial sessions the practitioner meets with all those members of the nuclear client family who are willing to participate in treatment. The practitioner bonds with the family, adopting their language and style. He functions in a basically affirming and benevolent manner and allies with each family member.

The practitioner assesses and schematizes the marital, rearing, and independent transactions, and gains an initial understanding of the adult clients' self-system structures. If needed, he or she then modifies the transaction(s) in which the presenting problem takes place.

The practitioner points out areas of deficiency in each spouse's own rearing that are being replicated in the here and now. In contrast to these deficiencies, the therapist meets positive transference expectations by assuming a remedial/healthy parental demeanor tailored to each spouse. The clients then contract for a reparental relationship with the therapist.

Phase Two

In the intact family such a contract begins phase two, in which the therapist begins to see each spouse individually, or the couple conjointly, on a weekly or bimonthly basis, with other family members brought in as needed for diagnosis or direct therapeutic input. The practitioner develops the structures in the spousal self-systems, while continuing to monitor and elevate the familial transactions.

In these meetings the practitioner develops and refines the remedial/healthy parental posture with each spouse, so that he or she meets their developmental needs at deeper and deeper levels of the self-system. This gives the therapist greater therapeutic leverage in the continued work toward optimal marital, rearing, and independent transactions, which is conducted in a coherent fashion in order to avoid family disorganization or fragmentation.

Working further on the heart of the holon, the practitioner elevates the marital transaction. First he or she completes any further transactional work that is required to bring the relationship to an asymptomatic level. In order to promote the regressive trend in the marriage, the practitioner encourages spouses to emotionally resonate with one another in a context of mutual support and understanding. Simultaneously, the practitioner promotes the couple's positive ambition and competence. The spouses set new standards and goals for themselves and their children, and the practitioner assists them in attaining these goals in a step-by-step fashion.

With the single-parent family and the single adult, the practitioner has worked to elevate the adult client's self-system structures, as well as his or her mastery of career, courtship and/or rearing demands. At the same time, clients are involved in a regressed dependent relationship with the therapist in which they become deeply identified with him or her and introject him or her as an idealized object. They have been asked to change their behaviors not only in the presenting transaction, but also in the courtship and independent transactions.

As the parent/childlike involvement with each spouse or adult client continues, the client matures in a manner paralleling the normal developmental sequences of childhood. The practitioner adjusts the reparental posture accordingly.

Phase Three

When clients achieve enough ego strength and demonstrate that they have incorporated the therapeutic inputs sufficiently to creatively use them on their own, phase three begins; and the thrust changes to mastery of separation. Clients begin to be pushed out of the nest therapeutically in order to further promote self-sufficiency. Clients may attend sessions less frequently. Single clients may be asked to leave treatment on a temporary or permanent basis in order to find and bond with a mate who is growth-promoting.

With intact or remarried families, the practitioner elevates the marital relationship so that it can fulfill the needs that the therapeutic relationship is satisfying. One spouse, or both, may be given a vacation from treatment. Also, during this phase, each mate is encouraged to achieve a healthy degree of psychological separation from the other, so as to be able to function as a quasi-independent growth agent. The therapist will often move the marital system to a more open position, which allows for greater autonomy and individuation for each mate. In this maneuver, the mates undertake independent and risk-taking activities in which they grow in self-appreciation and self-reliance and master their fear of loss of the mate. As they develop as separate individuals, they relate with less conflict or enmeshment and experience greater mutual respect and appreciation. This sets the stage for them to become effective growth agents for each other.

The therapist then actively cultivates PAR growth patterns in the marriage. Enlisting each mate as a therapeutic ally, the practitioner educates each spouse in regard to the partner's psychodynamics and teaches the necessary regressive and progressive inputs that the partner needs to grow and develop. Additionally, both partners are taught how to use the marital relationship to transmute typical negative trans- actions in the family.

Because of previous systemic work, the marital relationship at this time already manifests improved bonding, as well as more extensive and honest communication. The mates are more willing and able to parent intramaritally and thereby help each other overcome personal immaturities that weaken teamwork and stifle achievement. The practi- tioner inspires and encourages the altruism of sincere lovers and de- velops a sense of responsibility on the part of each spouse to help the other toward self-contacting and emotional growth, on one hand, and psychosocial effectiveness and achievement on the other. Consequently, the marital transaction becomes characterized by heightened reciprocal growth pressure and the mutual provision of remedial nurturance, pro- grams, and discipline.

Thus, at the beginning of the final phase of CFT treatment, each spouse has two growth agents: practitioner and partner. As the build- ing of love and work continues, the mates increasingly take over the therapeutic function, and their relationship takes on the charged posi- tive feeling that they had toward the therapist. Easing out of the paren- tal position, the therapist begins to distance him- or herself from the couple. This distancing further promotes the introjection of and identi- fication with the practitioner in a process paralleling that in the healthy young adult leaving home. The spouses become more adept at being mutual growth agents, and the practitioner's role is now that of con- sultant to the client couple. Finally, at termination, the spouses leave on their own path of actualization (Stein, 1980).

CHAPTER 4

Techniques

From the seed grows a root, then a sprout; from the sprout, the seedling leaves; from the leaves, the stem; around the stem, the branches; at the top, the flower . . . We cannot say that the seed causes the growth, nor that the soil does. We can say that the potentialities for growth lie within the seed, in mysterious life forces, which, when properly fostered, take on certain forms.

—Mary Caroline Richards (1964, pp. 36–37)

The CFT practitioner, in dynamic interaction with the client, attunes him- or herself to the client's growth needs. He or she functions as the flexible and healthy parent would, in interaction with the child at different developmental stages. Thus, all techniques emanate from a core of benevolent concern for the client, and much of the therapist's behavior typifies the parental functioning found in nature.

Clients actively seek the correct remedial/healthy reparental inputs and will provide verbal and nonverbal releasers to elicit them. The practitioner adjusts his or her inputs in accord with these releasers, building a reparental stance in a careful manner that is attuned to the clients' signals. There is a specific admixture of remedial/healthy interventions that forms the stance in each case. A stance is usually more nurturant or more disciplinary, but this changes over time as clients mature.

The therapist creates a therapeutic alliance with each adult client through bonding with and regressing each client. He or she then refines the reparental stance by developing the progressive and regressive strategies. Finally the therapist chooses nurturant, programming, transactional, disciplinary, anger-releasing, and paradoxical techniques to implement these strategies. This chapter will present all of these basic CFT techniques.

All techniques in CFT are aimed toward specific goals, based on the clients' needs and desires. Short-term goals include intermediary steps from presenting dysfunction toward more optimal family process. The long-term goal of CFT is healthy family functioning. These goals shape and influence the practitioner's progressive and regressive strategies and techniques.

BONDING

Bonding begins at the initial family interview. When the practitioner meets with the client family, he or she must first engage them in such a way as to be accepted as a quasimember of the group. Then the therapist utilizes regression techniques to foster the needed child/parent bonds.

The practitioner begins by observing the family and then adopting the behavioral style and language that characterize its members. All family members will utilize to some extent a common style and language based on their own particular heritage and shared experiences. As the therapist follows suit, he or she gains status as a quasimember of the group. The therapist interacts in a warm and empathic manner with each family member. This demonstrates that he or she is flexible and dedicated to health, which is independent of any alliance with a particular family member.

The adult members of the family are, of course, the most important figures targeted for bonding. Each spouse will have his or her own sensory processing modes (Bandler & Grinder, 1975). He or she will tend to process experiences with greater emphasis on the visual, auditory, or kinesthetic modalities. Primary sensory modes are indicated by the spouses' particular use of verbs and other parts of speech. The client may "be in the dark, and unable to see things clearly," "hear the death knell sound," or "feel the weight of the family problems." The practitioner, in order to deepen bonds with these critical family members, must be highly attentive to and speak in a manner congruent with these personal characteristics. He or she must use tailored sensory-based terminology, i.e., describe things in terms of visual, auditory, or kinesthetic aspects when addressing members who are respectively visual, auditory, or kinesthetic processors.

Nonverbally, the practitioner must use similar vocal tones and expressions, and mimic the behavioral movements and breathing patterns of each spouse. Such symmetry and relatedness forms the bedrock of a parent-child relationship. Stern (1971) has demonstrated this in the sequences of mother-infant interaction that he videotaped and observed in slow motion. In his study, mothers and infants related in a highly synchronized dance with accompanying vocal patterns.

Another way to establish a reparental therapeutic alliance is by providing a smorgasbord of mild nurturing, disciplinary, and programming techniques. The practitioner then observes the clients' responses closely, alert for nonverbal tropisms and verbal reactions. Clients will indicate that the therapist's input is correct by orienting toward the therapist, making eye contact, and becoming attentive and receptive. Delighted laughter or further self-disclosure are often additional cues. Verbalizations that are essentially affirming of the practitioner and indicative of need fulfillment also point to the correctness of the therapeutic posture.

However, if clients orient away from the therapist, continually avoid eye contact, or change the subject, they are signaling the practitioner to change or modify his stance. Laughter or verbal comments that are invalidating toward the therapist are further confirmations of a "miss."

Tears, coupled with the clients' verbal messages, orient the therapist to recognize his success or failure in meeting clients' needs. Clients may cry and indicate that they are shedding tears of gratitude for a specific input, which is clearly a "hit," or they may begin to disclose real grief and pain. For example, a nurturant approach with a man who was abusive to both his wife and son elicited his slumping down in his chair and looking out of the window. No releasers from the client were provided to the therapist and this was read as a "miss." Later, disciplinary confrontation with the man provoked tears and disclosure of self-hate and feelings of inadequacy. This was the first time that the client had given the therapist congruent nonverbal and verbal messages. These behaviors indicated that he could benefit from some confrontation.

Of course, this method of calibrating therapeutic interventions is utilized throughout the treatment process to refine and develop the therapeutic stance. Reparental interventions that are repeated "hits" result eventually in the client's ability to deliver the same types of input to a spouse or a child. There is a chaining effect in which the therapist's stance is internalized as a model by the client, thus broadening his or her behavioral repertoire.

REGRESSION

The second stage of the bonding process is regression. As the therapist's directives to the family are accepted and change occurs, he begins to gain status in their eyes. He is perceived first as authority, then as a part of the family, and finally as a parental figure. The type of regression desired is always initially one with a positive transference. Thus, almost all regression techniques are done in a nurturant and benevolent manner. Most clients are regressed both indirectly and directly by the therapist's programming. Indirect techniques are generally utilized in the beginning phase of treatment with direct techniques added later. Some clients who experience childlike feelings or needs as weak, bad, or reprehensible, or those who are fearful of engulfment can only respond to indirect regression.

Techniques for Indirect Regression

There are three basic techniques for indirect regression: the "if" icon; the therapist/client transactional techniques; and role play or decentering.

In the "*if*" *icon* technique, the therapist verbally describes inviting images of remedial/healthy parent-child interaction that could have taken place between them. Special attention is paid to sensory-based detail in the imagery, with emphasis on the client's own major sensory modalities. Thus, a single mother who had been emotionally abandoned by her mother and processed experience auditorially was given the following icon: "If I had been your mother, we would have baked chocolate chip cookies together in the afternoon. I would have sung a little song to you while we waited for them to finish baking." This type of an icon immediately elicits longings for and participation in the experience as if it were happening or had happened in the past. The client may respond with a comment like, "I wish you had been my mother!" Whereupon the therapist can reply with something like, "I could be like a mother to you."

Transactional regression is an indirect technique that occurs in at least part of every CFT session. The therapist assumes a parental manner, both verbally and nonverbally, in dealing with clients. Body language is generally authoritative, and gestures are made with parental concern and involvement. A therapist might, for instance, pat a client's head, or put an arm around the client's shoulder. Verbally, clients may be given diminutive pet names that are special and delightful to them. At times, the therapist may use vocal tones that are higher and more musical and intimate, much like a mother might use in addressing her child. Or the therapist might use childlike terminology and say things like, "No one kissed your boo boo." The therapist, of course, uses these methods experimentally, gauging whether clients are ready to go with the suggestions or not. Clients often quickly respond to such transactional regression in a warm and inviting manner.

Decentering is the third indirect regression technique. The spouse is asked to take on a child role in a demonstrative role play with the therapist. The client may be asked to play the part of his or her children or a subordinate at work. The therapist then moves in, impacting on the client in an intimate and powerful manner. The client, who is decentered from a normal role, finds him- or herself in a safe, "not real" situation. In this state the client can directly experience the practitioner as a parent, without the fears that such a relationship with a therapist might bring up. In the hypnotic state of the role play, the client can find that plasticity of role is not as difficult or uncomfortable as anticipated. Often, the client quickly finds the role play enjoyable. He or she can then absorb parental inputs and regress further into a more trusting relationship.

Techniques for Direct Regression

A more direct method of regression is the technique of direct suggestion, which is usually used somewhat later in treatment. The therapist gives a direct suggestion to the spouse (and him- or herself) regarding their roles in the therapeutic transaction. Thus, he or she can say to a client, when appropriate, "You're only five years old" or "I am your father and your mother!" Or, building up positive transference, the therapist may say, "I'm the best father in the whole world for you right now." The spouse will usually indicate verbally and nonverbally that he or she is willing to participate in this shared fantasy.

Since the experience is hypnotic in nature, the therapist can take the role of either a father or a mother, regardless of his or her actual gender. If clients require corrective homoaffiliative or heteroaffiliative interventions, the therapist, calling upon those more masculine or feminine aspects of him- or herself, can create the proper therapeutic stance in spite of biology.

For example, a female therapist took a more masculine posture in conjoint and individual sessions with a depressed 34-year-old man who had lost his father at an early age. She was more forceful, more demanding, and louder in her therapeutic role, using male mannerisms that were more intrusive, sharp, and direct. In one conjoint session, she used her pen to make a point and told him that someday, as the chairman of the board of his own company, he might use a cigar in a similar way.

The therapist must be especially alert and sensitive to signs from the client that indicate whether or not he or she is on target with regression techniques. Attempting to regress a client can backfire on the therapist if the client feels belittled or insulted. Signs welcoming regressive input include more verbal and nonverbal relatedness, i.e., greater eye contact and body mirroring, more self-disclosure, or at times direct verbal reinforcement (as in, "I love it when you say you're my mother"). Most indicative of successful regression, of course, is childlike behavior, which the client usually demonstrates for short periods directly after regressive inputs. A client may become wide-eyed, free, and giggling, call the therapist "Mom" or "Dad," or verbally report that he or she feels like a son or daughter to the therapist. At times, a client may remain regressed throughout an entire session, curled up on the therapist's couch, or otherwise maintaining a childlike demeanor. Of course, in these instances the therapist makes a particular effort to promote mature behavior outside the office.

NURTURANCE

Nurturance is an important tool in the regressive strategy. The paradigm of nurturance is to be found in the mother-infant dyad. It is similar to bonding. The practitioner functions in a fully attentive state, examining the client with delighted discovery. Meditating on the client, he or she enjoys the innocence and beauty inherent in the client's being. Unconditional positive regard forms the bedrock of nurturance.

However, validation of the client is limited as a technique in elevating self-esteem if the therapist does not understand the client. The practitioner must explore the client's inner reality, going over intrapsychic programs and models with him or her. Exploration of dreams and fantasies is an important aspect of this process. The therapist may offer interpretations that are analytic in nature. Client and therapist explore hidden impulses and affect. The practitioner identifies with the client and resonates empathically with feeling states he or she experiences with regard to these issues. For instance, the therapist may cry with a client. Through such inputs, the client feels deeply understood and accepted as a human being.

Active behavioral inputs are also needed to nurture most clients. These components are largely nonverbal and affirming and affectionate in nature. Active nurturant acts such as beaming or smiling at the client, or stroking a client's cheek can go a long way toward enhancing self-esteem and quelling basic terrors. Nurturance remediates foundation deficits. The client experiences a sense of oneness and psychological fusion with a significant other, which assuages abandonment terrors and gives a sense of belongingness in the world. As successful nurturance takes place, engulfment and annihilation terrors ebb.

In nurturing clients, there is some courting on the therapist's part.

The courtship is the nonsexualized or quasicourting of the parent (Scheflen, 1974). The therapist maintains warmth and rapport, defining their relationship as a nonsexual "love affair of the heart."

At times, however, clients become involved in oedipal or electra fantasies and can become seductive with the therapist. The therapist's job with these clients is similar to that of the opposite-sex parent's task in the family. He or she must reassure the clients in terms of their attractiveness, but must firmly establish that their involvement will never be sexual, primary, or permanent.

With the few clients who require a very nurturant stance at the beginning of treatment, the therapist functions much as a mother would with a very young child. He or she is psychologically fused with the client, looking at the world from the client's point of view. A more protective stance is taken in which others are viewed more critically in terms of their interactions with the client. The client is oriented to be with people who strongly appreciate and value him or her. Of course, over time, as the client matures, the practitioner will be more demanding in terms of the client's taking responsibility for creating negative interactions with others.

PROGRAMMING

Programming is much like the kind of informal hypnosis that occurs in all families. As Laing and Esterson (1971) have pointed out, children are raised in a trancelike state vis-à-vis their parents. In this state, they are programmed regarding themselves and the world. One artist illustrated the process of programming well when he said, "When I was a child my mother said to me, 'If you become a soldier, you'll be a general. If you become a monk, you'll end up the Pope.' Instead, I became a painter and wound up as Picasso" (Gilot & Lake, 1964, p. 60).

In CFT, positive programming actually involves the practitioner's highlighting of the morphogenic thrust inherent in symptomatic behavior. Symptoms are the result of a combination of homeostatic mechanisms aimed at maintaining the pathogenic status quo and growth-seeking behaviors that are ineffective in promoting change. By focusing on and fostering the growth-seeking aspects, the practitioner allows them to come to the fore.

Programming can be targeted toward three areas: the definition of the self; the description of the world; and one's behaviors, attitudes, and values. In CFT, the therapist helps redefine the client's self-image in the direction of enhanced value, competence, and attractiveness. The world is described in a positive, yet realistic fashion. Clients' negative view-points are worked with and transformed in the direction of a healthy view of the world – as a place that is basically safe, challenging, and full of opportunities and stimuli for growth. Programming of behavior can involve the giving of advice, instruction, or tasks. All of these programs are used in the progressive strategy to remediate dysfunction in the marital, rearing, or independent transactions.

Programming elevates clients step by step toward optimal transactional functioning. For example, the father who is distant from his son might first be programmed to simply spend time with him. He would then be given a task that involved instructing or guiding his son in one or two areas of living, such as teaching him how to drive a car. Finally, he would be instructed to fully assume the role of programmer and disciplinary parent with his son. His wife would then take a complementary role as nurturer and facilitator.

First-Order and Second-Order Programs

Programs can be first order or second order in nature. First-order programs include direct education, task giving, and advice, as well as more elaborate direct hypnotic suggestions. In these elaborate suggestions, detailed pictures or icons are depicted for clients. Attention is paid to accentuating aspects of the program in the client's primary sensory modality. For example, a client who processes experience auditorally might be provided with the following: "You can lead your business people like an orchestra. A swish of your baton and the horn section rings out beautifully. A gesture to the back of the orchestra and the cymbals resound!"

Second-order or implied programming consists of verbal and non-verbal messages given to the client that are based on the therapist's own experience of the client. Second-order programming is indirect. The therapist develops an inner model of the client as he or she might be if fully actualized in a competent and relational state. The therapist then relates to the client as if the latter had in fact achieved such a level of functioning. Often the therapist gives the client-as-he-could-be a name that summarizes the special and attractive qualities he or she could possess.

For instance, a passive and shy young father might be dubbed "Rocky," after the cultural boxing hero. During a session, the therapist might engage in a mock boxing match with him, ending with an interaction in which he holds the young man's hand aloft in victory.

In attempting to provide positive programming for a client, the practitioner must be adept at reading cues that indicate a hit or a miss in his interventions. When programming is being incorporated into self-system structures, the client enters a hypnotic reverie, manifesting certain behavioral signs. These include unconscious and conscious eye and body movements, which "dance" along with the imagery. Verbalizations that follow from the imagery are important indicators also. When a client provides such cues, the practitioner's programming is correctly aligned with the client's own dreams and visions for the future.

Inspiration

When the practitioner finds the right type of programming for a client, he or she can become inspirational with it. Inspiration is provided by a high degree of affect. The client follows the therapist's lead and attaches a high emotional cathexis to the suggestions. The intensity of the programming is amplified, which facilitates a client's recreating the scene in the world in a symbolic or real way. For example, if the therapist working with "Rocky" allows loud and intense excitement into his voice while lifting his client's hand high "in front of the cheering crowd," the client is likely to become excited and thrilled emotionally by the scene. He will be more motivated to go out and symbolically create it in his life.

Relabeling and Reframing

Relabeling and reframing (Watzlawick, 1978) are programming techniques that are especially effective when used in sessions attended by more than one family member. Reframing involves the redefinition of a context or a relationship in the transaction. Relabeling involves the redefinition of a family member and his motivation or goals. Usually these techniques redefine negatives into positives, although the reverse also occurs with regularity. For example, a wife who was actively psychotic was relabeled as the caretaker and guardian angel by the therapist. He explained to her husband that she actually wanted him to feel more comfortable and not threatened by issues in their marriage. The wife became more lucid and agreed to take care of her husband in a more competent manner.

Similarly a chaotic family with out-of-control children received a reframe of their situation as a rudderless ship which was really meant to get to journey's end. The reframe enhanced their interest and motivation to connect to each other and to the therapist, as captain.

Appropriateness of Programming to Client's Developmental Needs

Programming, as with all other reparental interventions, must be appropriate to the client's developmental needs. For example, we can follow the progression of second-order programming through the provision of gifts from the therapist to a single woman who had no deeply nurturant relationships. In the initial phase, programming for bonding with the therapist, and acceptance of attachment needs was done by giving the client a small teddy bear, "which could go everywhere" with her. Later in the treatment, she was given a large piece of cheese, which was "milk" that she could take with her to "eat." A year later, she was given a pair of earrings and a manicure, which programmed her for a positive female sexual identification. She was then given a second teddy bear to reassure her that rapprochement needs would still be met. Finally, two-and-a-half years after starting treatment, the woman was given a champagne toast to celebrate her marital engagement, a rewarding event that carried the program for the successful resolution of oedipal level issues – a message to go forward and celebrate life as a mature woman.

Anchoring

Programming, in order to be effective must be anchored, or congruent with some aspect of the client's self-definition. The client must be able to believe in the possibility of the programmed behaviors and self-system definition, even if only in terms of entering a pleasant hypnotic reverie with the practitioner. If this is not the case, the therapist's programming will not be accepted. Thus, programming must always start with some aspect of the client's behavior or family-of-origin programs. This material is elaborated on or reframed to become new dreams for the client.

For example, a depressed mother and housewife was raised by a woman who was an aspiring actress turned alcoholic. When this client was younger, her mother had a series of modeling photographs taken of her daughter. She later was unable to actualize this dream for her daughter in any way. The therapist asked the woman's husband to find the photographs and bring them to one of the couple's sessions. The therapist then propped them up around the office and repeatedly discussed the "fact" that this was the "real" client, a "star of life." She went on to describe how she had visions of the wife walking into the room, radiant, poised, alive, and vivacious, so that all eyes were on her. As the therapist allowed herself to engage in this reverie, the client laughed delightedly and began to behave playfully as though she were actually in the scene, offering her hand in a gracious manner to the therapist. Over time the client's identification as the star was repeatedly played out in interactions with the therapist and the woman's husband. As it became incorporated, the woman's demeanor and affect became lighter, more poised, and vibrant.

When clients have little in the way of positive programs from the past for the therapist to draw on, the therapist may use an associative technique in which the pathogenic behavior or self-definition is paired with healthy behaviors or definitions, often using relabeling. For example, a negativistic and self-critical father, obsessed with his own inadequacy as well as that of his children, was programmed to be the "champion loser." The concept of champion was then tied to his obsessive negative ruminations. Over time the "champion" aspects of the self-definition were redeveloped into a purely positive self-definition.

Use of Programming in the Regressive and Progressive Strategies

Programming is used in both the regressive and the progressive treatment strategies. In the regressive strategy, the programming is used to regress clients in relation to the therapist and to promote positive transference. The positive transference facilitates both the identification with the therapist and the development of positive self-system structures.

In the progressive strategy, the client is given tasks and programmed to seek success and love in the various behavioral transactions. Sexual identification is transformed so that the client experiences him- or herself as more competent and relationally able. Triangulation models are moved toward the optimal configuration. This progressive thrust results eventually in the client's maturity and independence from the therapist.

TRANSACTIONAL TECHNIQUES

In CFT, structural and strategic family therapy techniques (Stanton, 1981) can be given from either a nurturant or a disciplinary stance. With the added reparental overtones, these interventions have an amplified impact on the client family. Family therapy techniques include: transactional vivification; task giving, either in or outside of sessions; role play; role reversal; role prescription; and the paradoxical techniques of symptom prescription or amplification.

Transactional Vivification

In transactional vivification, a description is given to the family in the form of an image or picture of the members and their current interactions. A symbolic metaphor is used to summarize information about the family as a whole, its members, and their interaction, so that family members can view and experience themselves in a different way. Metaphors are particularly useful because they speak to the unconscious as well as the conscious mind. For example, an ineffective, weak mother, who presented with two older girls who fought each other with kitchen knives, was told after she minimized the problem that she was "Little Bo Peep who doesn't realize that her sheep have turned to wolves — snarling, snapping, and on the attack! Out for blood!" This statement was delivered in a strong disciplinary stance, with the therapist face to face with the client. After the therapist continued on in this vein, the mother was able to see the gravity of the problem and contracted for therapy.

Task Giving

Task giving, an important technique in the progressive strategy, involves the prescription of certain behaviors that are to be performed in a time-limited fashion. Tasks are aimed at restructuring or strategically changing transactions, and usually involve new and ego alien behaviors. For example, in a case in which marital disagreements were manifested through a scapegoated child, the parents were encouraged to jointly script out a five-minute show to be put on by the problem child every day at the time that was usually most problematic. Or in another case, the parents were instructed paradoxically to be sure to have horrible fights with the child precisely at bedtime. In both situations, the presenting problems were alleviated and the couples' marital issues surfaced.

Clients will usually offer resistance to a task through reality-based and/or habitual excuses. Both must be overcome by the therapist so that there is firm agreement, generally from all parties involved in the transaction, that the task will be accomplished. The therapist, with the spouses, proposes solutions to reality-based problems. If agreement about performing the task is not reached, the therapist might proceed to confront the clients in order to forge the mini contract.

For example, a disengaged father claimed that he worked a swing shift and could not make time for his son. The therapist insisted that his son needed him and found 15 minutes in the morning for them to spend together. When the father still protested, the therapist raised his voice and said, "Don't be self-centered like your father was with you! Your son needs you!" Resistance to performance of the task was already weakened because it was to be only of a short duration. The therapist took full advantage of this, pointing out to the father that only 15 minutes of his time was required. The father agreed and followed through on the task.

After the task is agreed to, the interactions will often take place, although not entirely as prescribed. In some instances, natural morphogenic processes take over, and the prescribed behaviors last beyond the time limit. For example, when the disengaged father mentioned above was instructed to play baseball with his son for 10 minutes, he often played for 30 or 40 minutes because he found that he enjoyed the activity so much. Similarly, when a husband is given the task of courting his wife with gifts of flowers and candy on one evening, he may repeat it for several evenings.

On the other hand, the new behavior may appear in some halfhearted or even negative fashion. It is the therapist's job to provide adequate follow-through by discussing the experience and providing educative refinement of the interaction. If needed, he or she may use disciplinary techniques to help the clients integrate the interaction into the natural routine of family life. If such follow-through is not given, the new behaviors, even if enjoyed and pursued initially, will be extinguished by the homeostatic forces in the family.

In the independent transactional progression, tasks are often given out sequentially, so that clients master higher and higher level challenges. So, for example, a father who works as a laborer may first be instructed to take a night course at a high school, and then to study for a high school equivalency diploma. Next, he would be asked to take the equivalency test, and then to take one course at a trade school. The next task would be the challenge of completing a full course of training in the trade school. Finally, he would have to find a job where he could use his new skills.

Role Reversal and Role Prescription

Role reversal can be extremely useful in the marital work. Such a progressive maneuver throws homeostatic contracts into a full-tilt reversal, loosening up rigid sequences of behaviors and jarring rigid and delimiting sexual identifications. Two family members cannot occupy the same position at the same time in the family script. As one mate usurps the other's role, he or she helps the other to change as well.

Role reversal can result in much transactional and/or intrapsychic growth. Each spouse views his or her own behavior from a different perspective and is awakened to new possibilities in the mate's behavior. Intrapsychic strengths and weaknesses are discovered, and the stage is set for new levels of knowledge of self and other, as well as new patterns of behavioral exchange.

For example, a constricted and intellectualized husband was instructed to react impulsively when his feelings were hurt, by throwing dishes around, emptying drawers, and threatening to leave, as his wife typically did. The wife, on the other hand, was encouraged to sit quietly and knit. As they began to do this, the spouses started talking to one another instead of repeating a useless transactional pattern. The wife felt pleased and powerful in her new position of self-control. By being controlled and steadfast, she had integrated a part of her masculine identity. The husband, on the other hand, began to get in touch with the feminine part of himself. He cultivated an appreciation for the depth of his own emotions and his need for relatedness.

Role prescription is a progressive strategy in which the spouses are instructed to assume ongoing complementary roles with each other and/or the children. The therapist describes and models these roles for the spouses.

Role reversal and prescription are similar to task giving, but the behaviors are less discrete and not time-limited. Rather, the behaviors are ongoing and subject to the client's own interpretation of proper role function. Therapeutic follow-through, with educative refinement and, if needed, discipline, is necessary to ensure that role prescriptions are actually carried out.

For example, a husband agreed to function as a remedial father figure in assisting his wife with her independent transactions. He obtained a night school brochure and helped her enroll in a psychology course. However, he accused his wife of being lazy when she received a C as her first grade. The therapist, upon hearing this sequence, applauded the husband for his efforts, but stepped in to correct and educate him in regard to his abusive disciplining of his wife.

Often clients are instructed to play a role at school or at work in their independent transactions. A young woman who was a student in graduate school was asked to function as a star pupil. She sat at the front of her class but made no comments on the professor's lecture. The practitioner learned of this, and instructed her to participate in class and also engage the professor in less formal discourse before or after class. They agreed that if she did not complete this part of the role prescription at a given class, she wold be fined $25.

DISCIPLINE

Discipline is the provision of punishment and rewards aimed at assisting clients to achieve behavioral or intrapsychic goals. It is a potent therapeutic technique when utilized by a well-trained and supervised psychotherapist.

Discipline has been discussed in the family therapy literature most recently by Haley (1984), who described his work along with that of Milton Erickson. In Haley's "ordeal therapy," the therapist functions as a skilled technician who chooses and prescribes ordeals, such as scrubbing floors, which are to occur after symptomatic behavior. The client will often give up the symptom to be free of the ordeal. The technique rather than the relationship is considered by Haley to be paramount in helping the client.

Benefits of Discipline

In contradistinction to Haley, discipline in CFT is viewed as an integral part of the therapeutic relationship. It is utilized to both deepen the relationship with the practitioner and help clients mature. Discipline shapes clients' ego functioning, just as it does that of children. This is a particularly important process with clients who are dissociated from reality. They find that their actions have real consequences and that they truly exist in the context of interpersonal relationships. Their relationship with the practitioner then becomes more real, and more of a focus for them. Additionally, when discipline occurs, a host of reactive feelings, including sadness and anger, may erupt in clients, which tend to add intensity to the therapeutic relationship.

Discipline promotes self-reflection and introspection. For example, as the therapist delineated the nature of a broken agreement with a father, the man marshalled excuses and defensive arguments. The therapist then helped the client view and understand more clearly the process by which he shirked responsibilities.

Discipline also functions as a very powerful means of indirect programming. If the therapist disciplines a client in regard to accomplishing a task, this conveys an embedded message that he or she truly believes that the client can, in fact, accomplish this feat. The client, in turn, comes to believe in him- or herself in a similar manner.

Discipline is a particularly important technique in CFT work. Because clients are gratified in terms of the needs for dependency and nurturance, they can easily become "stuck," relating to the practitioner and fearful of growth in their behavioral functioning in the world. When nurturance and positive programming fail to produce change, discipline is needed. Clients make use of the programming received from the practitioner and move to new levels of mastery. When a client is successful, he or she finds a new level of identity with the practitioner. Positive transference experienced toward the practitioner becomes turned toward the self. Self-love and self-esteem rise.

The therapist's use of discipline in treatment also proves constructive for clients in another way. The practitioner must demonstrate bulldogged determination and follow-through in order to discipline successfully. This provides an important modeling experience for clients. They learn to be assertive and achieve results in endeavors in the world.

Preconditions for Discipline

Discipline is never given to clients unless certain preconditions have been met. These include: bonding with the practitioner; a solid contract for ongoing treatment; and a firm parental relationship with clients in which the practitioner is seen as a benevolent agent assisting the clients to achieve their goals.

If these conditions have not been met, discipline can have adverse or even disastrous clinical effects. Clients can experience the discipline as an attack or an abandonment, or fall into strong negative transference, where the practitioner is seen as the bad, hateful, or destructive parent. Clients can suffer lowered self-esteem or increased symptomatology. And they may terminate treatment.

This almost never occurs, however, if the therapist has first bonded with and nurtured clients and then slowly introduced the discipline. The practitioner sets the stage by defining discipline and describing how such input will help. At this point clients are usually very quick to indicate their acceptance or rejection of discipline from the therapist. Often they will directly ask for discipline with statements like, "I need a kick in the pants" or "I wish I was held accountable." The therapist can then promise to fulfill these needs, agreeing to verbally admonish or otherwise discipline clients when needed.

In order for discipline to be effective, the problem behaviors must be well-defined and clear, and the clients must be committed to changing them. The therapist must also be committed to altering the dysfunctional behaviors. He or she must maintain vigilance past the testing-of-limits stage, during which clients may fail to do agreed-upon tasks, and then look to see whether there will be therapeutic follow-through.

Disciplinary Approach

Of course, disciplinary interventions, along with all other reparental techniques, are provided in a fashion tailored to compensate for deficiencies and dysfunctions originating in the family of origin. Clients who have been abused will generally receive little or no discipline, or discipline through fear of loss. Clients who have received little discipline growing up need a variety of disciplinary interventions.

Effective discipline does not involve rejection of the client, but rather rejection of unwanted behaviors. There is ongoing positive regard for the person of the client while discipline takes place.

Forms of Discipline

Punishments can range from verbal confrontation and expression of the practitioner's displeasure and anger, to the fulfillment of unpleasant punitive tasks, or the loss of attention or contact with the practitioner. In verbal confrontation, the practitioner delineates in vivid fashion, often using unpleasant metaphors, the client's self-destructive behavior. For example, a self-absorbed and undermining woman might be told that she is acting like a black widow spider in her marriage.

Displeasure, sadness, and disappointment are other forms of discipline. Clients who are in positive transference often react with feelings of guilt and a wish to do better when the therapist honestly indicates a sense of being let down by them. Induction of guilt is another disciplinary technique, often used with more psychopathic clients. The therapist delineates their destructive behaviors at great length and ends with programming them to develop a sense of conscience and mortality.

Anger can be a useful disciplinary tool. Many clients are frightened of the expression of anger and so it serves as a good motivator. In addition, the practitioner's use of anger provides clients with a role model who can be honestly and constructively angry. In order to be effective, the practitioner must allow real feelings to emerge, which he or she can then amplify in a controlled fashion.

Thus, when a masochistic wife reported that she had slept with her husband who had mentally and physically abused her, the practitioner paced around the room, loudly exclaiming, "I'm furious with you! Absolutely furious!" She then moved in face to face and shouted, "You're too good for that! Too good!" Or, after a fearful client refused to attend a job interview, the practitioner yelled out suddenly, "You were afraid! Now I'm so angry with you, my anger is bigger than your fear. I am seething! Don't you ever, ever, ever pull this again!"

In another form of discipline, the therapist may ask for an agreement for fulfillment of a task, which carries a specific punishment for non-compliance. The therapist may simply propose the agreement outright or may suggest, as Haley (1984) does, that he or she knows of something that will definitely solve the client's problem, but refuses to discuss it unless the client agrees beforehand to comply. The client is tantalized with the promised solution and agrees to cooperate with the plan. The task can be an unpleasant activity, which is something the client feels he or she should be doing, or it can simply be an unpleasant task that is morally acceptable and not self-deprecating.

For example, a client may agree to stop buying marijuana, with the understanding that if he breaks this agreement he will have to donate to charity double the amount of the money spent on drugs. Often the therapist will write up these agreements on his or her stationery and have the client sign them. This clarifies both the nature of the problem behavior and the task, in addition to giving the contract a formal and legal quality. It also provides the therapist with a tool to hold the client accountable when and if he or she attempts to rationalize forgetting or bowing out of the contract.

Fear of loss of the therapist provides another avenue for discipline that is extremely potent, since the practitioner's attention and nurturance are highly valued. Thus, removal of attention, refusal to discuss certain issues, abrupt termination of a phone call, or even cancellation of a session can become potent maneuvers. Fear-of-loss techniques are very useful with clients who ruminate obsessively in unproductive monologues. The practitioner may inform the client that he or she is bored or may proceed to stare out of the office window.

In one clinical situation, a fearful client clung to phone contact with the practitioner, claiming that she "couldn't" ask her boss for a raise — a task she had agreed to complete. She was told to "Do it!" with a resounding hang-up of the phone.

Techniques such as these are, of course, potentially dangerous, and are not to be used without proper supervision. When the practitioner utilizes these maneuvers, clients often become extremely angry. However, if the technique is used in a sophisticated fashion in the context of a benevolent treatment framework, clients usually become remorseful and quickly correct their behaviors. Later they are quite thankful to the therapist.

ANGER-RELEASING TECHNIQUES

In addition to providing nurturance and rewards, the therapist usually must, at some point in treatment, help release the clients' anger and negative transference. In order to do this, the therapist has to be in touch with his or her own countertransference. The practitioner needs to feel in control of the clinical situation and to deal with his or her own anxiety regarding anger and verbal attack. He or she must also be ready and able to deal with feelings of inadequacy that may arise from the clients' confrontations.

Finally, the therapist must be ready to honestly admit error, while sorting out clients' distorted accusations and thinking. Only when the therapist has satisfied these criteria should he or she actively encourage expression of anger and negative transference in the relationship. Preparation for this has occurred throughout treatment. The therapist frames anger as a feeling that is healthy and helpful to the treatment process.

Clients are told that they will not be allowed to injure either themselves or the practitioner or destroy anything in the practitioner's office. Anger is to be felt and verbalized, complete with violent terminology or imagery, but not acted upon. The therapist discusses how the therapeutic relationship will not be destroyed by the honest expression of anger. The practitioner explains how primitive fears of annihilation of self and/or others, or feelings of rejection and abandonment will flare, and that he or she will help the clients overcome them.

Another potent strategy in bringing out anger and negative transferences is echoing the client's inner reality. This technique is used only when the client has developed sufficient ego strength and self-love to allow him or her to permit the therapist to become his or her alter ego. Usually this strategy is used in the latter part of treatment when the client is deeply bonded with the practitioner as a benevolent, reparental figure.

The practitioner, then, in a paradoxical maneuver begins to voice some of the negative inner dialogue of the client. This has freeing and widespread benefit. The client can emerge from his or her private inner sanctum and explore those impulses and feelings that he or she formerly dreaded and kept hidden. The client generally becomes angry and ventilates these feelings to the practitioner. Finally, the client, no longer having to assume the self-accusatory role, starts to argue with the practitioner about all the positive qualities he, the client, actually possesses. Often there is a complete role reversal, whereby the client argues that he or she is worthwhile, good, unselfish, and so forth, while the practitioner verbalizes some of the exact deprecating words the client had used to describe him- or herself. The client then comes to own his or her own valuable qualities in a firm and real way.

For example, a female client came a half hour late to a session, bearing a large gift-wrapped box for her therapist. She reported that she was so excited about bringing this gift that she had lost her way coming to the session, even though she had been to that office at least 30 times. The practitioner suspected that the gift was not being given wholeheartedly, but rather as some type of reparation. She refused to take the gift and began calling the woman mindless, a quality of "craziness" that the woman was terrified about manifesting. The client yelled back, in a transference reaction, accusing the practitioner of being like her mother, cold and rejecting. She then went on to say that the therapist had been 10 minutes late for several sessions, which in her distorted thinking meant that she was "worthless and like a dog" to the therapist. She kept the gift and stormed out of the office.

The therapist phoned her later, discussed the realities of the therapeutic interplay with her, and applauded her for being brave and real. Three months later, the therapist had a session with the woman in which she referred to her as a "dog." The woman immediately defended herself, proclaiming her strength and importance. Once again, the therapist congratulated her for asserting herself.

PARADOX

Inherent in the separation/individuation process, in which the individual moves away from parents and into the world to define himself as an autonomous person, we find natural oppositional tendencies. Paradoxical techniques that play on these tendencies can be extremely useful in promoting change and are generally used in CFT when direct programming and disciplining have met with failure at remediating behavioral or intrapsychic problems. At that point, symptom prescription or symptom prediction and amplification may be useful.

As with all CFT techniques, paradox emanates from a reparental stance and can be either disciplinary or nurturant in nature. A disciplinary paradox carries the bonus of the clients' anger to help propel them full force into the countervailing position. For example, the practitioner used symptom amplification in a powerful fashion when she told a single mother who maintained a relationship with a dependent drug addict, "You go waste yourself on that man. Go on! Make sure you spend every last penny on him. Sell your favorite gold necklace so he can buy some smack! And be sure to have your son call him dad. That way, your son will wind up like him." Or with another family in which a father refused to control his alcoholic, acting-out adolescent son, the therapist predicted the symptom in a disciplinary way, exclaiming, "You'll be at his funeral soon! He'll crash his car head on into someone else one night after a rock concert. You'll be there with blood on your hands when they lower his coffin into the ground!"

Nurturant paradoxical interventions come from a nurturant benevolent mode and are often infantilizing in nature. For example, a therapist told a "helpless" and indulgent mother that her defiant children were too difficult for her to handle and that she ought to stay in her bedroom and rest all day rather than interact with them. The woman rebelled, insisting that she could handle the children.

When clients "bounce back" from paradoxical interventions, they may simply start acting in a healthy manner. At other times clients may ask the therapist for assistance. The therapist can then recontract with them for change in a more potent manner. The therapist may not agree to discuss the matter until the clients prove their intentions by fulfilling specific, healthy tasks. Or the therapist may have clients sign agreements regarding the new healthy behaviors which carry punitive tasks for nonperformance.

For example, when the indulgent mother who was paradoxically told to ignore her misbehaving children wished to "emerge," she insisted that the therapist show her how to interact with and discipline her children. The therapist then asked her to prove her intentions by removing the children's toy chests. He agreed to discuss further disciplinary measures only at that point. When the mother complied, he then had her sign an agreement that she would post their chores on the refrigerator and chart their performance daily, with the stipulation that if she missed a day she would be fined $15. This money was to be sent to the local reform school each week in expectation of her children's future enrollment there.

THE USE OF TECHNIQUES IN CFT

In general, the practitioner must be extremely flexible and will use most of the above techniques to various degrees with every client. Only a small percentage of the client population requires a stance that is purely nurturant or disciplinary in nature. In these cases there has been extreme pathology or indulgence in the family of origin.

A technique or stance is correct when it produces results. Effective nurturance results in increased self-esteem and congruent changes in behaviors. Correct programming produces positive behavioral change, although this is often accompanied by intrapsychic upset. And proper disciplinary follow-through results in positive behavior change and the clients' gaining a sense of accomplishment, although they may experience some intrapsychic conflict. If clients manifest increasing anxiety, depression, or other symptomatology, with no constructive behavioral movement, this indicates that the practitioner has taken a stance that is fundamentally incorrect. When a reparental stance is on target, there is usually behavioral movement, or flowering of the self, from month to month. Clients come to sessions with increased poise, vibrancy, and warmth.

All techniques have both systemic and individual impact. Even the provision of nurturance to a single family member has systemic repercussions, because the practitioner, as a reparental agent, functions as a model for the individual. As such, techniques have a chaining effect throughout the family holon.

CHAPTER 5

The Initial Interview

We may our ends by our beginnings know.

— Sir John Denham (1928, p. 197)

There are four tasks that the therapist must accomplish in the opening phase of treatment: bonding as a reparental agent; assessment and mapping of the client or client family; beginning transactional work; and contracting for change through treatment. Ideally, all four goals should be achieved to some degree in the initial interview. Each of these goals, of course, contains the seeds of the whole regressive/progressive treatment process. Thus, the initial interview is a microcosm of the CFT treatment. Before looking at these four tasks to be achieved, let us first examine family attendance at this critical interview.

ATTENDANCE

During the intake phone call, the practitioner bonds empathically and asks about the presenting problem and the composition of the family. He or she then requests that particular members of the client family attend the initial session. At times the client who requests treatment will insist that only he or she, or the identified patient, need come in. If the practitioner meets with much resistance, he or she keeps the focus on the presenting problem, but explains that the other family members are needed to provide information and help with its resolution.

If the presenting problem concerns a child, all nuclear family members are asked to attend the initial sessions. The family is seen as a whole, with special effort made to ally with both parents. The children may be left out of part of the session to deepen the bond with the parents or in order to get more information about the marriage.

When the presenting problem concerns the marital transaction, both mates are asked to attend. The practitioner spends time with the mates together to observe and diagnose the marital transaction.

When a married adult presents alone for treatment, the spouse will be asked to attend the first or second session. Conjoint and concurrent meetings are also held with these cases. If the presenting problem is in the marital transaction or in the mate's independent transactions, the children are not asked to attend the first three or four sessions. They are brought in later, however, to complete a full evaluation of the family holon.

When a single adult presents for treatment, he or she is seen alone initially. Later in treatment, the family of origin may be brought in for sessions. Extended family members who are integrally involved with the family may occasionally be included in a few initial sessions as well.

When family members are adamant about who should or should not attend initial sessions, the practitioner goes with the resistance and meets with those members who are willing to attend. However, the practitioner still schematizes and focuses on the entire family holon as a unit of treatment. Nonattending members are contacted directly or worked with strategically through the participating family members.

BONDING

The practitioner becomes a quasimember of the family group, and then builds rapport with each adult member by mirroring body postures, breathing, and movements. He or she begins to introduce regression techniques (see Chapter 4).

ASSESSMENT AND MAPPING

The practitioner elicits information from each family member about the transaction in which the presenting problem takes place. He or she then attempts to widen the exploration to other transactions, tying this information back into the presenting problem. Asking relevant questions and noting the behavioral patterns, the practitioner begins to schematize the marital, rearing, and independent transactions. He or she formulates hypotheses about each mate's self-system structures as well.

All the while, the practitioner focuses increasing attention on the spouses (or on the adult client in the case of the single parent or single adult). He or she empathizes and bonds with each one, mirroring behavioral style, affect, and language usage. The therapist begins to develop a remedial healthy reparental stance with each one of them. Regression is developed and promoted through direct and indirect hypnotic suggestions, and the use of verbal and nonverbal parentlike behaviors.

Assessment of Transactions

In terms of the rearing transactions, family members are interviewed in regard to the family's daily activity pattern. Information is elicited from each family member about who spends time with each child, who disciplines, who is affectionate and nurturant, and who programs for success or failure. The family is questioned regarding coalitions and alliances. The children's academic performance and peer group activities are ascertained. Responses are also cross-checked with other family members to discern agreement or disagreement, particularly between the spouses.

The marital transaction is assessed directly when clients permit access to the information. The mates are asked about the amount of time spent together, typical patterns of conflict, areas of satisfaction and dissatisfaction, angers and hurts, and the history of the relationship. Often, aspects of the relationship will be metaphors reframed by the practitioner. Reporting these metaphors back to the couple then leads to a correction and refinement process, a fine tuning of the clinician's understanding. For example, in an exploration of power relationships, the therapist mentioned that the wife in a family "wore the pants." At that point, both husband and wife chimed in to add, "only with the children."

Most importantly, in transactional assessment the patterns of behavioral interaction in the room are studied and noted by the practitioner. He or she observes who talks with whom; the manner in which each family member is addressed; and when members speak or are silent. The power hierarchy is noted, along with patterns of enmeshment, conflict, and distantiation. All of this information gives the therapist the most critical and real sense of the rearing and marital transactions.

The independent transactions are explored through the questioning of both spouses about the activities of each. Questions are asked regarding job titles, duties, and their performance. Often a spouse will round out the picture of the other spouse's functioning in a particularly helpful way. For example, in one case a wife reported that her husband, a young MBA, was underpaid and overworked in a large company for which he worked. She described how this situation paralleled that in which as a youth he had worked diligently in the family business for little pay.

Assessment of Self-system Structures

Self-system assessment begins with an analysis of the way in which each adult presents for treatment. Dress, behavioral style, and physical posture provide the first clues to sexual identification and foundation issues. Dress and behavioral style suggest gender as well as age identification. Clients can present with the style and vocal tones of a male or female child, adolescent or adult, regardless of biological gender or age. These attributes indicate particular types of sexual identifications.

In assessing the sexual identification, the clinician is examining the client's self-concept as a separate and discrete person in relation to significant others. In contrast, foundation assessments have to do with the more primitive, fusional sense of self-and-world. When the client manifests tight muscular constriction and behaves in a rigid way or seems without life and expression, there may be terror of engulfment or annihilation of self or other at the foundation level. If the client is physically sunken in and depressed in expression, fears of abandonment may predominate.

Transference in relation to the therapist provides further information about all three levels of the self-system. Competitive behavior that occurs with the same-sex therapist, or seductive behavior with an opposite-sex therapist, may indicate that the client has a triangulation model involving an oedipal win. Seductive behavior toward the same-sex therapist may indicate that sexual identification is basically contrary to gender and that the client's homoaffiliative needs have been unmet.

When clients avoid relating to the therapist – refusing eye contact, maintaining physical distance, withholding verbally, etc. – there may be at the foundation level a fear of engulfment or annihilation of self or others. When clients aggressively seek verbal or physical contact or an excessive amount of attention, fears of abandonment usually predominate.

In order to further the practitioner's understanding of self-system structures, the clients are also questioned directly about how they experience themselves and significant others in the world; what their parents were like as role models; and the nature of their relationships with their parents. Introspective and self-disclosing clients are often quite clear about their internalized introjects and identifications. With clients who are more guarded or who are blocked, the clinician must function more as a detective, gathering information and building hypotheses about the self-system structures. Because of the unconscious nature of much of the self-system structures, symbols that recur in dreams and fantasies, and frequently utilized expressions and associations can be extremely helpful in enlarging the clinician's understanding. For instance, a husband had repetitive dreams of a young boy who was stalked by a monster. This suggested a foundation terror of annihilation, an identification of the self as masculine and young, and anxieties typical of an oedipal winner who is terrified of the "monster" father. As these symbols emerge, they can also be reported to clients in a manner that promotes change through insight.

Clinical interventions as assessment tools

The therapist also uses clinical interventions as diagnostic tools in assessing self-system structures. Behaviors or transactional tasks are offered by the therapist, and clients' reactions to them are noted diagnostically. For instance, in exploring introjects at the foundation level, the therapist might physically move toward a client and note his or her reaction. Fear and withdrawal, along with expressions like, "Stop if you value your life!" which may be consciously expressed as jokes, unconsciously signal the client's deep fears in connection with hurting others who become intimate. Or, at the level of sexual identification, the therapist may suggest that a female client wear makeup, whereupon she might reply that she really should not or could not because it would not be right for her. Such a reply might suggest that she views herself either as more masculine or as childlike.

Transactional tasks can generate a great deal of information so that the practitioner can refine his or her understanding of particular transactions and self-system structures. When a father refuses to spend time with his son, there is indication that his triangulation model involves parental or paternal distantiation from the child. His style in reporting that he broke an agreement with the practitioner is indicative of the level of moral development inherent in his sexual identification. Questioning him and his wife regarding their interaction around the broken agreement, refines the therapist's understanding of the way in which the marital transaction maintains his difficulties as a father and as a man.

Compliance or noncompliance with transactional tasks also sheds light on the family's PAR process. In general, as part of that process, a progressive push on the part of the therapist, through tasks, for example, will elicit the spouses' dysfunctional models and programs in an abreactive regressive countermovement.

Using the Optimal Family Model for Assessment

In making assessments, the practitioner is aided by the CFT model of healthy family process. Comparing the family's functioning to that of healthy families helps the therapist to identify gaps and pathogenic trends more clearly. Working so closely with clients, the CFT therapist can easily be misled in his or her perceptions of the client family. Actually imagining family members in optimal, growth-promoting roles quickly provides the sharp contrast that outlines deficiencies in the family's current functioning.

Mapping

As part of the assessment procedures, the practitioner sketches a family map at intake and refines it as treatment progresses. Family maps summarize information about the three familial transactions, the spousal self-system structures, and the therapeutic relationship. They help to demarcate the direction of the therapist's efforts.

In such a map, a female member is denoted with an O, a male with a □. Adult symbols are larger than child symbols. Ages are included below each symbol. The therapist is placed at the top of the map as part of the configuration. Positions of power in the family are noted by placement of a member's symbol at the top of the configuration.

Normal interactions are indicated by a straight line (−). A normal relationship indicates that there is some nurturance, positive programming, and discipline in the dyad. If the normal line is drawn between figures who are in different power positions, these inputs tend to flow from the parentified figure to the child figure. Enmeshment is indicated by a double line (=). This line indicates that there is psychological fusion, a lack of differentiation between self and other in the dyad. Distantiation, or lack of interest or involvement, is represented by a dotted line (....). Conflictual relationships or those characterized by angry and oppositional reactions are represented by a crossed-off line (+). Oscillation between two modes of relating is indicated by two separate notations drawn next to each other. For example, (+) indicates that a relationship is characterized at times by distance and at times by conflict. Divorce is indicated by a doubly crossed-off line (#). Spousal self-system structures are denoted within the spouse's symbols. Independent transactions are described next to each members' sign. See Figure 2 for the model map outline.

Diagnostic assessments, as well as history taking, continue throughout treatment. The practitioner continually enlarges his or her understanding of the clients' self-system structures and the family's transac-

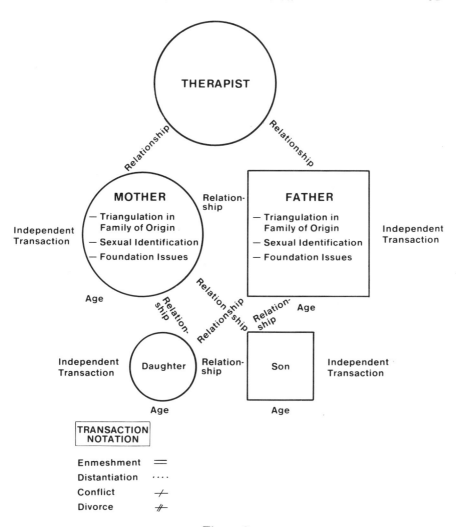

Figure 2

tional dynamics, and adjusts the remedial/healthy reparental position accordingly.

TRANSACTIONAL WORK

The practitioner moves into a parentlike mode with each spouse, and works on the transaction that governs the presenting problems. Often change begins with the therapist's use of transactional vivification or reframing, followed by a task. If possible, the practitioner also works on the other transactions, particularly on the marital transaction, which is so important in family life. The network of behaviors from the marital transaction are more readily available in the therapy than are the self-systems of each spouse.

For instance, the therapist may reflect back to a nonrelational couple that they are like "two mummies" with each other, and then reframe the same behavior, indicating that they are "two mommies" taking care of and protecting each other from anger. The practitioner might then give them the task of having marital arguments.

Since there is an ongoing interplay between the self-systems and the marital transactions as the therapist changes overt marital behaviors, he or she will also impact on the psyche of each spouse. Moreover, by stopping defensiveness and aggression in the marriage, there is a tendency for each spouse to experience underlying needs, deficits, and longings for contact that had previously been suppressed. These needs and wants then become manifest in relation to the therapist, furthering the regression process.

CONTRACTING FOR CHANGE

The therapist delineates and closes the contract for treatment by the end of the initial interview. The therapist agrees to function as a benevolent reparental figure who will work with all persons and on all problems in the family as needed. He or she allies with the health-seeking parts of the individual's self-system structures and the latent growth trends already present in the familial transactions. Inspiring hope, the therapist programs for the solution of the presenting problem, as well as for healthier functioning in the whole family. He or she asks for a clear agreement on the part of adult clients that this contract for growth is to be honored as a serious commitment. The therapist solidifies the contract by asking for repeated confirmation, both verbally and nonverbally, that the clients will work together toward these goals.

CASE EXAMPLE

Returning to the case of Bill Jones, which was described in the Introduction (see p. xv), we will examine how the therapist conducts the initial interview.

In the initial interview, the therapist, Sam Kirschner, met with Bill, his 15-year-old sister Pat, Bill's parents, and his probation officer, David Miller, M. A. Bill was surly, defiant, and uncommunicative. At first, he repeatedly fled the consulting room and tried to break out of the detention facility in which the session was being held. During the final escape attempt, Bill was restrained from kicking in the glass panel at the front door. He collapsed on the floor, sobbing, and brokenly admitted that he hated himself and felt no good for anything. Bill was brought back into the consulting room and the initial session began.

Segments of Transcript of Initial Interview

Therapist: (to father) What's happening in this family? There's something really wrong here.

The therapist begins assessment procedures. He is somewhat confrontive and strong in the face of Bill's acting out. He uses a barking tone that mimics the vocal qualities of both father and son in this family.

Father: Well, I don't know where it started . . . somewhere. I don't know.

Father demonstrates in this remark that his sexual identity is unauthoritative and weak, i.e., "I don't even know what the problem is, or where it started."

Therapist: You've been married how long?

The therapist takes charge in conducting the session, beginning his assessment and mapping procedures.

Father: About 18 years.
Therapist: 18 years. When did people start having problems here?
Father: When did that start? Well, we had problems, but we stayed together. Guess maybe I should have left, I don't know. Maybe, it'd been better.

The client indicates that there are severe difficulties in the marital transaction and that it is available for the therapist's exploration.

Therapist: Things were rocky right from the beginning, right?
Father: No, no, not from the beginning.
Therapist: No?
Father: No, no. *(to mother)* Wasn't that bad, was it?

Therapist: Well, your wife will have her opinion. She has her own mind on things. You know that.

The therapist, maintaining control of the session, stops the couple from further interaction. He begins to subtly reprogram the father to be more authoritative, i.e., "You know that."

Father: No. It wasn't from the beginning. No, we was . . . we got along good for quite a while.
Therapist: After both kids were born, in between, it started going wrong?
Father: No, no, no. Whatever happened happened after the kids were born.
Therapist: Right. What happened?
Father: I don't know. We just didn't click, didn't agree on things, I guess.
Therapist: Like how to raise them?
Father: One thing.
Therapist: Your wife's a little too soft?

The therapist explores the rearing transaction.

Father: Nah, nah. I'm the one that's soft.
Therapist: You're the soft one?
Father: Yeah.
Therapist: Mom was a little too tough on them, you thought?
Father: Well, we didn't agree on things.
Therapist: Like what?
Father: Well, for one thing, she used to side with him all the time.
Therapist: Uh, huh.
Father: That . . . that might've been a problem with him. I was never right as far as she was concerned.
Therapist: Right.
Father: And uh, she'd back him up all the time.
Therapist: In other words, you would try to discipline him and she'd take his side.
Father: Right. She'd take his side.
Therapist: She'd be the lawyer.
Father: Right. That's it.
Therapist: Right. And how about your daughter?
Father: Well, we'd click a little better.
Therapist: So, uh, you were saying your wife was siding with your son.
Father: I'd say so, yes. Yes, against me, in most everything.

From a triadic point of view, Bill and mother seem to form a coalition against father. The therapist formulates a tentative map of the rearing transaction in his mind as shown in Figure 3.

Therapist: I mean, if a man can't run his son, what's the point of being there?

The practitioner begins to restructure the rearing transaction. He programs the father to be a powerful force in his son's life by suggesting this role as a fundamental and necessary one in family life. He also introduces a fear-of-loss maneuver by suggesting a vague threat to the marital transaction. This mobilizes anxieties in both husband and wife in regard to the loss of the other, thus setting the stage for change.

Father: Well, I guess I thought about it, always. I don't say I was right all the time, but I was never right . . . as far as he was concerned.
Therapist: Uh-huh.
Father: But she always sided with him.
Therapist: Uh-huh.
Father: No matter what.

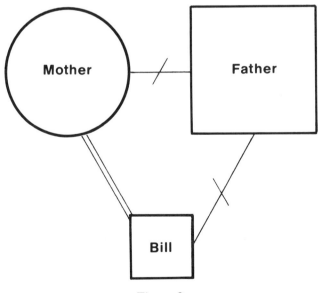

Figure 3

Therapist: Uh-huh.
Father: I don't know whether you remember, Pat, either. You don't, you
    was too little.

Father's readiness to look for support from his daughter indicates there
may be a real enmeshment here, a coalition of father and daughter
against mother.

Pat: I don't know.
Bill: (sigh) Can I tell you somethin'?
Therapist: In a second. *(looking at mother)* Well, I know you're a foun-
    tain of information.

The therapist prevents the son from interrupting, thus modeling paternal discipline. He begins to focus on the other critical family member,
the mother, programming her to produce information.

Mother: Why?
Therapist: I know you know a lot of things!
Mother: How do you know that?
Therapist: You have very, uh, your eyes tell me a lot.

The practitioner is bonding as a nurturant reparental agent by making
eye contact and being attentive to mother.

Mother: (giggles)

Mother indicates that this bonding technique is welcome, exciting, and
correct.

Therapist: Your eyes tell me a lot. So? Can you fill in the missing pieces
    for us?
Mother: Well, I don't have all the answers either, even if my eyes say so.
Therapist: Well, I think that if all of us put our heads together we'll get
    all the answers.

He moves toward a contract to work together.

Mother: Well, let me just put it this way. I raised three children before
    these two came along.

Mother refers here to a previous marriage.

Therapist: Right.

Mother: Now, I don't say I'm perfect. I never had any problems with them and me and their father were divorced. They saw their father every other weekend.

Bill: You gonna start crying?

Mother: No, I can't help it if I cry, Billy.

Therapist: That's OK!

Bill: I'm walking out if you cry.

Mother: Well, I can't help it.

Bill: 'Cause, I can't take it!

This segment suggests that Bill has a strong relationship with his mother. When his mother begins to cry, he becomes agitated and threatens to leave the room. Apparently, the enmeshed mother/son dyad is in some way connected with Bill's impulsiveness and possibly his acting-out behavior.

Therapist: Hold on . . .

Mother: Well, then, just look the other way!

Bill: No. you always start like it's some big soap opera or something.

Therapist: Hey, listen . . . your mother has a right to cry. I know it bothers you.

Mother: I have as much to cry about as you do.

Therapist: Hold on . . .

Bill: There you go again! Just be quiet if you're going to cry!

Therapist: Hold on! *(to mother)* What happens when you cry is that your son feels it. It upsets him. That's what happens. He's very close to you. You know that. OK? So, he has a right to be upset also. . . .

The therapist describes their symbiosis and then stops their interaction. His tone and style remain nurturant toward the mother.

Mother: And I remember when we were married six weeks – six weeks we were married and you didn't like the way your eggs looked.

Father: That's right.

Mother: And you took the plate and slung it across the floor.

Father: That's right. That's exactly what I did.

Mother: No, it's not the right thing to do!

Father: That's what I did.

Mother: You slung them across the floor.

Father: I don't like all burnt eggs.

Mother: And who cleaned it up?
Father: I didn't.
Mother: You know damn right well you didn't.
Therapist: So?
Father: She shoulda knew better.

The in vivo marital transaction manifests a cycle of anger, invalidation, and recrimination.

Pat: She used to cook us breakfast. Bacon and stuff. Have the cereal
    ready. She didn't cook eggs.
Father: When, Patty?
Pat: We never ate them. We didn't like the way she cooked eggs.
Father: Maybe she did a few times. I had to make the eggs for her 'cause
    she didn't make the eggs right for Patty.
Mother: That's 'cause I didn't know how to make them right.

Mother's remark may suggest that her sexual identification is that of an inadequate woman.

Pat: She doesn't know how to make them.
Father: That's right. *(to Pat)* So you make them right.
Pat: So?
Therapist: I've seen people fight about things like that.

The practitioner suggests that such disagreements are normal, so that the spouses will continue to divulge information without self-consciousness.

Father: Now, I like my eggs over well. But I don't like 'em burnt.
Therapist: I understand, me too.

A bonding maneuver, mimetic, aimed at promoting father's identification with the therapist.

Father: Now, Patty likes nice scrambled eggs, light, no brown stuff, and
    that's the way she made 'em.
Therapist: Everybody in this group had to have custom-made eggs.

The beginning of a reframe, which also lightens the mood.

Mother: I mean, this is ridiculous, fighting over how eggs are cooked.

Father: That's the way it was.
Therapist: No, but it's interesting.

The practitioner functions as a noncritical model, while programming the family to continue describing everyday interactions.

Father: That went into a lot of other stuff.
Therapist: That's right, like what? Like what?
Father: I don't know, but it did. You don't do nothin' right.

The negative programming in the marital transaction emerges. Father has reinforced and maintained mother's inadequate sense of self.

Therapist: That's what it ran into?
Mother: See, see.
Therapist: It ran into that you felt that your wife was not doing anything right?
Father: Well, she . . . I don't say everything.
Therapist: Well, a lot of things.
Father: Well . . .
Mother: There are two things I'm good for. I can make good potato salad.
Father: Yeah . . .
Mother: (voice breaking) And I can make good iced tea.
Father: Yeah . . .
Mother: And clean the house. That's all I'm good for as far as he's concerned.

Mother describes how her model of herself as an extremely incompetent woman is maintained.

Therapist: Is that right?
Mother: But I know better, I mean I know what I'm worth. *(begins to cry)*

Mother's affect confirms that this is indeed her model for herself, in spite of her verbal protestation.

Therapist: You know what you're worth?
Bill: Then why you getting ready to cry?
Mother: You're darn right well I do.
Therapist: Well, because her feelings are hurt. You know why she's getting ready to cry.

Mother: There are things I would like to do right now . . .
Bill: My feelings should be hurt, nobody else's.

As the marital tensions break out to the surface, Bill calls attention to himself as the identified patient. His actions tend to defuse the marital disagreement, as both mother and father join to focus on him. His acting-out behavior may serve to protect and preserve his parents' marriage.

Therapist: Why's that?
Mother: Billy, everybody's feelings are involved here, not just yours!
Bill: Well, I don't want to hear no crying, 'cause if I don't have to cry, nobody has to cry.
Father: You never cry.
Bill: That's right.
Father: Maybe it would do good if you did.
Mother: And the reason why Billy came to me, because he couldn't go to you, because you'd scream and you'd holler and everything else. And that's the reason why I don't always come to you.
Father: Hum.
Mother: Because I don't get a chance to finish my sentence. Right away you've got the conclusion made. That's you.
Therapist: Sounds like what I'm hearing is everything is Dad's fault. Dad was this, Dad was that. You know, I don't believe that.

The therapist avoids scapegoating father, in order to hold both parents responsible.

Father: No, no.
Mother: No, I don't either.
Therapist: Sure sounds that way. Bill couldn't go to his dad. You can't go to his dad. Dad complains about little things and throws dishes, and who knows what else. What other kind of things?
Father: That's the worst I ever did.
Therapist: Is that the worst? Did you ever throw a dish at her?

The therapist continues to explore the marital transaction.

Father: No, I never did. She wouldn't take that. She'd throw me the hell out.
Therapist: You were the one who threw the dishes at him?
Mother: Many a time I felt like throwing.

Father: No, she's not excitable like I am. I'm the excitable one.

Therapist: Right. Well, when you were excitable, like with Bill, what would you do? How would you discipline him?

Assessment of disciplining in the rearing transaction.

Father: Well, I'd threaten to hit him. I never hit him though.

Therapist: You never hit him?

Father: Rarely, if I ever did.

Bill: (nodding his head)

Miller: He did.

Father: Did I ever hit you?

Mother: Now see. You know what the trouble is?

Father: Maybe a few times.

Mother: Now that's a good man sitting there. Don't misunderstand me.

Therapist: I hope I'm not misunderstanding you.

Mother: He's a good man, but when it comes to raising kids, he's all talk. He's all talk, he never takes any action.

Therapist: He would threaten, but he wouldn't do it.

Mother: And if I wanted to take action then, I was, you know, I'm the hardhearted Hanna.

In the rearing transaction, it becomes clear that neither parent provided adequate discipline/guidance for Bill.

Father: I'm a very affectionate person. I don't get no affection, love and affection. I have to talk to somebody, so I used to go to my sisters.

The lack of nurturance in the marital transaction surfaces and leads to further disagreement. The children are then organized into the marital struggle.

Mother: You don't give any either, so you have to give it to get it.

Father: Well then, you don't give any either, so you didn't give none to the kids for that matter.

Mother: Well, that's another thing. You always said I never gave them any . . .

Father: Oh, that's right.

Mother: . . . affection, and that's a lie. That's a lie!

Father: When did you ever put your arm around Patty?

Mother: Ask her.

Father: Now tell her, Patty.

Mother: Ask them.
Father: Tell her, Patty. Tell her the truth.
Mother: Ask the kids.
Father: Tell the truth, Patty.
Pat: You did it, but you always was with Billy.
Father: That's right.
Mother: Why? When?
Pat: It was always Billy, and I was always with Daddy.
Bill: I can't hack this baby shit.

Billy clearly feels infantilized in his relationship with mother, and this embarrasses him. This sense of himself as infantlike is probably an integral part of his identity.

Therapist: Will you hold on! This isn't baby shit at all.
Miller: It isn't baby stuff.
Father: You didn't get no affection. I was the one who always worried about 'em.
Pat: She did, but it was always Billy.
Father: So, that's what I'm telling you.
Mother: And you know why?
Father: Why?
Mother: Because Billy kinda needed it a little more, because he didn't have you to go to.
Father: I needed affection, too. I never got any.
Mother: He had to have somebody to come to.
Father: Patty's the only one ever showed she even liked me. You didn't want me, he didn't want me.

The rearing transaction is clearer. Basic outlines of the marital and rearing transactions are mapped in Figure 4.

Mother: That's in your head.
Father: That's why . . .
Therapist: Hold it. Hold it. Is it? That's in his head? I don't think so.

The therapist again focuses on the marital transaction, keeping the discussion away from the children.

Mother: That I didn't want him?
Therapist: That's not in his head.
Mother: All right. I wanna tell you something. I mean that's what he thinks.

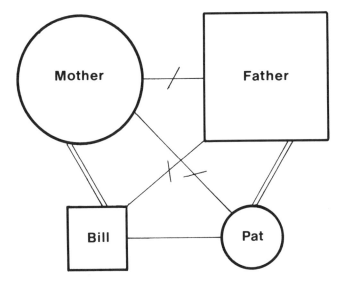

Figure 4

Therapist: Is it different?

Mother: That's what I mean. If I didn't have some feeling for him, do you think I'd still be with him?

Father: Yeah.

Mother: Do you?

Therapist: Why would she stay with you?

Father: On account of the kids.

Mother: All right, let me put it this way. Do you remember when we moved over into the house? We moved over in '66.

Father: Yeah.

Mother: And by the time '68 rolled around, Julie and Johnny gave us an electric blanket for Christmas.

Father: I don't remember.

Mother: And Julie says, "Mom, it's a dual control, so that if Pop doesn't want it too hot, he can turn it where he wants and you can turn it where you want." Now, this may sound silly . . .

Therapist: No, it sounds good.

Mother: I mean it may sound silly, but we slept, we were sleeping together, naturally.

Bill: Not anymore.

Mother: No, not for years. That's the point I'm trying to get across.

Pat: She's in my room.

Bill: Yeah, but she still had her own room. The house is a pig pen.

Mother: That's the point I'm trying to get across, Billy.

Therapist: So, what happened?

Mother: So, we'd each sleep with the electric blanket. He'd put it up to #9. I can't stand the heat, and he has to have the heat.

Therapist: Right.

Mother: And I'd say to him, "Well, it's a dual control, so that I can turn my . . . you know." Well, he gave me such a damn hard time, it got to a point where I thought, "I can't take this." I mean when I go to bed at night, I want to lay down and go to sleep. I want to relax, not be, you know, like this. So I thought, all right, I'll stay in the same room, but I cannot sleep in that bed like that. So, we had an old chair that opened down into like a cot. It was like a chair bed. So, I fixed that up, and I thought, I'm still in the same room with him. You follow me? So, I went and slept on that. Well, he happened to be out one night, didn't come home till two in the morning.

Therapist: I'll bet he didn't like that.

Mother: And he comes . . . Didn't bother him.

Father: (laughing)

Mother: Didn't bother him.

Therapist: Didn't bother him?

Mother: No, it didn't. He came in, "Oh, look where sleeping beauty is." I mean that's the way he is. He's a real comedian, he thinks. So I slept in there OK. Everything was fine. Nothing was going on.

Therapist: Right. I guess not.

Mother: But nothing was going on even the other way, so don't misunderstand me. And then he wonders, then he wonders. So, anyway then, after a while, I was snoring one night.

Father: One?

Mother: I can snore. I mean I can snore loud.

Bill: Oh, Jesus.

Pat: She can snore.

Mother: And you know, when you're snoring, you don't know you're doing it, right, OK? So, I'm in a dead sleep and I'm snoring. He says, *(loudly)* "Turn on the other side." And I mean that's the way he said it, and he shook me all up. So I turned. And then, I thought afterwards, I can't stay in here if I can't go to bed and not worry about being screamed at.

Father: Well, how 'bout me now?

Therapist: And that was 10 years ago?

Father: Yeah.

The extent of the schism in the marital transaction emerges.

Therapist: You both could really be living life nicely now. And instead of living it together, you live it separately. That makes people older faster, you know that, right? You know what they say about living together.

The therapist programs for a healthier marriage with more vitality.

Mother: Well, he walks around, he complains. Any little thing that happens, he gets all shook up and he says, "This is a house of hate! This is a house of hate!" Well now, how can anybody feel good?

The positive program brings up the negative family programs in sharp contrast. We see here how the marital disagreements have set up the emotional climate in the family.

Bill: It is. We live like a bunch of animals.
Pat: Well, where am I gonna put all my stuff? She's in my room. I don't have my own room.
Therapist: That's right.
Mother: I don't have any place to go.
Therapist: What are you doing in her room?
Pat: Because she can't sleep with him.
Mother: I have no place to go. He doesn't want me in his room.
Therapist: I understand that. But why aren't you sleeping together with your husband?
Mother: Ask him.
Therapist: Why aren't you two sleeping together?
Father: I can't sleep with her.
Therapist: Why not?
Father: She keeps me awake. There's no way.
Therapist: She'll make you younger. You're getting too old.

The therapist continues to work on the marital transaction, programming for change in one target area: the sleeping arrangement.

Mother: I can't sleep with him either because . . .
Father: We just had a natural . . .
Therapist: You remember Charlie Chaplin?

The therapist, who is considerably younger than the father, selects an alternate role model for the father, one who had remained more sexually active in his later years.

Father: Yeah.
Therapist: Well, he had a kid when he was 80 years old.
Father: I know.
Therapist: I think it's gonna be a big problem when these kids are gone. You're gonna be looking at the four walls together.
Father: Not me. I'll be gone out. Get myself a young chick.
Therapist: Is that right? You've got a young chick right here. She's a young chick right now.

The therapist begins to reprogram and enhance mother's sexual identity, and models this process for father. He hopes that the chaining process will ultimately help father perceive and relate to her differently.

Father: Who? Patty?

The oedipal win becomes clear here. Because of the failures in the marriage, both children have been organized to fulfill the parents' needs.

Therapist: No, not Patty.
Mother: Yeah, see what I mean.

The therapist again makes eye contact with mother, while mirroring her breathing and body positions. He assumes the demeanor of a prizing mother.

Therapist: Not Patty. You. You with that sparkle in your eyes.
Mother: You see what I mean?
Therapist: Patty's gonna be gone.
Mother: Patty's his wife.
Pat: I'm not even allowed to have a boyfriend.
Mother: He had Patty sleeping in the bed with him when she was a little girl.
Father: Aw, now don't, right.
Bill: Yeah, it's the truth.
Father: It is the truth, that's right.
Mother: All right, then, now what are you saying "Oh" about?
Father: I didn't ask her to.
Pat: What do you want? Thunder and lightning's going on, or the air conditioner!
Father: She gets scared, and came in, and snuck in with me.
Pat: (to mother) Well, you wouldn't let me.
Mother: How could you sleep with me in a little single cot?

Pat: Well?

Father: Because you wouldn't let her sleep, you'd tell her, "Oh, it's too crowded." I could hear you.

Mother: I have a single cot, you have a double bed. Now, how's she gonna sleep on the cot with the size of me?

Therapist: So, listen. You still have your double bed?

Father: Yeah.

Therapist: How come half of it's missing? How come it's not being used?

The therapist uses the word bed as a metaphor for the marital relationship.

Mother: He came in. (*Before* I moved to the other bed.) I was in the bed, sound asleep. He comes in 3 o'clock in the morning. He gets in the bed, and the bed falls down. "It's your fault," he said. It's all my fault!

Therapist: That's right. You two need a new bed.

Father: That's right.

Mother: I told him that years ago.

Father: That's what we need, a new bed.

Father takes in the therapist and his program.

Mother: We need a new everything, Dr. Kirschner. We need a new everything. We really do.

Mother recognizes the severe deficits in the whole family system and invites the therapist to help.

Therapist: I'll tell you what you need most of all. You need some new teamwork here because if you don't pull together, I don't know what's going to happen with Bill. Because he doesn't like it there at all. And when Bill doesn't like where he's living, he's gonna go out and do something that he doesn't want to do. So, I want to know . . .

Here the practitioner uses symptom prediction as discipline to prod the parents into the teamwork that underlies good parenting. Also, he programs Bill by avoiding the family's use of the nickname of "Billy," and calling him by the more adult name "Bill."

Father: We've been getting along pretty good.

Therapist: Can you two work with us here so that we can get this situation straightened out?

The practitioner ignores father's defensive remark and asks for a contract to work together on the rearing and marital transactions.

Mother: I'm willing to.
Father: Yeah.

The parents agree to the contract. Note that up to this point there has been little interaction between the therapist and Bill, the identified patient.

Therapist: There's going to have to be some changes. *(to father)* You're going to have to give a little bit. *(to mother)* You're going to have to give a little bit. A little compromise.

The practitioner programs for morphogenesis. In the following segment, the family flows with the therapist's suggestions naturally. His thrust seems to take the family where it wants to go. Note the daughter's and mother's immediate verbalizations, followed by the father's affirming chuckle.

Pat: Is she gonna get out of my room?
Therapist: She's gonna get out of your room, that's one of the problems.
Mother: Where am I gonna go?
Pat: You're gonna go with him.
Therapist: You're going to go into Dad's room.
Mother: Well, he better get moving in the front room then.
Therapist: Why does he have to go into the front room?
Mother: Because that's the bedroom with the double bed.
Therapist: Oh, I see.
Mother: You better get that old rug off the floor. And get that other old piece and put it down or do something with it.
Father: *(chuckles)*
Mother: Listen. You'd have to be in our house to understand what's going on.
Therapist: I may take a visit there someday.
Father: Oh, geez.
Mother: You'll have a heart attack.
Therapist: I'll wire myself.

The therapist bonds with the family by jokingly agreeing with their sense of the family reality.

Mother: You better bring some pills.

Note mother's program for the family in regard to dealing with unpleasant realities.

Therapist: Hey look, we need some teamwork here. Your son's out in the cold.

The therapist has cut into the family's homeostatic mechanisms and focuses again on the first morphogenic step, the development of teamwork. He also uses the identified patient's situation as a verification of the family's emptiness and lack of affection and direction. Again, the family goes along easily with the therapist's push for growth.

Father: So, what are we gonna do?
Therapist: A couple of things.
Mother: I know what you can do. You get rid of the double bed and you buy twin beds, that's what you do.
Pat: And you give me the double bed in my room.
Mother: And Patty can have the cot in the middle of her room.
Pat: Naw, I don't want the cot, I don't have a bed. That cot's so uncomfortable.
Mother: No, I mean the one I'm in, Pat.
Therapist: What a man does here is to get everybody new beds. I want you and your wife to start living together as a husband and wife.

The practitioner cements the growth trends with direct paternal input to father.

Therapist: You know that your son feels like he doesn't have a family.

He again identifies the emptiness of the family unit with Bill's problems. This tends to cohere the group members as they can empathize with each other's emptiness.

Mother: Well, I'm glad you . . .
Therapist: You know who his family is? Those gangsters he was hanging out with. That's his family.

Mother: Well, do you want to know something? For a long time I've been wondering where I belong. Really.

Mother, the primary role model for Bill, indicates that at the foundation level she feels a sense of abandonment, a lack of relatedness in the family.

Therapist: That's right. Everybody in this family. It's like a man without a country here. It's a very, very sad situation.

The practitioner again generalizes the problem to the whole of the family, using a vivid metaphor.

Mother: I'm just wondering what my purpose in life is.
Therapist: Your purpose in life right now is to work with me and Dave and get this situation straightened out. That's your purpose in life. 'Cause believe you me, if we work successfully on this, there's going be a whole lot of difference in your life. It's never too late! You know, I've worked with people who are older than the two of you.

The therapist is being a strong parental figure here. He moves in, takes charge, and gives a basic life program to the mother. He is hammering home the therapeutic contract by suggesting positive rewards inherent in its fulfillment. The therapist is parenting the parents and relating to them in ways he wants them to relate with each other and with Bill in order to control his acting out.

Mother: Well, we've needed a change for a long time.
Father: Who the hell was around there for me to talk to, for me, for years? Myself. I sat there by myself. She's out, he's up in his room. She's either up in her room or down the cellar! This went on for years. I sat there like a dummy.
Mother: No, it didn't go on for years either.
Therapist: That's what happens when a bull doesn't have his mate. He becomes more ornery.

The therapist uses a metaphor to vivify the transaction and its effect on the father's sexual identity as an angry, ineffective man.

Father: I don't know why I deserved that.
Therapist: I didn't say you deserved it.
Mother: It's not what you deserved. It's the way you made a person feel.

Father: Oh, yeah.
Mother: I didn't feel that you wanted me around.
Father: I have feelings, too, you know.
Mother: I know you have feelings. We all have feelings. But you better remember that you're not the only one with them.
Therapist: You mean, you told your wife your feelings.

In a judo-like maneuver, the therapist reframes the father's statement in order to work with the morphogenic component there, i.e., his longing for intimacy.

Father: Oh, yeah.
Therapist: Really? You told her you felt hurt, you felt rejected by her?

He begins to educate the father (and the mother) in the area of self-disclosure in the marital transaction, a component necessary for the PAR process to take place.

Mother: No, he hasn't.
Father: Well, years ago I did. I told you. You didn't want me.
Mother: When was this?
Father: Well, you don't have a good memory.
Therapist: Well, tell it to her now.

The therapist tries to build the self-disclosure into the immediate marital transaction.

Bill: I'm gonna take one of my pills.

The son threatens to act out here. We would hypothesize that this serves to block marital relating, which might lead to escalating tensions.

Father: She don't *(have a good memory)*. What, now?
Therapist: Tell it to her now.
Father: We've been getting along better than we had been.

Note the family's homeostatic processes in maintaining a distantiated marriage. When the son's attempt to block marital relating proves unsuccessful, the father takes over by denying problems and being defensive.

Therapist: Yeah, but you're still not in the same bedroom.

Father: No, I can't sleep with her.

Bill: You can say it, but they ain't gonna do it.

Therapist: I understand that's a problem. You two don't go to bed relaxed. That's the problem.

The therapist also begins to work on the lack of nurturance and successful rapprochement in the marriage.

Mother: Nobody ever goes to bed relaxed.

Therapist: You're a bundle of nerves when you go to sleep.

Father: I am. That's what I am.

Therapist: You know what you need? You need your woman to massage you at night.

Father: Oh, yeah?

Therapist: That's what you need, that's right.

Father: Won't catch her doing that.

Therapist: You won't catch her doing that? Hey, why couldn't she do that?

Mother: Because I'd have to have some more feelings for him before I could do that. And I don't have that much right now because . . .

Therapist: I understand.

Mother: I don't feel like . . .

Father: That's right.

Therapist: I understand. But you could do it if you had more feelings, right?

Mother: If I had more feelings, yeah. It's not like turning off a cold water spigot.

Therapist: Absolutely. How could you get more feelings for him?

He validates the mother but moves forward anyway. The goal is to first generate hope and then nurturance in the marriage.

Mother: If he treated me like I was a human being, and not just something that went around the house all day.

Therapist: How about if he treated Bill differently? Would that make a difference to you?

The therapist ties the rearing and marital transactions together. If the father is more appropriately involved with Bill, whom mother perceives as an extension of herself, then she would be more affectionate toward her husband.

Mother: It doesn't matter to me. As long as he treats him decent, that's all.

Father: You think I've mistreated Bill?

Therapist: Would you love him?

Mother: I didn't say that.

Father: Maybe I didn't go about it right, but I tried.

Therapist: Hold it. Would you have more feelings for your husband if he treated your son differently?

Mother: No more than I would if he treated her right, too. I mean I want him to treat them . . .

Therapist: . . . yeah, the same. But I'm saying if he did that, if he treated Bill . . .

Mother: Certainly.

Therapist: . . . you'd have more feelings for him.

Mother: Yeah. I mean, after all they're father and son.

Mother supports the father-son dyad, echoing the therapist.

Bill: (to father) I don't need you to help me, I'll do it myself.

Father: How you gonna do it?

Bill: That's why I did that stickup, to get money to buy a car and get my license and all.

Father: Oh.

Therapist: Smart.

He disciplines Bill directly, and father follows the modeled behavior immediately.

Father: Yeah, real smart. The next time you'll think about it. You know where you'll wind up, don't you?

Mother: There'd better not be a next time.

Therapist: Hey, Bill, it's because of that kind of thinking, without your Dad's help, that you've been in the kind of trouble you've been in.

The practitioner, using the optimal rearing model, begins to shape father to guide son in terms of his independent transactions.

Bill: Well, he don't help me.

Therapist: I know he doesn't.

Bill: Well?

Therapist: But, that's what we're trying to work on.

Bill: Well, you know, I don't give a shit.

Therapist: (to father) You never had a trade, right? And your father never discussed a career with you. What you need to do now is to be a real father and discuss with your son about looking into some trades with him. We'll *(therapist and Miller)* be behind you and help you. Now, what's this program that we've been thinking about for Bill?

The therapist programs the father to parent his son and offers him direct parental support.

Miller: We've been trying to get him into a vocational school.

Bill: I am into that.

Miller: OK.

Therapist: All right. Now what, is there a high school diploma that goes with that?

Miller: We can set him up to take his equivalency exam if he sticks with it.

Therapist: OK. So he doesn't have to go back to regular school. All he's gotta do is stay there. They help him with his stuff?

Bill: I ain't sticking with it. It's a bunch of bull, diplomas.

Miller: You don't want to go back to school though, so how you gonna get this thing? How you gonna get this diploma?

Bill: I don't know. I don't need one. I stole one from. . . . I'll fill it out.

Therapist: (to father) Now, your son. You see, here's the problem. Your son is getting absolutely no direction whatsoever. Nothing. It's like you fold your hands, you throw your hands up in the air and you say, "Well, I don't know." But there are ways for you to find out. You're an intelligent man. You're retired now, right? OK. Now, I need to show you how to father your son — here. He needs direction from you, and you need it from me. A father leads his son, right? You go down there with your son, to this program, and see what the score is.

The therapist confronts the father about his lack of involvement with Bill and, like a good parent, encourages and guides him in remedying the problem.

Miller: You're going there Friday, right?

Therapist: Find out what's available.

Father: Yeah.

Therapist: OK. You find out. You ask questions. You find out what the score is, what he needs.

Bill: All I want is a job.

Therapist: Listen . . .

Bill: I'll be all right with a job.

Therapist: Hey, listen.

Bill: All I need is a job.

Therapist: All you need is a job? You need something more than a job, otherwise you're going to be stuck pumping gas for the rest of your life. And one day you're going to be unhappy about making $2.25 or $2.50 an hour, Bill. And do you know what you're going to do then? You're going to bump somebody's head off.

Again the therapist fathers the son directly, confronting him about the nature and probable consequences of his immature program for living. He continues to program the son and the whole family to elevate themselves.

Mother: Can I say something?

Therapist: Hold on.

The therapist blocks the mother here to allow for his own, and later the father's, parenting of Bill.

Mother: All right.

Therapist: And you know damn well what I'm saying. The fact is, Bill, you're headed for a life of being a loser, and you know it. And without a trade, you're going to be stuck. And I don't want you to be a loser. And your Dad doesn't want you to be a loser either, except he doesn't know how to help you right now. And I want people in this family to stop being losers. Everybody throws up their hands. They say, "I don't know, the hell with it."

Bill: I never had things other kids had.

Therapist: That's right. You didn't. I want to make sure that you have those things. But you're not gonna get them by saying the hell with school, the hell with a trade, the hell with this, the hell with that. The people with trades and the people with education, they're the people who make money. Not the guys who pump gas. And you can't get any kind of a decent job without at least a high school education. That's a minimum. The guy who works on my car makes $12.00 an hour. The guy who does . . . you know, the plumbers or

the electricians, they make good money. And all of them have high
school educations. Every one of them. Except the real old-timers.
(looks at the father) The real old-timers, you know, that was then . . .

The therapist, continuing in a parental mode, educates and disciplines
the son, bonds with the father in a validating way, and models for both.

Father: They worked themselves up.

Father joins in to father Bill.

Therapist: They worked themselves up, but you can't do that anymore.
Those days are gone. *(to father)* You have to take, you have to go
down there with your son tomorrow.
Father: Yeah, right.
Therapist: And you have to start asking some questions. Maybe by ask-
ing the right questions, you can help him. By making suggestions.
But you can't expect him to listen to everything you say, you just
can't. Otherwise, it's going to be two bulls again.

Note how the therapist continually refers to Bill as "your son" when talking to the father in order to program for more of a father-son relationship. The therapist begins to disengage the son from mother while engaging him with father.

Therapist: You don't need your wife to go down. You can give her the
day off. Why don't you two just go. See if you can keep a quiet
car, and go down there and see what the story is.
Miller: (to Bill) Did you hear what he said? Quiet car, you two don't fight.
You talk.
Therapist: You two are going to have to learn how to talk to each other.
It's like a new skill, like learning roofing.

The therapist bonds father and son together by using a metaphor to
which they can both relate. He also programs in a trade for them to consider for Bill.

Father: He wants everything at once.
Therapist: Hey, Dad, you wanted everything at once at one time in your
life, too, you know.
Father: I don't know.

Therapist: We all did, we all did! Remember how your mother used to talk to you?

The therapist promotes the father's identification with Bill. He looks for other role models that father can use in order to be more empathic with his son.

Father: Yeah.
Therapist: Was it nice?
Father: Yep.
Therapist: You think you can imitate her when you're talking to your son?
Father: I don't know if he'll listen.
Therapist: Well, he may not listen the first few times. But you know how you do it? You keep trying.
Father: He don't like to be bugged.
Therapist: I think if you're being sweet with him, he'll take it. He needs a little sugar, if you know what I mean. A little honey?

A direct program for the father to provide nurturance for the son.

Father: Um. *(to son)* Well, what do you think? You listening?
Bill: I'm listening.
Therapist: *(to father)* Tell him that you want to help him.
Father: I do want to help him. You know what he'll say, "Well, will you let me drive the car? And get that, and get that."
Therapist: Now, you see what you're doing?
Father: No, I don't see.
Therapist: Well, you see, you're already making up your mind for him.
Mother: You're negative.
Therapist: You're making up your mind for him. That's not how your mother talked to you. Come on. What would your mother have said? What would your mother . . .
Father: I don't know.
Therapist: *(very softly)* Come on. What would your mother have said?

The father now has two role models for relating to Bill: his biological mother and the therapist.

Father: I can't think that far back. It was a long time ago.
Therapist: Oh, I'll bet she's in the back of your mind somewhere.

The therapist regresses the father back to childhood. Using his voice and body language, he puts the father in trance.

Father: Yeah. You know what? She is . . . among other things.
Therapist: OK, well?
Father: (very softly) Put your rubbers on, son. Put your rubbers on, son.
Bill: I don't need that.
Therapist: Right, that tone. But that's not. . . . What do you need from your Dad? Tell your Dad what you need from him.
Bill: I don't know what I need.
Father: What about the car?
Bill: Yeah.
Therapist: OK. So, talk about the car. *(to father)* Talk about how you could help him with the car.

Here we reach a task in which a microcosm of the desired rearing transaction will take place. Father will help son in an area where he needs and wants help.

Therapist: OK, now, I want you to talk with him about how you're going to be with him in the car. Tell him how relaxed you're going to be.
Father: I'm relaxed, but, well . . . I don't know about relaxed.
Therapist: Tell him how relaxed you're going to be.

The therapist programs optimistically for appropriate fatherly behavior.

Father: He does pretty good, but he don't . . . I drive in a different style than he's driving.
Therapist: Well, you have to get used to his style.
Father: He's got, you know . . . he really moves.
Therapist: Tell him how good he's been driving.
Father: I have.
Therapist: Have you told him? *(to son)* Does your Dad tell you how good you're doing? *(Bill shakes his head)* He doesn't?
Bill: He says it to my Mom.
Father: I told you, you done good. Now don't say I didn't tell you.
Bill: Well, I don't remember.
Father: Well, you don't remember, but I did.
Therapist: I think he doesn't.
Father: Your mother's told you, and I told you.
Therapist: I think he doesn't hear it enough from you, then.

Father: Maybe he don't listen. He don't listen to me.

Therapist: No, I think he expects you to be angry with him all the time.

Father: Maybe that's it.

Therapist: So, then, when you sneak in those nice things, he doesn't hear it, you know. He kinda tunes them out.

Father: Could be. I got my style of driving, and he . . .

Therapist: Well?

Father: Don't drive like me.

Therapist: Well, is it all right if he doesn't drive like you, as long as it's safe?

The remark refers directly to the task at hand, and is also a metaphoric program for a differentiated yet positive relationship between father and son.

Father: If it's safe, yeah.

Therapist: OK.

Father: He can drive, but he's got a lot to learn.

Therapist: Why don't you wait until he asks you.

Father: Asks me what?

Therapist: He's driving with you in the car and let's say he pops a question to you. Well, what do you do now?

Father: Well, yeah. I'll be glad to help him. He won't ask. He knows it all. He won't ask.

Therapist: Well, if he doesn't ask you, then don't bother telling him.

Father: Well.

Therapist: You know why? It's just a fight.

Father: That's right.

Therapist: OK.

Father: That's right.

Therapist: But I think that if he knew that you were on his side, he could ask you some questions.

The therapist moves the father and son toward a healthy relationship in which the father will function as a coach and mentor for the boy.

Father: Yeah. Well, I'm on his side, but . . .

Therapist: He doesn't know that.

Father: He won't let me be.

Therapist: No, he doesn't know that.

Bill: I want somebody to go out and help me find a job.

This is a morphogenic signal, a wish for fathering.

Therapist: Well, your Dad's going to help you find a job, that's what he's going to do. He's going to go down to the trade school with you tomorrow. He's going to . . .

Bill: He ain't gonna do nothing.

Miller: But you have to go there tomorrow, Bill. Start there.

Therapist: That's where we're starting. *(to father)* Now listen, do you have any friends in the neighborhood he could also work for?

Father: Not really, no.

Therapist: Nothing? Well, you go with him in the car. Try some different places. Try to help him find a job. *(pause)* Now listen, I want to guarantee you something. You get involved with this kid in the way we talked about, and your wife's going to be nice to you these days. She's going to be nicer to you than she's been in a long, long time.

Father: Yeah?

Therapist: Guaranteed.

Mother: Yeah, but you better get those single beds in the front bedroom. *(laughing)*

Miller: There's another project for you.

Therapist: There you go. That's something else. You going to help him get those twin beds?

Mother: Sure.

Therapist: You should go out together to buy them. That's right.

The therapist programs again for the fulfillment of the marital task.

Miller: (to Bill) You two have the whole day together, don't you?

Father: Yeah.

Therapist: You willing to work?

Father: Yes, I am.

Therapist: Yes? Mom? You willing to work?

Mother: Yes.

Therapist: OK. Settled. We'll meet here again next week.

The therapeutic contract is resolidified.

Summary of Initial Interview

Summarizing the therapist's assessments from the initial session with the family, we have the following information:

An extremely distant and hostile relationship between mother and father set the tone for family life, (" . . . a house of hate"), destroyed any hope of a parental team, and amplified the need for nurturance in each spouse. This state of schism severely undermined the rearing transaction. Instead of being nurtured for their own sake and oriented toward successful lives, the children were used to fill the parents' needs and were caught up in their marital battles. The illicit coalitions that were then formed – mother-son, father-daughter – further undermined the parents' executive functioning in the rearing transaction, and their bonding as a marital pair.

Divided leadership in the rearing transaction generated and supported Bill's incompetence in his independent transactions. With no adult to educate, guide, and discipline him, he never learned to tolerate frustration, or to be goal-directed and self-disciplined. As a result, he dropped out of school and turned to criminal behavior. Bill's failures in turn affected his parents' marriage. His incompetence served to join them together, as they focused on his problems rather than on each other.

Bill's self-system structures were largely based on his mother's self-system. At the foundation level, Bill experienced a great fear of rejection and abandonment, based on the introjection of his mother, who felt totally alone in the world. His primary role model also was his mother, a woman who experienced herself as a weak, inadequate and masculine female. He experienced himself as her infant. Because he essentially "won" mother from father, he felt anxiety in relationship to all women. His triangulation model was to maintain an emotional marriage to mother, to combat or distance father, and to function as a marriage-preserving scapegoat for his parents. Bill's other role model, his father, was a man who, at the foundation, felt alone and abandoned. His sexual identity was that of a loud, weak, ineffective and feminine man. Thus, the marital transaction/spousal self-system dialectic in this family was extremely dysfunctional and tended to reinforce and maintain Bill's symptomatology. Figure 5 illustrates the dynamics, along with the beginning of a therapeutic relationship.

All major aspects of the overall treatment plan generated from this diagnostic assessment began to appear in the initial session. The therapist would continue to unite the parents and to develop mutual nurturance and positive programming between them. Thus, the necessity to organize the children to fulfill affectional and relational needs or to pull the parents together at the children's expense would be diminished.

Follow-up

In the ensuing weeks, the therapist continued to promote the relationship between father and son, coaching and mentoring father so that

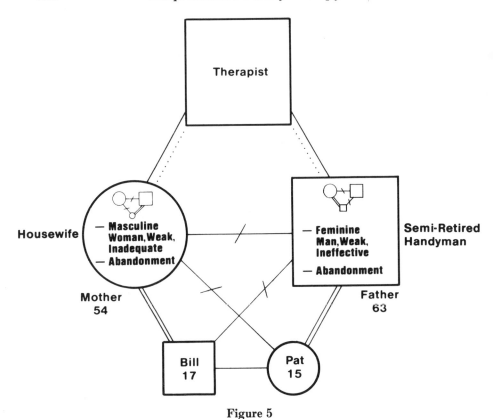

Figure 5

he could do the same for his son. The therapist simultaneously disengaged mother and son and promoted mother's role as coach and mentor for her daughter. Since Bill was an older adolescent, the practitioner and the probation officer supplied some of the fatherly inputs directly to the boy. They helped program him in the areas of work and dating, and facilitated maturation and competence.

Four weeks after treatment began, the couple moved back into the same bedroom. An atmosphere of lightness and levity pervaded the consultation room as they discussed how they had rearranged furniture and had bought a new red rug for the bedroom. The therapist nurtured and prized the couple for their efforts.

Father helped Bill to learn how to drive. In one family session, the therapist had father talk to Bill about specific points on which he would be tested for his driver's license, while mother took notes. The therapist became firmer with father, and would not allow him in sessions to be disrespectful of his spouse. Bill observed this process and became more respectful of his father.

Because this was a training case, the therapist turned the family over to the probation officer for continued treatment, moving behind the one-way mirror for ongoing supervision. The probation officer facilitated further growth in the family. For instance, in one of his maneuvers, he promoted both Bill's independent life and the marital transaction. He assigned the father the task of driving Bill to his date's house, and then having him take out his wife afterward. This quasi double-date promoted both father's and son's identification with the male therapist. The parents' date was their first in 10 years and went very well.

A year later, Bill obtained his high school equivalency diploma. He secured a job and was saving up money to leave home and go out on his own. Bill's career plans included becoming an air-conditioning and heating contractor, a trade suggested by father during one of the sessions. He was dating and staying out of trouble. Two years later, the family was still doing well and Bill was released from probation.

CHAPTER 6

The Child as the Presenting Problem

You are the bows from which your children as living arrows are sent forth. The archer sees the mark upon the path of the infinite, and He bends you with His might that His arrows may go swift and far. Let your bending in the archer's hand be for gladness; for even as He loves the arrow that flies, so He loves also the bow that is stable.

—Kahlil Gibran (1983, p. 18)

When a family presents with a child as the identified patient, the practitioner typically begins treatment with all members of the nuclear family present at the initial interview. At times a family member refuses to attend, and the practitioner meets only with those who will. He or she will then try to engage the resistant member either directly by phone or strategically through other family members.

For six to eight weeks the therapist works with the family as a whole. All members attend each meeting, although the children may be asked to leave the consulting room for brief periods. This is done to foster executive alliance between therapist and parents, or to elicit information about the marriage. The therapist bonds with the spouses, schematizes and maps the family holon, and begins to strategically change or restructure the rearing transaction. Concurrently, the therapist becomes a reparental agent for each spouse.

The therapist discusses the problem with each family member in order to both widen his knowledge and "spread the problem" by eliciting various viewpoints about its development. From the beginning, he or she works to open the spouses' eyes as to the etiology and maintenance of the problem in the rearing transaction. The therapist questions both spouses and the child(ren) closely about all the attempts they have already made to deal with the problem, and also why they think their approaches have failed.

In addition, the practitioner observes the family's nonverbal interactions very closely, in order to ascertain their behavioral patterns. When the practitioner suspects a large discrepancy between what a spouse reports and how he or she acts, he may ask for an in vivo demonstration of the interaction the spouse is describing. If, for example, a father reports in a soft-spoken and smiling manner that he's tried every type of discipline in the world with his son and nothing works, the therapist might ask the father to show him exactly how he disciplined his son after the last problem episode. The realities of the behavioral patterns in the rearing transaction can then become quite clear to the practitioner.

The therapist observes the parents to discern how they disagree about raising their child. Generally, a child's symptomatology is maintained, at least in part, by parental disagreement about how to discipline or guide him or her. For example, one parent may undermine the other's authority either overtly or covertly. Or one parent may use the child inappropriately as a surrogate spouse, while the other competes for a place in the dyad. In both types of configurations, the dysfunctional rearing transaction is organized in such a way as to prevent any meaningful collaboration between the parents. The child's problems will remain, and his or her growth and maturation will proceed in an atmosphere of divisiveness.

Parental disagreements usually occur in a homeostatic cycle in which each parent maintains a predictable position vis-à-vis the other spouse and the child. Disagreements about the children are usually part and parcel of the marital conflict. These disagreements are brought out directly in the consulting room. For example, a seven-year-old boy was referred for therapy after he had poked a child in the eye with a pencil. At the initial interview, his parents enacted for the therapist how they had dealt with the boy after they were told of his misbehavior. The boy's mother screamed hysterically at him, while his father made excuses for his behavior. The father blamed the other child and the school authorities. This infuriated the mother and she accused the father of not giving a "damn." The son began to yell at his mother saying that she never believed him. The father withdrew from the fracas while mother and son continued to argue.

The therapist interrupted the interaction at this point. He hypothesized that this sequence was a repetitive one, in which mother would try to discipline, father would intervene, and then mother would continue to interact with son in a disempowered role. Father and son were

involved in a coalition from which mother was excluded. Viewed maritally, father was sending son to do battle with mother on his behalf. Mother
engaged this "weaker" emissary as the enemy. No wonder, then, that
his son's victim had been a girl.

In addition to enacting and schematizing homeostatic sequences that
typify the rearing transaction, the therapist also will begin to explore
each spouse's upbringing. The practitioner asks the spouses about the
parenting they themselves received. As the practitioner discusses this
with the couple, they generally begin to open to him as a potential reparental agent. Also, the responsibility for the current failures is partly attributed to problems in their own upbringing. This has a freeing
effect on the parents, in that they can dissolve some of their guilt in
connection with the child's failures.

THE REPARENTAL CONTRACT

As the spouses begin to apprehend the deficiencies in the rearing
transaction, they also start to understand the relationship between this
dysfunction and their relationships with their own parents. Thus, it is
easier for them to contract with the practitioner for reparental intervention.

Therapeutic interventions may not be described initially as reparental
to the client, but similar metaphors may be used. For example, the practitioner said to a disengaged father who reported that his son was withdrawn and out of control:

> Your son is floating all alone in space. He could be piloting a
> wonderful spaceship, with you behind him at the controls. He
> would love that more than anything, but your father was not at
> ground control for you, so you hardly know what that's all about.
> So, I can help you. I've put in some time at Cape Canaveral and
> I know how to blast off and land. Your son could really be dyna-
> mite out there, instead of depressed and withdrawn. And you could
> be, too! Do you want me to be there for you like that?

At that point, the father contracted for reparental contact and positive programming, which in turn would chain down to his son.

The therapeutic contract calls for remediating the rearing dysfunction plus intervening reparentally with the parents. The therapist seeks
to extend the contract in a nonthreatening way to include work on the
marital and independent transactions as well. If the practitioner has
carefully calibrated his healthy/remedial stance with the spouses, they

will eagerly agree to this extension of the growth contract. When the practitioner is in the correct reparental stance, the clients begin to be receptive to his or her suggestions almost immediately. For example, in the case just described, the practitioner shook hands with the father at the end of the session and added, "When I'm behind you, I'll help you with your work and your relationship with your wife, too, if you'd like." The father lit up at this.

In the formation of the therapeutic contract, both parents should experience the therapist as an available ally. The therapist inspires hope by pointing out that with his help, there will be a team of three adults to work on the problems of the child. If the parents feel extremely overwhelmed and hopeless, the therapist minimizes the problem and discusses how their particular type of rearing problem has been effectively handled in other families. If the parents deny and underestimate the problem, the therapist maximizes it through the use of vivid metaphors that predict and amplify possible negative outcomes, should the dysfunction continue.

For example, if parents present with an anorexic teenager and insist that she has only a minor problem, the therapist might describe how the adolescent could easily wind up "an emaciated skeleton laid out in a coffin." These techniques are used in accord with realistic future possibilities. Through these techniques, the spouses' willingness to perform tasks in the rearing transaction is enhanced, and the practitioner can forge a strong contract to remediate the presenting problem.

As in all CFT work, the contract for treatment must be closed with a firm verbal and nonverbal commitment on the part of the spouses to work together with the therapist toward their goals. This contract shapes all future interactions and generates the expectation of hard work on the part of both therapist and clients, and the probability of a positive outcome.

In rare cases, spouses may be particularly rigid and unable to accept any share of responsibility for the child's problems. Defensive organization may be extreme, with all pathology projected onto the child who is described as a truly defective person. The parents may want to abandon the child, asking for placement in a foster home, etc. Or they may wish to dump the responsibility for the child onto the therapist. They may ask him to medicate the child or see the child individually. Often these parents claim that they have tried everything in working with the child, and are no longer willing to try anymore. Or they claim extreme impotence and inability to deal with the problem child.

In these instances, the practitioner must initially "go with the flow" and join with the resistance. Then he or she can paradoxically amplify the pathogenic rearing transaction in such a manner that the parents' natural protective impulses emerge. At that point, parents will choose to work on their behaviors in the rearing transaction and open themselves to the practitioner for his assistance.

For example, in the Adams family, Jonathan, age seven, presented with hyperactive behavior. Mrs. Adams, age 27, was a depressed woman who "couldn't" control Jonathan in any way. Mr. Adams, age 30, who worked long hours selling real estate, could control Jonathan somewhat, but he tended to be abusive in his interactions with his son. Mother was enmeshed with Jana, aged five, who functioned as her companion while her husband was away.

After consulting with and defeating three therapists, the family presented for treatment with one of the authors. The parents were rigid and resistant to changing their positions in the rearing transaction and asked the therapist to meet alone with Jonathan. Both parents said they were fed up with Jonathan and could not take him any longer. The practitioner said that such an arrangement would not help the boy, and he amplified the problem with the following nurturant paradox:

> Mom and Dad, you look so tired. This child is really draining the family. Let's put him in foster placement for a while. Now I know those horror stories they tell about the foster homes and what happens to children in them, but we have to do what we have to do.

Later in the interview, the practitioner sensed that the mother had remained unmoved, while father was upset. The therapist then began to notice how Jana, mother's favorite, seemed similar to Jonathan. Spreading the problem, the therapist talked about how Jana would probably have to be placed, too, when she got older. At this point, both parents pleaded with the therapist to come up with an alternative plan. The practitioner told the parents that they would have to turn themselves inside out to help the boy. They agreed to this and asked the practitioner to help them. This paved the way for the establishment of a re-parental contract with each spouse.

INITIAL TASKS

After contracting, the therapist begins to move the rearing transaction one step at a time from the presenting configuration toward an optimal one. This usually involves prescribing gradual realignments in role allocation such that, over time, the same-sex parent becomes the primary disciplinarian and the opposite-sex parent the primary nurturer and facilitator. In order to achieve this, the marital and independent transactions, as well as the spousal self-system structures, must be developed. Initially, however, the rearing transaction is the main transaction targeted for work.

In a presenting configuration where a parent is enmeshed in an overprotective way with a child, the initial tasks involve promoting the child's individuation and bonding him or her with the disengaged parent. For example, a mother who hovered anxiously over her six-year-old son was instructed to send him out two times a week to ride his bike alone. Her husband was given the task of working with his son on a construction toy set.

In families with this enmeshed configuration, mother's interest and attention must be engaged in an alternative activity so that she can let go of the child. Often these women are severely deficient in healthy self-caretaking. They project all of their needs into the caretaking of children and find vicarious fulfillment in the satisfaction of the child's needs. When this is the case, the therapist draws attention in an empathic manner to the fact that mother is overworked and emotionally drained by her child. Taking a nurturant stance, the therapist offers or implies that her needs could be filled more appropriately by her husband and by the therapist. Upon experiencing sincere interest and attention, such a woman begins to withdraw some of the energy she had invested in her child(ren) and to open up to her spouse and therapist for attention and caring.

The therapist can then insist in a caring fashion that mother take time for self-nurturing activities like taking bubble baths or joining a health club. Or she might be instructed to call a night school in search of an interesting class to take while her husband plays with the child. If the woman has sufficient ego strength, a powerful maneuver to produce positive self-involvement is to accelerate her in a new career or work endeavor. Of course, if there is another child from whom mother is disconnected, the therapist will assign the task of focusing her attention on that child.

Often the presenting problem with an enmeshed-disengaged parental configuration is that the child is out of control at home and at school. When a family presents with a child who is a discipline problem, there almost never is true disciplining of the child in the family. True discipline implies parental teamwork, consistency, and dedication to change behavior. When parents of an out-of-control child report that they have disciplined their child, they may be indicating that they get angry at the child, abuse the child verbally or physically, or reject the child. But, in reality, they have never been able to have the self-discipline and/or teamwork necessary to sustain their efforts with the child.

Thus, a discipline-problem child in a family is an indicator that the parents themselves require discipline in a kindly, sustained fashion from the therapist. When this is provided, the parents will learn to discipline the child in a benevolent way. Follow-through is a critical ingredient which must be modeled for the parents. When a task or role is agreed upon with the practitioner, he or she must check in subsequent sessions to see that the agreed-upon behaviors are being carried out. By holding the parents accountable, the therapist teaches the parents to hold the child accountable.

When a parent is attacking and verbally abusive to a child while the other parent remains in the role of passive nurturer, the nurturant parent, regardless of sex, is put in charge of the programming and disciplining of the child. The negativistic parent is encouraged to connect with the child by spending time together in pleasurable activities. A critical maneuver in such cases is one in which the therapist empathizes with the plight of the punitive parent. For instance, in the case of 12-year-old Tommy, the father, an army officer, was extremely reactive in a negative way to the boy's every move. The therapist pointed out what a lonely and disadvantaged position father was in as the "heavy" or bad one in the family. She offered to help him with his own problems at work, while he left the burden of the disciplining of their son to his wife. He agreed. The therapist then suggested that he get to relax and enjoy his son by going for short walks with him.

When the rearing relationship presents with one or both parents disengaged and/or overinvolved in their independent transactions, the initial tasks might involve simply providing contact, attention, and nurturance to the children. The practitioner might ask that the parent(s) spend a half hour of special time with each child, in which they engage in a pleasurable and age-appropriate activity.

When family problems concern adolescents, the practitioner may, at times, see the teenager in individual sessions. This is especially important if pathology is severe or individuation issues are paramount. The practitioner then gives needed reparental inputs to the child directly to speed the growth process. He or she nurtures the adolescent and helps him or her to formulate career goals, handle peer pressures, and build social skills. The therapist also puts constructive pressure on the adolescent to develop positive contact with and receptivity to his or her parents.

SEVERE PSYCHOPATHOLOGY

Children or adolescents who exhibit serious antisocial behavior or dangerous acting out must quickly be controlled by the practitioner and the parents. If the child engages in criminal activities or drunk driving, or puts himself or the welfare of others in jeopardy, the practitioner attempts to have the parents clamp down and assume an extremely powerful position with the adolescent. Usually parents of these children are either indulgent or uninvolved, or discipline sporadically and inconsistently.

With these cases, parents are made aware in graphic detail of the dangerous consequences and future life failure awaiting their child. Dedication to remediation of the problem and cooperation with the practitioner are thus enhanced. At that point strong disciplinary measures are instituted in the child's life. The child may be grounded. Privileges are severely restricted. Time is structured and chores increased. The practitioner is consistent in orchestrating this state of affairs, which fosters consistency in the parents' involvement. Thus, parents move into and stay in the proper hierarchical position in the family.

When adolescents are runaways and parents function in a weak or indulgent manner, they may be instructed to empower themselves by first giving the child the number of a neighbor to call in emergencies, and then locking the house when the child is out beyond curfew. Of course, if the adolescent runs away to avoid physical or sexual abuse, it is these parental behaviors that must themselves be corrected.

PHYSICAL AND SEXUAL ABUSE

When there is physical or sexual abuse in the rearing transaction, the therapist must control and stop the abuse as soon as possible to protect the child. The therapist vivifies the horrible nature of the problem in front of the family so that defensive denial on either parent's part is dispelled. Guilt, shame, and the like are cultivated as motivators to change behavior. The therapist then calls for a contract to protect the child, which includes powerful consequences for noncompliance. For instance, in a couple in which the father had committed incest with his daughter, the couple was told to swear to the therapist and their daughter that such behavior would stop. The therapist then had the wife tell her husband that if it did not, she would institute divorce proceedings. The incest stopped, and the couple began to work on their marriage.

Although the option of separation may be mentioned strategically to induce parents' cooperation, in general, fragmentation of the family is avoided. Placement of children in hospitals, group homes, or foster homes is done only as a last resort to protect the child.

In general, the practitioner also does not remove a parent from the family. Such moves are experienced by the children as a frightening abandonment, which adds psychological pain to the injuries they have already suffered. Additionally, when the family stays together, parents can learn how to raise their children more effectively. The therapist can also help the parents make reparation for physical/sexual abuse. Of course, the child's safety comes first, and in some cases it is necessary to place a child or exclude a parent temporarily from family life.

BEYOND THE PRESENTING PROBLEM

When gross misalignments and severe dysfunctions are corrected in the rearing transaction, and both parents have proper involvement and balanced interest in the children, enhanced parental teamwork becomes the goal. The practitioner teaches the parents to spend time discussing and planning for the development of each child. He or she teaches them to negotiate agreements and make contracts with each other for coordinated role performance with each child. The therapist emphasizes that contractual agreements made regarding the children should remain as firm commitments. Thus, the parents are organized to develop a hierarchical boundary around themselves as a benevolent executive team that is devoted to actualizing each child's potential.

The therapist then begins to optimize the rearing transaction. All along, the therapist has worked to reprogram and relabel the role definition of the children in the client family. He has focused on the real assets, talent, and attractiveness of each child, presenting these images of the children to the parents in such a way that they can perceive them. The parents are organized to help the children optimize school performance, to develop peer group interactions that are stimulating, fun, and fulfilling, and to excel at sports and hobbies that promote physical health, self-esteem, and learning. The parents are guided into the SSP-OSP rearing configuration.

In order to optimize parental teamwork, the marital transaction must be enhanced. Marital issues often surface when the presenting problems concerning a child clear up. The therapist then works with the spouses on their own individual and marital growth processes, so that they become better equipped for providing healthier nurturance, programming, and discipline for their children.

CASE EXAMPLE #1

Jack and Linda Smithson came for treatment, to the senior author, when 10-year-old John, their only son, was threatened with expulsion from school. John was defiant and disobedient both at home and at school. Initially, the treatment revolved around the amelioration of this presenting problem and bonding with Jack and Linda. The Smithson's rearing transaction showed an enmeshed mother/disengaged father pattern.

John, a bright and verbal blond-headed boy, sat close to his mother. Their movements tended to be synchronized and symmetrical. His manner was that of an entitled young man. Often he would interrupt the adults to brag about his baseball exploits. Father, who sat quietly in an observant position, with his arms folded, made no attempt to correct John and, in fact, did not even address him directly during the initial interview. Mother, who was also very verbal, tended to join John in his bragging behavior. She admitted that John would not cooperate, and yet she tended to minimize the problem. When the therapist questioned Jack, he described how he felt there definitely was a problem with John. He said that he could not understand his son.

In the first interview, the therapist worked to disengage John from his mother and to build a relationship between John and his father. Initially, she had Jack interact with his son, both within and outside of the sessions. In session, she asked the two to sit close together and had Jack ask his son questions and listen to his answers. Out of session, she asked Jack to play baseball with his son for 15 minutes, three times a week. In order to disengage Linda, the therapist began to pique her interest in developing her own independent transactions. Linda, a homemaker, was quite bored with her role. The therapist suggested that she send for a catalog from the local community college to explore taking a course there.

In the second session, Linda and Jack reported that they had followed through on these initial tasks, although Jack had been somewhat haphazard with his performance and Linda had tended to intrude herself into Jack and John's time together. The practitioner continued to meet with the family for the next several sessions. During this time, she assessed the spouses' self-system deficits, while she continued to restructure the rearing transaction.

Thirty-year-old Linda presented as an overweight, yet attractive woman, whose depression was masked by rapid and anxious verbalization. Her childhood was characterized by a profoundly symbiotic relationship with a depressed, anxiety-ridden mother who undermined the father-daughter relationship. Her father was a quiet alcoholic who had little interaction with Linda. Linda had identified with her mother and thought of herself as a weak little girl who was afraid of the world. According to her triangulation model, intimacy was to be obtained in a parent-child relationship rather than in marriage. Her parents' marriage was characterized by emotional distance and isolation, punctuated by physical battles.

These self-system structures were mirrored in Linda's contemporary family transactions. She was reclusively overinvolved with John, emotionally distantiated from her own spouse, and unsuccessful in a career. The therapist hypothesized that at the foundation level, Linda experienced profound anxiety about being in a world that she experienced as unsafe and hostile. Her basic terror, like her mother's, concerned abandonment by significant others.

Based on these assessments, the therapist assumed the role of a strong, warm, prizing, and programming mother figure. This stance increased the potential for emotional connection with Linda, as the symbiotic mode of relating was familiar to her. In order to bond in this manner with Linda, the therapist utilized a number of hypnotherapeutic techniques during the family sessions. First, she mirrored Linda's body positions and breathing patterns, which relaxed her. Then, making eye contact with her, the therapist was warm and strongly validating. In this atmosphere, she challenged Linda to dream about her own future and not exclusively about her son's. Linda became excited about her relationship with this new role model. Seeking more approval from the therapist, she began to follow the therapist's directions in regard to promoting the father-son relationship in the family. She also began to follow up on the therapist's suggestions about developing a new career.

Jack presented as a quiet, noncommittal 32-year-old man who chain-smoked. He described himself as having a minor drinking problem. Jack's identity was formed in the context of a family in which his parents were typically frozen in icy conflict with each other. Jack's mother turned to him to meet her needs for nurturance and affection. His father was either uninvolved with, or rejecting and disapproving, of both Jack and his mother. Jack's mother discouraged any connection between Jack and his father. This triangulation was replicated in the relationships with Linda and John.

Jack's mother was a depressed woman who became alcoholic when Jack reached puberty. With his mother as his primary model, Jack seemed to have developed a confused sexual identity, experiencing himself as an impotent boy/girl. The therapist suspected that at the foundation level, Jack felt terrified of being engulfed or annihilated by significant others, as a result of the relationship he had had with his mother, who was alternately fused with him, or infuriated by and threatening with him. Consequently, he had developed a schizoid interpersonal position, which had adversely affected his functioning as a spouse, a parent, and a professional salesman. Based on these clinical hypotheses, the therapist assumed an intrusive disciplinary role initially, in order to strengthen Jack's weak sexual identity.

The therapist began to bond with Jack through the use of a decentering technique, which was also aimed at elevating the rearing transaction and the concomitant alleviation of the presenting problem. In the third session, the therapist asked the boy to leave the session. Then she cast Jack as John in a dyadic role play and fathered him. Grabbing him by the shoulders and looking into his eyes, she said, "I expect the best from you, and I won't accept anything less! You're a bright, creative, and talented boy. You have to do your best in life." Being cast in this regressive role vis-à-vis the therapist allowed Jack to experience an intense interaction with the therapist that he himself needed. This also gave him a vivid model to follow in relating to John.

The therapist assigned Jack the task of reproducing this interaction with his son, which was to be backed up with a chore and homework schedule. Continuing in a role-play format, the therapist then modeled an array of disciplinary actions that Jack could utilize. She had Jack set up a permanent grounding of John, where peer involvement and outside play were contingent on his completing chores and homework. She also had Jack remove John's tape player, radio, and toy car collection, with the stipulation that the boy could earn them back only one at a time through cooperative behavior at school and at home. By the fourth session, it became apparent that Jack's follow-through on this assignment was weak and the therapist took Jack by the shoulders again and disciplined him directly, saying:

> What is this weak, negligent, and useless fathering? John needs you to be what you could be – loving and dynamic, a real assertive man in the world! Not like that distant father you had who didn't even notice if you were coming or going! That judgmental father who hid from the world! I'm going to be a father to you! A good one who won't let you off the hook! I'm instituting a fine system. You owe me $10 for every time John forgets his chores or homework and you let him go out and play!

Jack chuckled in response and agreed to this contract with the therapist.

The therapist had suggested that Linda take the business course that interested her at the community college, but she proved resistant to suggestions regarding elevation of her independent transactions. Linda protested that she was afraid to take the course because she was too stupid and slow (as per her earlier programming.) The therapist then switched to a paradoxical approach. In a family session, she suggested that Linda stay at home and perfect her marriage to John. She suggested that Linda should be at John's beck and call and should chauffeur him to four afterschool activities. Linda rebelled by enrolling in the course.

By the sixth session, father and son were much closer and John's behavior was improving at school. The therapist contracted to continue meeting with the spouses conjointly and individually. In subsequent sessions, she monitored their parental involvement with John and, on occasion, would see him in family sessions. Six months later, a report from John's teacher indicated that he had shown dramatic improvement in his behavior and schoolwork.

CASE EXAMPLE #2

The Johnson family presented to the senior author with a complaint regarding seven-year-old Carol Ann who had a bedwetting problem. Forty-year-old Steve, the father, was a successful physician. His wife, Jean, age 35, worked as a medical researcher. The couple also had a five-year-old child, Kimberly. The couple rescheduled their initial appointment twice to accommodate the father's busy schedule. At the initial interview, the parents were rather reserved in manner and both appeared haggard and worn. Carol Ann sat apart from her parents and quietly chewed her finger nails. Kimberly also sat quietly, but with an almost doll-like demeanor.

The practitioner bonded with each member and asked each one about the family's daily activities. She discovered that Steve worked 10-12 hours a day, six days a week. Jean, who had a computer terminal in her office at home, as well as at the university, reported that she worked full-time. The girls reported that she worked all the time.

A live-in housekeeper got the girls ready for school each morning and took care of them every afternoon after school. The parents described Carol Ann as a little mother with Kimberly. Mother was involved in working with Carol Ann around her symptom. She had tried various methods, such as prohibiting liquids at bedtime and waking her at night to urinate. Carol Ann had been seen in play therapy with a child psychiatrist for two years. She still wet the bed two to four times a week. The therapist mapped the rearing and marital transaction (see Figure 6).

Steve explained in the initial session that he would no longer attend

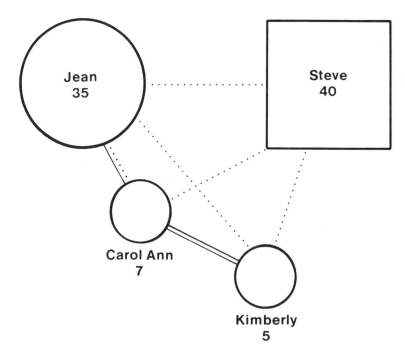

Figure 6

family sessions because of his busy schedule. His wife made no comment about this. The therapist decided to amplify the problem with a vivid metaphor in order to properly engage the father.

"Steve, I really wouldn't do that if I were you. Your kid is drowning. Drowning!" she exclaimed dramatically. Carol Ann began to weep.

"What do you mean?" he asked. The therapist then explained that Carol Ann was drowning in sadness, and was "starving to death for attention." The therapist used auditory-based imagery tailored to Steve. The therapist continued, "She's crying. Listen! Can't you hear her crying? She needs you now."

Steve's eyes began to fill up with this metaphor. He admitted that Carol Ann sounded like a girl in trouble.

The therapist asked Steve if he was really going to cop out on Carol Ann. His eyes moistened and he said, "No." The therapist clapped him on the back in an approving and fatherly way. Steve agreed to participate in the family sessions.

The therapist asked Steve to talk about his own childhood. He reported that as a child he had felt alone. Steve's parents were both physicians and he had been raised by a series of maids and housekeepers. The practitioner asked Steve about the manner in which he had cried out. Steve reported that he had also been a bedwetter as a child. Then, the therapist put her hand on Steve's shoulder in a fatherly way, and said, "Does she have to go through the same shame and cry out the same way to get your attention, Steve? I don't believe you want this!"

Steve admitted that he did not want this for his daughter. The practitioner then held out her hand to contact Steve, saying, "Let me help you."

Steve asked how.

"By showing you what a father is. And how about Jean? She looks like she's crying in the desert, too. You're not really here in this family!"

Steve received this with a downcast and sad expression. The therapist continued, "But I think you're really a good boy. You don't seem to want this. It's just all you know. But I can show you another way."

"I can't hear the warning signals because I'm so driven with my practice," Steve said. "It seems to run me."

"Well, we'll just have to run it," said the practitioner.

"Great," said Steve.

The practitioner then began to focus on Jean, "I'm going to straighten out your husband and get him back in the family, Jean." Jean gave her approval to the plan.

The therapist continued: "We need some juice in this family. And not water." Here the practitioner made a symbolic reference to the symptom in a metaphor used to characterize the lack of relatedness in the family. Both spouses agreed with the practitioner. She then prescribed tasks that involved each parent spending 10 minutes of special time with each child every day of the week. They were asked to ignore Carol Ann's bedwetting. She also asked the parents to arrange for a babysitter so that they could go out on a date. The parents agreed.

By the next session, which was held a week later, both parents had carried out their tasks. Carol Ann had wet the bed twice. The practitioner asked Steve to make up a chart and put it on the refrigerator. Carol was to be given a gold star for each day she had a dry bed. Seven gold stars meant that she would go out for her favorite treat, a hot fudge sundae with Steve.

In this session, the practitioner focused on Jean. Jean discussed how she had more of a relationship with her father than with her mother. She was, in fact, pursuing her father's dream of working in cancer research. Jean's mother was described as a drudge, a housewife who was given little respect in the family. Jean had an older brother, the apple of her parents' eyes, who had become a physician. The practitioner hypothesized from this that Jean had problematic cross-sex identification. She began to program Jean in an indirect way for a positive feminine identification. Addressing Steve, she said, "Jean is a lovely, lovely woman. She looks so drained, though. I want her to get to enjoy herself and her children! She's the kind of woman who can have it all—motherhood, marriage, beauty, and success!" Jean chuckled at this, indicating she was interested in the positive programming. The girls were very attentive to this program as well.

By the third session, Steve was slipping in his fulfillment of the task. Jean, however, was spending more time with the girls. Carol Ann had wet the bed three times. Kimberly and Carol Ann appeared more relaxed. Steve had spent only one 10-minute session with each girl and had sabotaged the date with Jean.

The practitioner moved her chair close to Jean and began a fear-of-loss maneuver. "He's fading out, fading out again. Are you going to put up with this? I know he's your brother, the prince, who can do no wrong! But will you allow you and the children to die inside, sacrificed to medicine?"

"No," Jean answered.

"Well, how are you going to prevent it? I want you to straighten him out. You can do it better than me!"

"If he's going to abandon us, I'll abandon him first."

"You'll give him a dose of his own medicine."

"Yes, but I'm not sure how," said Jean.

"Not too severe, dear. How about staying with a friend for a few days?"

Jean agreed to this plan. Steve was quietly angry and resentful. The therapist encouraged him to spend extra time at the hospital since he wouldn't have to spend time with the family.

The next week, Steve carried out all his tasks. Carol Ann wet the bed only once. The practitioner organized the family to eat dinner together more often. In the following session, the therapist engaged Kimberly in a tickling episode on the floor. This modeling was followed by direct instruction to Jean to work in loosening up this child. Privately with the couple, this task was also prescribed for Steve who needed to loosen up Jean in their romantic life.

By the fifth session, Carol Ann proudly reported that she had a perfect week. Kimberly was more talkative and relational. Steve and Jean were pleased and happy about their childrearing successes. The therapist reviewed all the tasks and applauded the family's progress. The practitioner helped Steve revise his office schedule to allow for more time with the family. Jean discussed her longing for a Ph.D. in her field, which the practitioner encouraged.

At the sixth session, only Jean and the children came in. Jean explained that Steve had gotten bogged down in work and had missed several days of interaction with the children, whereupon she had left and stayed with a friend for two days. He had become quite angry and upset.

The practitioner worked with Jean and the girls, organizing a baking project and shopping trip for the three of them. Later, she phoned Steve. He ventilated some anger at the therapist and Jean. When the therapist accepted the anger, Steve cooled down. He then confessed that he worked so much because he really felt incompetent and like a fraud as a doctor. The therapist paradoxically suggested that he work harder to prove to himself that he was really competent. Steve replied that he was already doing that and that he wanted to change to a new approach. The practitioner then offered Steve an individual session, which Steve eagerly took.

At the seventh session, Steve spoke in greater detail about his negative self-image, that of a weak and incompetent boy. The therapist bonded with him more closely as a father figure and told Steve that she would help him grow up. But first she made him agree to certain conditions. He would have to honor their contract about his office schedule and time with the children and Jean. Otherwise, the therapist would let him get "swallowed up by the monster – his practice." Steve was frightened by the imagery, which he quickly associated with his father who had, in fact, been consumed by his practice.

The whole family attended the eighth session. Carol Ann's bedwetting had stopped. Steve and Jean sat closer to each other, and there was more physical contact with the children. Carol Ann appeared to be more distant and less maternal toward Kimberly. The parents asked the therapist if they could speak with her alone. After the children had left, Steve and Jean said that they wanted to improve their marriage. They spoke about the coldness that had crept up between them and how they were strangers to each other.

The therapist had constructed hypotheses about the spouses' self-systems. At the oedipal level, both Steve and Jean had lost the coveted opposite-sex parent (OSP). No matter how well they had achieved as children, they could not get the needed relationship with the OSP. Each experienced the triangle of relationships as disconnected – three people in search of a common ground. This pattern had been repeated in the contemporary rearing transaction.

At the level of sexual identification, Jean wanted to be a boy, a prince, like her brother. She devalued being a woman and a mother and prized her career above everything. Steve also felt like a weak and incompetent boy. He had grown up believing he would never become as good as his father. There was a powerful homoaffiliative longing that the therapist knew she would have to satisfy both directly in treatment and in Steve's relationship with Jean. The marriage of the two "boys" had of course satisfied some of these longings but neither spouse had known how to really fill the other's needs adequately.

At the foundation level, each experienced a tremendous fear of engulfment. The marital closeness that had been prescribed by the therapist had catalyzed a regressive process in which primitive terrors had surfaced. Yet each spouse preferred the anxiety that had been generated to the coldness with which they had lived. The family map at this point is schematized in Figure 7.

The session concluded with a contract to continue treatment with the couple on a conjoint and concurrent basis. The next phase of treatment involved providing corrective reparental inputs to the spouses and elevating their marital transaction. The children's progress was also monitored and they were included in the family sessions every few months.

Carol Ann's bedwetting problem recurred only one more time during treatment. One and a half years later, both children were doing well at home and at school; Jean and Steve felt much closer maritally and personally more fulfilled.

CASE EXAMPLE #3

A teenage girl, age 15, was referred because of excessive weight loss. The anorexic adolescent, Marla, had become a strict vegetarian as part of her "spiritual" development. When her weight dropped under 85 pounds, the parents called the junior author for treatment. At the therapist's request, the parents, Myrna and Josh, brought Marla and their two other children, Daniel, 17, and Roberta, 13, to the session.

Within 15 minutes, the siblings were verbally fighting with each other, especially Daniel with Marla. The parents said that they couldn't control these two and looked forward to their both leaving home and going away to college. The therapist explored the rearing transaction further and discovered that Daniel did not date any girls and was basically reclusive. His most consistent companion was Marla, whom he often teased unmercifully with obscene words and gestures.

His father, Josh, would alternately laugh or pay no attention to Daniel's behavior, while his mother, Myrna, would ineffectively tell him to stop. Marla expressed a sense of being unprotected in a crazy household. Roberta, on the other hand, sat close to her mother and seemed in synch with her.

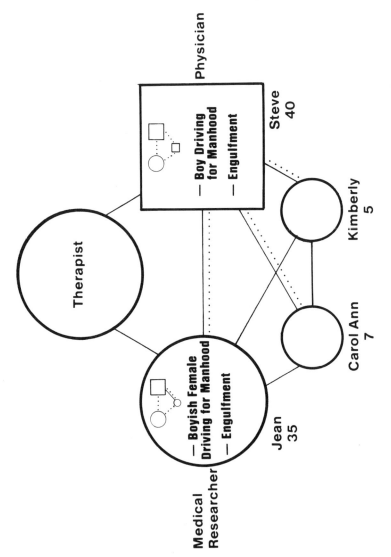

Figure 7

142

The therapist explored Josh's independent transactions and found that he worked for his father in a family-owned business. Josh said he hoped his son would join the business as well. The therapist then began to discuss a "minor problem" that would prevent this from happening. He suggested, however, that a solution did exist so that Daniel could possibly still join him in the business. Josh pressed the therapist to tell him what he meant. The therapist announced that Daniel could go to work in the business, but first Josh had to fire all the female personnel, since Daniel's presence among them would ruin the business.

Myrna, who had been relatively quiet to that point, began to cry. She talked at length about how she felt put down and helpless in the family, and how her housekeeping efforts went unappreciated. She said she wanted to quit at times, also. The therapist moved into a nurturant position with her and into a more demanding posture with Josh.

The therapist began to discipline Josh in front of his son and asked him how much he enjoyed watching Daniel "get it on" with Marla. Since Daniel had no other girlfriends, the therapist reasoned aloud that Marla must be his "one and only true love." The therapist began to arouse the paternal, protective instincts in Josh. He challenged him to be a real man and to raise his son to be one also.

As the interview proceeded, Daniel slumped in his chair, showing signs of shame and embarrassment. The therapist had regressed Josh in relation to him, but also had succeeded in putting Josh in charge of Daniel. As Josh opened up to the practitioner, Daniel opened up to his father. Encouraged by the therapist, Daniel told his father how he felt miserable and unpopular. He wanted to date but did not know how to act with girls.

The therapist told Josh to father his son, especially in the area of dating. He was to discuss different girls who might be available for dates, topics to talk about with the girls, places to take them, and so forth. He also told Myrna to accompany Marla to a meditation workshop at the ashram Marla attended, and to find out about her daughter's inner life. The therapist told the family that they needed to thank Marla for being the spiritual conscience of the family. This reframe especially appealed to Myrna, who viewed herself as a religious and sincere person.

The therapist's initial map of this family is schematized in Figure 8. There appeared to be a strong homoaffiliative coalition between Josh and his son, in which they berated Myrna and Marla. Roberta had apparently been spared from their wrath. She and her mother had developed a close relationship and had a few common interests. These included some crafts and domestic projects in which Marla did not participate.

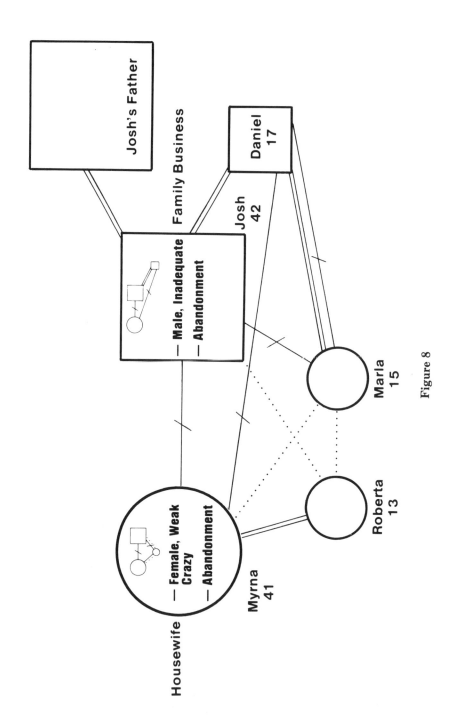

Figure 8

144

The therapist continued to see the whole family over the next three weeks. At the end of each session, he reserved time to work with the couple alone. Josh described a childhood in which he worked for hours after school in his parents' store. His happiest times were spent playing cards with his parents. During these "fun" times he recalled that he and his father would together deride his mother's playing skills, and she would get annoyed with him and his father. Josh still worked with his father in the store, although he claimed to hate every minute of it. He was simply afraid to go out on his own.

The therapist schematized Josh's self-system as follows: At the oedipal level, Josh had "won" his father, and perceived his mother and all women as the common enemy to men. Josh had repeated this coalition with Daniel vis-à-vis Marla and Myrna. Although Daniel was identified with his father, this identification was based on a mutual hatred and fear of women. Father and son really had nothing positive in common. There was no warmth in the relationship, and Josh longed for a father who would appreciate him just for being himself. At times, it appeared that Josh would look to Daniel to be a father to him. At the foundation level, Josh had profound fears of abandonment. He remained enmeshed with his parents and wanted to bring his son into the family quagmire out of his own fear of letting go.

Myrna's childhood was characterized by serious physical abuse at the hands of her father, who later abandoned the family when Myrna was 11. Her mother could not handle the strain of raising three children alone and had to be hospitalized for what Myrna called a nervous breakdown. Myrna, as the oldest child, was called upon to hold the family together. The three children were eventually placed in institutions, as the mother never recovered. Myrna's closeness with her mother was, in part, based on a common fear and hatred for men. She experienced sadness, but also relief at the loss of her father. Myrna grew up with the paradigm that one loses first the hated parent and then the parent with whom one sided. She experienced herself as a weak, ineffective woman like her mother, and was terrified that she would also go crazy. At the foundation level, like Josh, she had a profound fear of abandonment which had grown over time. While she had thought of quitting the marriage, her fear of loss was overpowering. She reported she had sworn to herself not to do to her children what her parents had done to her.

The therapist met with Marla in a few individual sessions in which he was prizing and validating with her. He lent her several books on Eastern philosophy that Marla had wanted to read. In the next several family sessions, the therapist continued to father Josh and had him work with Daniel. Marla and Roberta chimed in to give their opinions about which girls Daniel could date. The therapist asked Myrna to learn macrobiotic cooking, so that she could make special vegetarian meals for Marla.

Marla seemed very pleased by this, but at the fifth session reported that she had gone out for a hamburger. The therapist reacted in a very puzzled way to this and confronted Myrna about her "lousy cooking" in much the same way Marla had in the past. Marla defended her mother, saying that she really was a fine cook, but that she was sick of rice all the time. Marla also reported that she had gained five pounds, and that she and her mother had set a target weight of 100 pounds for her. Daniel had gone out on his first date with one of Marla's friends. The fighting between Marla and Daniel had subsided considerably. The therapist asked the teenagers to leave in the middle of this session, which gave the couple more of an opportunity to discuss their marriage.

As is typical in these cases, when the presenting problem in the rearing transaction is alleviated, the marital problems begin to surface. The therapist's dilemma at this point often is how to hold the couple in treatment to work on the underlying and more troublesome issue. Couples like Josh and Myrna are often quite relieved that their children are doing better and quite apprehensive about opening up the Pandora's box of their marriage.

In this case, the therapist had, in the previous family sessions, paradoxically praised Josh for giving Roberta "his share" of Myrna's love. Similarly, the therapist wistfully validated Myrna for making sure that at least her son had a close relationship with his father. The therapist said that some families have to sacrifice their marriage for "the sake of the children," while other families manage to have satisfactory marital and rearing relationships. Myrna and Josh insisted that they, too, wanted both. The therapist warned them that 20 years of marriage had given them many excuses to dig up from the archives of their marital records. And he said that he was hoping to hear the best of these excuses in the forthcoming sessions. The couple convinced the therapist that they wanted to start anew, and he agreed to help them.

A year later, Marla's weight had stabilized at 105 lbs. Marla had become less spiritual and considerably more materialistic. She was dating and was involved in a school sports activity. Daniel left home for college and was dating there. Roberta had made new friends, and Marla and mother had become significantly closer. Myrna had gotten a responsible position as an office manager in a law firm. The couple continued to improve their marriage.

CHAPTER 7

Marital Therapy

For even as love crowns you so shall he crucify you. Even as he is for your growth so is he for your pruning. Even as he ascends to your height and caresses your tenderest branches that quiver in the sun, so shall he descend to your roots and shake them in their clinging to the earth.

— Kahlil Gibran (1983, p. 11)

This chapter focuses on the challenge of enhancing marriages. First the spousal self-systems/marital transactions dialectic is presented. Then life-cycle issues are discussed, followed by the beginning stages of treatment, and the format of conjoint and concurrent sessions. Next, a special section deals with engaging the resistant spouse. Beginning and intermediate treatment foci are then discussed, after which there is a section on techniques. The chapter closes with a description and case example of the ending focus of treatment: the development of the intramarital therapeutic coalition.

SPOUSAL SELF-SYSTEMS/MARITAL TRANSACTION DIALECTIC

From a psychological perspective, the marital couple can be viewed as one organism. Each spouse extends his or her self-definition to include the other. Parts of the self and/or parts of the personalities of parental figures are projected onto or unconsciously assigned to the mate. Interior dramas are played out on the behavioral level in the marriage in beautifully coordinated complementary roles. These transactional dramas then feed back to reshape self-system structures.

147

Marriage also involves a thrust toward completion and integration of the self. Spouses are chosen not only on the basis of congruency in self-system structures, but also out of a longing to promote growth of self and other. Spouses choose partners similar to parental figures who are also able to provide the reparental inputs they need.

However, due to immature or pathological development, each spouse can become stuck and therefore unable to help the other grow. Destructive behavioral patterns become entrenched and needs remain unmet. Anxiety, depression, and the like also increase. When symptomatology is no longer tolerable, the couple may present for marital therapy.

Spousal self-systems are completely congruent, and this congruency helps to maintain behavioral homeostasis in the marriage. At the foundation, both mates can tolerate intimacy up to a certain intensity, or psychological distance to a degree or for a certain duration, before foundation terrors erupt. These limits are generally the same for both spouses. The terrors themselves are often congruent and shape the behavioral dance that controls intimate contact.

For example, a wife may have a greater fear of annihilation than the husband, whose primary anxiety revolves around abandonment, and to a lesser extent engulfment. The couple's typical sequence would show that the wife behaves in a cold and nonresponsive way, which in time triggers the husband's fear of abandonment. He will become angry and argumentative in an attempt to regain contact. The wife's annihilation fears will then escalate and she will flee, whereupon the husband will pursue her. The husband then may become extremely sweet and conciliatory, whereupon the wife might feel safe and signal the husband to have sex. Sex involves the 15 minutes of intimacy that they both can tolerate. The homeostatic dance then repeats itself, with the wife pulling away after sex is over. Although couples may present with one spouse saying that he or she wants more marital intimacy, in general both spouses are at the same level of object relations.

At the level of sexual identification, most mates function homeostatically with complementary role division, based on role patterns they observed and experienced in their families of origin. The man and woman may function in a masculine/feminine dance, with one taking the domineering, controlling, and forceful role and the other taking the passive, receptive, and empathic stance. Or they may have a more homoaffiliative or chum relationship, in which they both function in one mode or the other, with the result that there is less sexual passion or excitement. Or they may experience themselves as two children in the world whose relationship is a form of parallel play.

Other aspects of functioning refine role division further. One mate may function as the identified patient, the "sick one," while the other is the "sane, strong caretaker." One may be frozen in the parent role, the other in the child role. There is also the victim and the abuser; and the hysteric who feels emotions intensely and the nonemotional schizoid. In each of these dyads, each mate acts out aspects of self rigidly and repeatedly for the couple. This process impedes each spouse from integrating latent, positive, and fulfilling aspects of his or her personality because these aspects are being played out by the other. For example, the man who is locked into the controlled, nonresponsive role is unable to integrate his softer more sensitive side because his wife plays the role of reactor for the couple. Thus, rigidity in role function is associated with dysfunction; flexibility, with psychosocial health.

The spouses' triangulation models are congruent and interlocking. The congruency of these models reflects the spouses' proximity/distantiation sequences and their role divisions. Spousal triangulation models are played out behaviorally in parental behaviors in the rearing transaction. The child is organized to play a part in the script emerging out of the spouses' triangulation paradigms. For example, a son may function as an extension of the father, who is the sane and perfect one in the marriage. The son is organized by the couple to help Dad with his crazy, disturbed wife. Or, in another script, the two spouses war with each other by hurting their child. The child is perceived as an extension of the other spouse and is, therefore, attacked as a way of hurting the spouse. This particular triangulation is played out behaviorally quite often in separated couples.

LIFE-CYCLE ISSUES

In order to refine goals for treatment, the therapist must first understand the life-cycle issues facing the spouses. The context for marital work with the newly married couple is usually substantially different from that of a couple with children, or an older couple who have already launched their children into the world. In either case, however, the therapist's role is to help the couple succeed in those tasks that are appropriate to their stage of the life cycle. Whatever symptoms they present must be understood in the context of fulfilling these tasks. Understanding the family life cycle, then, helps shape therapeutic goals and, thereby, the overall process of therapy. The therapist operates with various blueprints about healthy family functioning along the stages of the life cycle and encourages the family's development in accordance with such templates.

The Young Couple

The young couple confront several major tasks in establishing their relationship. Each spouse must individuate and help the other individuate from his or her family of origin. Thus, goals for young couples often involve greater emphasis on the formation of a boundaried relationship. Newly married couples also need to develop and refine role division to provide for both socioeconomic security and the creation of a home. Each spouse must help the other develop appropriate sex role behaviors so that both can prepare for having and raising children. Spouses, at this stage, typically are learning to adjust to their new roles. Since they are often younger and more immature, there is less emphasis on generating the intramarital therapeutic coalition, which requires considerable spousal self-actualization. And since the formation of a boundaried relationship is so important for the young couple, a shorter term treatment is recommended. The CFT practitioner will often send young couples off on vacation from treatment for several years, so that they can mature and coalesce as a couple.

Couples with Young Children

Couples with young children generally organize themselves in more traditional role division, with the wife engaged in childrearing and the husband in a career outside the home. With such couples, the husband is worked with to improve his career, if appropriate, while the wife is encouraged to find fulfillment and success in her domestic activities. She is also helped to prepare for a future career. This may involve educational coursework, or part-time work. In addition, the therapist helps the husband assume a caretaking role with his wife, while she helps him move ahead in his career.

Couples with Older Children

In treating couples with older children, both spouses are encouraged to pursue careers, as well as be involved in childrearing. Older couples are more likely to have the maturity to become benevolent and responsible growth agents for each other, and this process then becomes a definite treatment goal. The spouses are challenged to help each other become more complete people both intrapsychically and behaviorally.

Couples with Grown Children

Couples with grown children are coming into the more regressive phase of family life. The earlier, progressive phases of childrearing and career building have been played out, and this life cycle stage is usually a time of relatedness and self-examination. The couple have the luxury of time to become more intimate, to pleasure and enjoy each other, and to complete unfinished business. Later on in this stage there is a quest for fusion with the other and for self-transcendence, which is a healthy preparation for death.

In the treatment of these couples, the intramarital therapeutic coalition can be generated with special emphasis on fulfilling these regressive needs. Furthermore, the coalition can be developed more quickly than with younger couples, who are more preoccupied with the progressive trend of marriage.

BEGINNING TREATMENT

In Stein's (1980) view, the therapist's task is to intervene in a remedial/healthy way with each spouse and amplify the growth trends in their transactions. When the couple presents for treatment, the practitioner assesses each spouse's self-system and maps out the interplay in the marital transaction. He or she bonds with each mate as a reparental agent and contracts to solve the presenting marital problem and promote a healthy relationship.

The practitioner, in addition to normal assessment procedures, questions the couple closely regarding their interactions, asking about how they spend time together, talk to and court each other, and give to and take from each other. He or she asks them about their sex life, if they seem open and willing to discuss it. The therapist asks about decision-making processes, areas and patterns of conflict, and conflict resolution. He or she also asks about how the spouses view each other and their relationship. Finally, the therapist questions them regarding their hopes and dreams for themselves and for each other, as well as how they have assisted each other to grow.

Often the therapist will ask the spouses to frame information as a metaphor, if possible, which can give a more complete picture of the couple, emanating, as it does, from a less guarded and more unconscious part of the self. Critical assessments are gained from body language, vocal tones, rhythm and sequences of interactions, and level of synchronicity in the partners' movements. This stance reflects more accurately than verbalizations the true nature of the spousal self-systems/marital transaction dialectic.

The couple are also questioned about their independent and rearing transactions, as well as the contact they have with their families of origin, in order to give the practitioner a rounded picture of the family holon. The therapist will, in general, also work on the independent and rearing transactions as needed. Both of these other transactions feed back to affect the mates' respect, esteem, and love for themselves and for each other.

The practitioner frames the information to the couple in vivid metaphors. The couple, in turn, reacts to these metaphors in a way that furthers the therapist's understanding. In order to clarify the assessment, the practitioner compares and contrasts the couple's current functioning with their functioning as it could be in an optimal marital transaction. The seeds of these healthy trends are usually latent in the current transaction. At times, the therapist reports this vision of healthy functioning in order to begin programming the couple and broadening the goals of the treatment contract.

For example, John and Louise Black presented with the problem of vicious fighting which would last for days at a time. The husband sat in a slumped position and looked beseechingly at his wife, who monopolized the interview. With a loud and strident voice, she indicated that her husband continually demanded attention from her with little annoying taps. Louise felt that John had no respect for her, as she had repeatedly asked him to stop this behavior. The husband added that she always exploded and then would be icy cold to him for days.

The practitioner vivified this transaction as follows. "So you're the bad little boy who nags his mother for attention. And you're caught being the weak ineffective mother who rejects her son!" And then contrasting this interaction with a healthy one, the therapist said, "You could be loving and growing this woman by showing her that her word is important, respecting her, and helping her to feel powerful in the world. She would love you so much for that. You would get the attention you really need, all the warmth and love you could want." Although the couple may initially reject these positive suggestions and their inherent programming, through repetition and indirect methods these become part of each spouse's self-system.

CONJOINT AND CONCURRENT SESSIONS

In CFT, sessions are held conjointly with both spouses and concurrently with each spouse alone. In this way the therapist gains access to the intrapsychic functioning of each spouse, the behavioral transactions, and the interface between psyche and system. The therapist can use the two formats alternatively depending on the focus of therapy.

Conjoint sessions are useful at the outset of treatment for assessing and restructuring the marital transaction. Spouses' interactional patterns become evident as they repeat the same basic sequences while relating to each other in the session. And they are open to direct therapeutic impact in the here and now during the conjoint meetings. Later in treatment, conjoint sessions are also useful in that they provide direct and immediate feedback about change that is taking place in the marital transaction as treatment progresses.

In conjoint sessions, the therapist can model appropriate behaviors with each spouse. These behaviors include communication and listening skills, as well as reparental interventions with each spouse. With modeling and other reparental inputs in the session, the spouses often experience new and positive marital behaviors that were "impossible" for them to manifest in the past. As these behaviors are materialized repeatedly in the consulting room, the sessions come to inspire hope and renewed motivation to work on the marriage together.

Seeing both spouses conjointly and individually allows for more information gathering. One spouse can be quite helpful in supplying much needed data about the other. In conjoint sessions, he or she can elaborate on or correct each partner's reports. In individual sessions each spouse can provide additional information from a different viewpoint in an uncensored manner. For example, in one case, the husband, Steve, was unable to recall details of his childhood. He could only describe his mother and father as OK. Steve manifested a false wooden smile which seemed to mask deep depression. He tended to deny any problems and spent time bragging about his business.

His wife, Lorraine, after 15 years of marriage, however, was able to paint a fuller picture. Whenever they would visit her in-laws, she observed that neither parent seemed to have much interest in Steve. His father was inclined to rattle off story after story about his own accomplishments. Lorraine told the therapist how Steve's mother would typically ignore Steve, while discussing the latest project she was creating for his sister. This information led the practitioner to better understand how cut off and alone Steve felt. She asked him how he managed to live like a man without a country. Steve responded that he was always a loner and that his life with Lorraine was an improvement over his childhood. Steve added that he really didn't expect much more out of marriage. He agreed, however, to work with the therapist since she seemed to understand him.

Individual sessions are used to deepen the reparental relationship with each spouse. During these sessions attention is paid to each spouse's individual needs and goals. By strengthening the bond with each spouse, the practitioner gains leverage in influencing the spouses' behavior. As such, the therapist will work through each spouse in the individual sessions to effect change in all the transactions and in each family member.

The Dynamics of the Triangle

Marriage therapy can be viewed as the formation of a family triangle. Sibling-like competition often develops between the spouses in relation to the new parental figure. They will then try to outdo each other to win more affection or approval from the therapist. The therapist can use these childlike longings to gain additional leverage with the spouses. For instance, a therapist talked with a wife about her husband's "disgusting" criminal activities as a drug dealer, activities which the wife was covertly supporting. Because the wife wanted to please the therapist and be the favored spouse, she went home and fought with her husband about his drug-dealing. In this case, since the wife also had tendencies to use and sell drugs, the sibling-like competition for the therapist promoted a rivalry between the spouses to curtail their illegal activities.

On the other hand, the triangle of potent relationships formed in the course of CFT treatment can result, in some cases, in splitting and the potential formation of illicit coalitions. When spouses are extremely disturbed at the foundation level, they may begin to split the partner and the therapist into the good object and the bad object. Sudden hatred and negativity erupt toward the bad one, coupled with an all-excusing and blind love toward the good one.

If the bad one is the therapist, the spouse may drop out of treatment. If the mate is experienced as the bad object, either spouse may threaten to separate or divorce. The therapist's goal at this point is to curtail any premature fragmentation and to heal the splitting. If the therapist is perceived as the negative object, he works directly with the spouse in negative transference, and through the other spouse to be perceived as benevolent. The therapist will talk with the spouse about being on his or her side and interpret the splitting reaction as negative transference. He or she will also send such information through the partner who is the therapeutic ally. The therapist might ask the allied mate, who is seen as the good one, to exaggerate his or her own faults or to emphasize to the other spouse how the therapist has really helped.

If the spouse is seen as the bad one and the therapist as the good one, the therapist may move into a very close alliance with the hated spouse, so that they operate as a team. If such splitting is out of control and the mate wishes to leave the marriage because of it, the therapist may have to threaten to cut back on sessions or even terminate the spouse who perceives the therapist as all good.

Engaging the Resistant Spouse

At times a spouse, often the wife, may present with marital problems, while the other spouse refuses to participate in treatment. If the wife enters treatment under such conditions, the therapist will bond with her and assess the marital transaction as far as possible, given the wife's biases. The practitioner can then follow three procedures to engage the resistant spouse: 1) reach out directly and call him; 2) work with the spouse in treatment to change the transaction at home so that the husband becomes less resistant; or 3) as a last resort, simply work with the cooperative spouse, impacting on her mate and the marital, rearing, and/or independent transactions through her.

The practitioner can often be quite successful in engaging a resistant spouse through direct phone contact. After securing the wife's permission, the practitioner calls and introduces himself. Generally, the therapist bonds with the husband, either positively through complimenting him on some aspect of his wife's personality or by being empathic about "how difficult she is." Then the therapist will explain that he or she requires some help in dealing with the wife, and will ask for information about her and how she treats her husband. The therapist listens empathically and identifies sympathetically with the husband's position in the marriage. As the man warms up to the therapist, the therapist firms up a position as the husband's ally. The therapist may offer to help control some aspects of the wife's behavior that particularly annoy the husband, or to help the man learn to deal with this "difficult" wife. The therapist then arranges for a meeting with the husband, or at least another phone call, either to continue hearing his side of the story or to help him with his wife.

Often these extremely resistant spouses become the most workable clients. Their rigidity and distancing function as a protective counterreaction to strong needs for dependency and self-disclosure, which they perceive as weakness. When they discover a reparental agent whom they can respect, who reaches out and allows these longings to emerge and be satisfied, they become quite cooperative. Often at this point, the wife may become uncooperative and may, in fact, try to terminate. The wife's resistance to treatment emerges as her husband relinquishes the oppositional role that he played out for the couple.

If the phone outreach fails or cannot be attempted because the wife is reluctant to inform her husband about her participation in treatment, or unwilling or afraid to allow the practitioner to call her husband, the practitioner must work through her to get the husband into treatment. In this case, the therapist emphasizes the importance of her husband's participation. He or she discusses how greater therapeutic gains will be achieved and how they will come more quickly if her husband is involved. Often the wife actually has conscious and/or unconscious reasons for not wanting her husband's attendance. She may want the therapist all to herself or may want to control her marriage either covertly or overtly without interference from the therapist. The therapist has to work with these issues and convince the wife that she stands to get more of what she wants, rather than less, if her husband comes in.

Once there is an agreement between them, the practitioner arranges for the wife to change the marital transaction positively and to convince her husband to come in. She often will know exactly how to handle her husband to get him into treatment, and the therapist should elicit this information from her. The therapist then formulates a plan with her. The wife may promise the husband that she will change in ways he desires if he goes into couple's treatment with her. She may start a diet if her weight annoys him, or stop complaining about his low income. Or the wife may be more attentive to the husband, while explaining that the therapist has helped her to change. This sets the stage for the husband to consult the therapist about his own problems or other difficulties he experiences with his wife.

If positive marital strategies do not meet with success, the therapist may work with the wife to exert pressure on the husband by amplifying negative tendencies in their normal interactional patterns. The wife might escalate arguments, stop talking to her husband, or walk out of the house. Instead of returning to the marital status quo after such incidents, the wife will amplify her argumentative or withdrawn behavior until the husband agrees to attend at least one session. These types of behaviors tend to stir up the husband's foundation terrors of annihilation and/or abandonment. As anxiety and discomfort rise, so does motivation for change. Of course, the husband may blame the therapist at this point for deterioration of the marriage. The wife, however, is encouraged to reorient her husband to the reality that their marital relationship is the true problem, and that the dysfunction is simply coming into view as a result of her amplification maneuvers. At this point, the husband usually enters treatment.

If all of these approaches fail, the therapist may continue to work on the marriage and the family holon through his or her efforts with the wife, but will be limited in effectiveness. Nonetheless, the therapist can continue to elevate the wife's self-system structures and to prescribe positive growth-oriented tasks, as well as growth-pressuring maneuvers and roles at home. Ultimately, in this type of configuration the marriage approaches a fragmentation point because the resistant spouse is not as supportive or validating as the practitioner. Thus, the wife loses interest in the mate and starts to outgrow him. At the fragmentation point, however, the husband's fear of abandonment may flare and bring him into treatment. He may then become quite cooperative and open to reparental and systemic interventions from the practitioner.

At other times, the therapist may choose not to work individually with the willing spouse because she or he may not be fulfilling the contract of working on the marriage. When this is the case, the therapist is being organized by the spouses to destroy the marriage. The practitioner will then usually send the spouse on vacation from treatment, until she or he brings in the resistant spouse. At that point, the couple, with the practitioner's assistance, contract clearly either for marital therapy or divorce mediation and counseling.

BEGINNING AND INTERMEDIATE FOCI

Goals in the marital work include preserving the integrity of the marriage, controlling abusive behavior and sporadic abandonment, the development of couple time for talking, courting, self-disclosure, and stopping extramarital affairs. Further goals include the completion of "unfinished business"; the equalization of power in the relationship; the enhancement of the couple's sexual life; and the fostering of constructive fighting. Final goals revolve around the formation of the intramarital therapeutic coalition. Goals are tailored to each couple with particular attention paid to the couple's developmental stage in the life cycle.

Preserving the Integrity of the Marriage

Because the couple is viewed as already evolving toward cooperation and personal integration, there is emphasis in the marital work on maintaining the integrity of the marriage. In most cases, breaking the couple up would simply slow down the spouses in their movement toward self/other fulfillment. The therapist will routinely tell spouses who threaten divorce that in order to remarry successfully, each will have to reexperience the stages of courting and attachment, followed by division of roles and responsibilities, and the resolution of power issues, etc., some of which have already been achieved in the present relationship. The therapist explains that each spouse will tend to become stuck in the growth process in approximately the same way in which he or she is presently mired. Since self-system structures will remain largely the same, selection of a new spouse will still tend to reflect the errors of the past. Homeostatic forces will emerge in the new relationship to maintain old self-system structures and repetitive dysfunctional marital sequences.

Thus, the first priority in most marital cases is the preservation of the marriage. Even if the couple is encouraged to separate for growth, the goal ultimately is to reunite them if at all possible.

If the couple presents on the verge of separation or divorce, the practitioner may still operate with a possible goal of uniting the couple if there is enough bonding between them. He or she may initially go along with their wish to separate or divorce, but will remain alert to, and work with, their longings and needs for each other that often arise when divorce is imminent. Great strides in personal development are possible at this juncture, which open new possibilities for relating in the marriage. At such a time, the therapist's vision of the couple's potential together may well determine whether the couple can transmute the crisis into a quantum leap in their growth, or will have to divorce.

Controlling Abusive Behavior

Physical and/or verbal abuse, when present, are prime initial targets for treatment. Abusive behavior that is repetitive in the couple's interactions reinforces and maintains sexual identities that are immature and incompetent. Strong disciplinary measures are needed when acting-out behavior looms as a threat to a family member's safety.

The practitioner's importance to both spouses enhances leverage in controlling or stopping serious acting out. For example, an abusive husband was told to stop hitting his wife because this behavior was "disgusting and reprehensible." Furthermore, the husband was told that if he physically struck his wife, he would lose a month's worth of sessions with the therapist. In another case, a wife who repeatedly threatened suicide to get attention was told by the therapist that she was acting like an ass. The practitioner told her that if she continued he would make sure that she would get virtually no attention from either him or her husband for at least a week. Both maneuvers were effective.

The therapist makes it abundantly clear to each spouse that as part of the whole therapeutic contract, dangerous behavior is absolutely unacceptable. He or she secures agreements with each spouse that abusive behavior will not recur without serious repercussions. The attacker agrees to a severe penalty and/or the victim agrees to a prompt and specific disciplinary action should the abuse recur. In one case, a husband, to whom money was very important, signed an agreement that he would pay his wife $300 for each angry outburst in which he physically hurt her. In another case, a woman was instructed to have her bags packed and in the car, with the understanding that if her husband became verbally demeaning and threatened her physically, she would leave the house immediately and go to a hotel to enjoy herself. In both cases, the abusive behaviors ceased.

Developing Couple Time

Couple time is extremely important as a precursor to the development of a full and rich rapprochement pattern. Spouses need to build in scheduled periods in which they can be spontaneous and open. In the process of discovering themselves and each other, they can learn to communicate, and develop romance, sensuality, and sexuality.

Both mates are given an inviting and detailed description of how they can build couple time into their lives. Couples are encouraged to have both "going-out" dates, where they have dinner, see a show, etc., and "going-in" dates, where they may sit in their bedroom and talk, or go for a walk together. They are encouraged to learn how to self-disclose and listen empathically. If need be, they are taught how to groom themselves so that they are attractive to each other, to give each other gifts, and generally how to act in an inviting manner with each other. They may be instructed to have romantic days in which one mate romances and takes care of the other, as well as getaway weekends and vacations.

Completing Unfinished Business

Unfinished business must be completed before the couple can move on to healthier and more fulfilling levels of relating. Old angers and hurts that stand in the way of intimacy must be honestly aired. Reparation, if needed, must be made, and contracts must be developed that prohibit any further manifestation of the wounding behavior. An atmosphere of forgiveness must also be cultivated.

For example, a wife harbored a great deal of anger over her husband's affair, which had ended three months before the couple entered treatment. She manifested her anger by being icy cold to and sexually rejecting of her husband. When this material was discussed, she reported that she really needed to get even with her husband to let go of her anger. The therapist agreed to a plan by which she disappeared for one full night to do as she pleased in a revengeful way. The therapist indicated to the husband that there was still hope for the marriage and thus steadied him. The husband experienced anxiety, abandonment terrors, and rage. Later in a conjoint session, the husband expressed his fears to his wife. She smiled and indicated that now, since she had left for the night, the ledger book was complete. The therapist had both spouses promise to protect each other from such pain in the future. They were now more free to proceed forward in the marriage.

Equalizing Overt Power

Power relationships in the marriage must be equalized in order to promote self-esteem for both spouses and to lay the groundwork for each spouse's ability to function as a growth agent for the other spouse. Each spouse should be able to initiate and shape various sequences or chains of behaviors in relation to domestic involvements, sexual activity, socializing, and so forth. In many cases, if the will of one spouse overly predominates, neither spouse will generally feel truly powerful or autonomous. The more willful spouse is generally overcompensating for underlying feelings of inadequacy and impotence that he or she experiences at a preconscious level. Usually, highly unequal power relationships are maintained in repetitive sequences in which the more willful spouse projects his or her own insecurities onto the partner. The "weaker" partner cooperates in the interaction by then playing out incompetent and ineffective behaviors.

Metaphors and detailed advice are given to promote powerful and benevolent roles for both spouses. Thus, a couple may be urged to be a wonderful and loving king and queen, instead of a king and his slave. Couples may also be encouraged to play out their control issues through a rich and varied sex life. Spouses may be urged to actively enjoy master-slave fantasies in sexual play rather than in their relationship as decisionmakers in other areas.

Enhancing the Couple's Sexual Life

The couple's sexual life is extremely important in meeting each spouse's primitive needs for self-transcendence and psychological fusion with the other. Sexual fulfillment results in increased energy, vitality, self-esteem, and attachment to the marital partner. As the therapist helps the couple to create an atmosphere of trust, validation, and satisfaction of self and other, deeply rooted tendencies that represent latent or undeveloped aspects of the personality will surface. These aspects can be played out sexually with great gain.

The first step in enhancing the couple's sexual life is, of course, dealing with any sexual dysfunction. In this case, the CFT practitioner integrates sex therapy techniques such as the Semans method or sensate focus exercises (Kaplan, 1974) into the overall treatment plan. However, if the spouses are profoundly immature, such that foundation terrors are extreme and sexual identities poorly formed, they may each first require a period of nurturance and grounding in a positive identity. Only after this can the couple's sexual interaction be considered as a serious focus of treatment. Generally, if this is the case, neither spouse is particularly interested in true sexuality anyway. Even if they express a desire for sexual contact, the deeper longings at this stage of development are for mothering. As they mature, interest in true sexuality and readiness to work for it increase.

When the sex therapy begins, in addition to the techniques described by Kaplan (1979) and others, the couple may be helped to surmount their sexual difficulties through the provision of role prescriptions that are in tune with their sexual identities and unmet needs. These prescriptions free up energies and desires that were formerly restricted by the spouses' concepts of stereotypical sex-role behaviors. A husband who tends to be more passive/receptive, but feels he must play the macho initiator role in the bedroom, may find new levels of sensual and sexual delight when his wife is asked to take charge in the sexual arena. She, of course, being in the reciprocal position, will experience new delights, too.

The practitioner also emphasizes the desirability of an open, playful, and creative interaction. Spouses are taught to discuss their sexual encounters and fantasies and to educate one another in regard to particular behaviors that are pleasurable and satisfying. Fantasy role play as the opposite gender, or sex with a homosexual flavor, or playful master/slave interactions, all can help the mates to integrate male and female parts of themselves. These role plays also help foster the acceptance of natural homosexual feelings, and the mastery of fears regarding dominance, submission, power, and surrender. As a result, fewer thoughts, feelings, and impulses need be suppressed or played out inappropriately in the independent or rearing transactions. Behavioral functioning can then be androgynous, flexible, and more fully goal-directed. With permission to be so free with each other, the partners begin to open up sexually, both in terms of exploring their own secret desires and in the range of sexual behaviors that they can allow and enjoy.

Fostering Constructive Fighting

Constructive fighting is a goal that promotes positive behavioral exchanges and prepares the mates to be powerful growth agents for each other. The therapist works in conjoint sessions to orchestrate constructive conflict and freer expressions of anger. Acceptance of anger allows it to dissipate so that warmth and loving feelings can emerge. The spouses must be able to ventilate anger and hurt to each other in an assertive manner, with "I" statements rather than blaming, "you" statements. Such ventilation allows them to become more individuated from each other and more in touch with their own sense of personal power. Both the individuation and the acceptance of anger that take place set the stage for the ability of each spouse to become benevolently disciplining of the other as treatment progresses.

With some couples, the therapist might foment anger in a conjoint session by magnifying one mate's failings to the other. Or the therapist might model the expression of anger toward one mate in front of the other. The therapist then directly instructs the couple to incorporate these experiences into their interactions.

TECHNIQUES

Interventions in the marital transaction, which in other treatment approaches normally meet with a good deal of resistance, can be implemented in CFT work because of the powerful position of the practitioner as a reparental agent. The mates look to the practitioner to guide them to relate more successfully with each other. Accordingly, the practitioner can work toward many of the marital goals in a direct manner, through education, confrontation, discipline, and detailed tasks.

When the therapist gives tasks, clients are often asked to assume responsibility for the completion of the tasks, rather than for simply doing them. This form of responsibility implies that they must overcome any interpersonal or intrapsychic obstacles that they encounter. In the marital transaction, such obstacles can be formidable. The therapist must predict homeostatic mechanisms that will arise in the couple to subvert the new behaviors. He gives specific and strategic suggestions in regard to dealing with the resistance that will erupt.

For example, when a husband in a distantiated marriage was asked to take his wife out on dates, he was apprised of the possibility that his wife might claim that she couldn't go because she had a headache, or that the couple might fight just before the date time, which would ruin the evening. The man was instructed to have the aspirin ready and some flowers to hand her in the middle of the fight in order to make up. He was then charged with the responsibility for ensuring that the couple went out on the date. This intervention was effective in initiating courtship.

The techniques utilized in the marital work also include bartering, role reversal, role play and modeling, indirect techniques, and a strategy centered around the spouses' fear of loss.

Bartering

If the spouses do not begin to change their behavior through direct suggestions, instruction, and other techniques, the therapist can often succeed through the process of bartering. For instance, a wife wanted to be courted and taken out on dates more often. Her husband wanted her to stop nagging him about making home repairs. The therapist promised the husband that if he took responsibility for ensuring that the couple went on a date each week, he would help to control the wife's nagging. The wife was told that if she stopped nagging her husband about the house, the therapist would get her husband to date her. Often the spouses will maintain that such change is impossible. If the therapist, with a daring twinkle in his or her eye, proposes that they try it as a test, each mate will often cooperate, half seriously and half in an attempt to demonstrate how impossible and rigid the other spouse really is. When the desired interactions actually do occur, each spouse becomes impressed by the therapist's abilities. Positive transference, hope, and motivation for change grow.

When the therapist is successful in work on the marital transaction, each spouse experiences a more positive self-image as a man or a woman. This change in sexual identity tends to create and reinforce chains of reciprocal positive exchanges in the marriage. On the other hand, a progressive step forward in the relationship also results in an abreactive regressive movement, in which the spouses experience primitive terrors and dysfunctional parental programs. When this process occurs, individual sessions with the therapist are useful in helping each spouse deal with the anxiety and fear that erupt when positive marital behaviors are initiated.

For example, in the case where bartering was used effectively, the spouses succeeded in initiating a date life together, whereupon the wife started to complain that she felt unattractive, unfeminine, and ugly. As this dysfunctional sexual identification surfaced, the therapist was able to explore this program with her and work more closely with her to change it. She began to dissociate these qualities from her own self-image. Thankful to her husband for courting and dating her, she began to become more sexually alive with him.

Role Reversal

Many systemic and intrapsychic changes can occur in the marital transaction/spousal self-systems dynamic through role reversal. Spouses discover, integrate, and refine latent aspects of their personalities. They also relate to each other in fresh and new ways.

For example, Heather and Joe had marital roles in which the wife was the parent, giver of time, attention, and food, while the husband was the child recipient. In order to reverse this, Joe was encouraged to be the good father and court his wife with gifts. The husband began to do this in part to please the therapist whom he had begun to view as a benevolent father figure. He gave his wife some expensive jewelry and took her shopping for clothes at a fashionable store. As he did this, Joe began to feel a little more potent and masculine in his sexual identification. The therapist validated this shift in identity. The husband became less needy of validation and attention from his wife. His wife, in turn, felt pampered and important to her husband. She learned about the joy of being more passive-receptive, and her behavior was less rejecting toward her husband.

Even when role reversals involve the assumption of a negative role, i.e., the crazy one, the weak one, or the victim, there is generally positive gain. The spouse learns to become more in touch with his or her own unconscious process or more empathic and helpful to the other mate. The spouse also learns about the more fulfilling and pleasurable aspects of the role he or she had feared to assume.

Role reversal can be used to equalize power in a relationship or to facilitate resolution of the couple's unfinished business, with benefit to both spouses. The less overtly powerful mate can be placed in charge of the couple's social activities for a time-limited period, or in charge of the sexual life, and so forth. For example, a domineering husband spent the day in activities developed by his quieter and more passive wife. She reported feeling more potent and creative in this role, and he, too, discovered the delight of nonplanning, the simple passive enjoyment of the moment. In another case, a woman had expressed almost all of her sexuality with an extramarital lover. Within the marital transaction, she was basically passive and cold while her husband tried to seduce her. After the wife confessed that she was having the affair, the practitioner asked the woman to make reparation to her husband by reversing roles and seducing and pleasuring him. The husband was instructed to be passive and let his wife come to him. This opened up new avenues of relating for the couple, and also helped to reduce both the man's anger and the woman's sense of guilt.

Role reversals can be particularly successful when utilized to deal with primitive fears of engulfment and annihilation. For example, a wife was very controlling with her husband, which assuaged her primitive terror of engulfment. The practitioner insisted at some point that she assume a passive role with him in the area of sexuality. As he took charge, her engulfment fears escalated. The practitioner held the couple to this new arrangement and processed the woman's fears with her in a reassuring mode. The woman was helped in this way to confront and master one of her basic terrors.

Relabeling and reframing can be potent tools for implementing role reversals. In one case, a woman who played the role of the dumb one in the marriage was relabeled the smart one by the therapist. She was told that she was doing a brilliant job protecting her husband from experiencing his own sense of intellectual inferiority. In conjoint sessions, the couple was told that every time she acted dumb, her husband felt smart. The wife's behavior was reframed as smart and loving protection, a superb way to build the husband's ego. Subsequently, the woman began to assert her own positions on various matters, rather than turning to her husband for his opinions. The husband appreciated the change, reporting that he, himself, felt less burdened with responsibility.

In another marital case, a husband's passive behavior was reframed as sadistic and aggressive. He subsequently became more active and his wife became more passive in their relationship.

Role Playing and Modeling

Role play, with one spouse in the role of the other, is an effective intervention both individually and interpersonally. The therapist takes the spouse's role, while the spouse takes the position of his or her partner. The therapist can heighten intimacy and bonding with the spouse and model healthy and remedial reparental interventions which the husband or wife can internalize and then play out maritally. Additionally, in taking the partner's role, a spouse experiences and plays out the opposite end of the homeostatically maintained continuum of behaviors, just as in intramarital role reversals. This process shifts the spouse's perspective to include the other spouse's point of view.

A loud aggressive husband, for instance, was asked to take the role of his passive and withdrawn wife. The therapist then played the man's role. First, he gruffly demanded his dinner, without so much as saying "hello," just as the husband usually did. This disconcerted the husband who was role playing his wife. As the wife, he asked the therapist about his day but the therapist turned away and ignored "her." The husband acknowledged that this was a typical interaction. The therapist stayed in role and demonstrated a different type of interaction. He asked "the wife" questions about her day in an inviting and interested manner. The husband responded warmly in the role play and a positive interaction ensued. The relationship between husband and therapist became closer, and the man was able in part to replicate the interaction at home.

Indirect Techniques

Indirect techniques are also quite useful in marital work. If direct techniques fail, symptom amplification, prescription, or prediction can produce transactional growth. Symptom amplification can be quite useful in stopping extramarital affairs. For example, one woman, who had had affairs during most of her 10 years of marriage, was given the following disciplining paradox: "Go ahead and live in a fantasy world. Take five lovers. They're all the same. It's the father you lost when you were seven years old. Spend the rest of your life looking for him in these men. Who cares if you feel dead, hungry, and empty inside? The search must go on! Why not five at once?" The woman promptly stopped her affairs.

In one case, symptom prescription was used to help a couple change a particularly nasty marital argument in which they engaged with great regularity. The spouses were instructed to have precisely the same argument every other day at 5:30 P.M. The couple responded by fighting less frequently and with less vehemence.

Symptom prediction, when it touches on fear of loss in the spouses, can be extremely powerful in changing marital interactions. If the therapist tells a spouse that the other will leave if he or she does not change attitudes and behaviors, and if this event seems the least bit likely to the spouse, he or she will often quickly change those attitudes and behaviors. This technique can, of course, be amplified into a strong paradox. The therapist might, for example, say, "Go on. Keep acting cold and rejecting toward your husband! Get him to dump you, so you can fall apart and really get into your pain!"

The Fear-of-Loss Strategy

A marriage bound together out of overly strong attachment needs cannot evolve and move forward. Growth of oneself or one's partner that might lead to independence is usually viewed as a threat to the marriage. In order to develop an intramarital coalition for growth, abandonment anxiety must be mastered. When these terrors diminish, positive morphogenesis can occur. Mates become less afraid to change homeostatic patterns and eventually can become powerful growth agents for each other.

The CFT practitioner utilizes the fear-of-loss strategy to help spouses master abandonment anxiety. This strategy is for use after the couple has been helped to develop their inner resources and have to some extent identified with the therapist. Considerable gains in well-being for each spouse can be made when such techniques are used. However, these techniques must be used with extreme care and caution. In the hands of a novice therapist or one who is not in supervision, these procedures could prove highly destructive to a marriage.

Fear-of-loss techniques have been used by spouses to discipline each other in normal family life. A common example is the "wife-going-home-to-mother" maneuver. Tactics that couples have used to trigger fear of loss fall along a continuum of potency. Least potent maneuvers are those where spouses refuse to speak to each other or cancel prearranged dates. At the next level, the husband or wife may sleep in a separate room or refuse to have sex. At the next level, one spouse may threaten to have an affair or to separate. An even more potent maneuver is for one spouse to leave for one day or night, a weekend, or even longer. Open marriage, actual separation, divorce proceedings, and divorce are progressively stronger tactics at the high end of the fear-of-loss continuum.

These maneuvers are also used in CFT, in a manner tailored to fit the exact dynamics of each couple. When a spouse has already used a fear-of-loss tactic successfully to bring about some changes, the therapist may suggest the next higher order threat to one or both mates. Or the therapist working with one spouse may begin to suggest progressively more threatening tactics along the fear-of-loss continuum.

In most cases, the therapist uses some of the fear-of-loss maneuvers and then works closely with the spouses in the ensuing crisis. Generally, the use of these tactics starts with the spouse who is less afraid of losing the partner. First, anxiety about losing the spouse has to be worked through and discussed. The therapist, who at this point has a strong relationship with both spouses, promises to work steadfastly to prevent divorce. He or she discusses and presents the maneuvers as strategic and powerful ones aimed at growth of the spouse and the relationship.

When the spouse agrees to the specific strategy and makes the fear-of-loss maneuver, the threatened spouse will usually become angry and frightened. This is quite useful in fostering the client's being in touch with and ventilating hidden feelings and transference distortions. The fact that the therapist is quite influential with the threatening spouse (and, thus, in a position to help quell the extreme anxiety and fear in regard to the situation) helps keep the threatened mate in relationship with the therapist. The threatened spouse ventilates his or her anger to the therapist, who needs to be receptive and understanding. Transference distortions that are aired are countered and dispelled. The therapist points out how the threatened mate really failed his or her partner and helped to create this state of affairs.

These inputs, coupled with the threatened loss of the mate, help the spouses to experience themselves more clearly as separate beings, with specific failings and shortcomings. The threatened spouse usually takes greater responsibility for the marital failures. This process, together with a strong desire to get back to the partner, produces a high degree of motivation for change. At this point, the threatened mate often moves into a very close relationship with the practitioner. He or she internalizes the therapist at a deeper level and can exhibit newfound maturity in the marriage.

For example, a couple married six years with no children had been in treatment with the senior author for one year. They presented with a devitalized relationship, in which the wife, who was a successful businesswoman, basically earned all the money and "ran the show." Her husband, who was a struggling psychotherapist, functioned as a rather passive and distant wife-child. After one year of treatment, the husband had made great strides in his independent transactions, having started a small private practice, and was feeling more self-confident. His wife was learning to relax and enjoy herself in a more relational and feminine way. They had begun to have sex and there was some courting and romance. However, despite the use of direct techniques, the couple still manifested the devitalized pattern of relating. The husband was overly passive and compliant, the wife overly active and demanding.

At a conjoint session, the wife said that she was fed up with the marriage and wanted to separate. The therapist suggested to the wife that she not sleep at home for a few days in the event her husband did not engage her in a courtly, active, and strong way. The husband jumped up and grabbed the practitioner by the arm, shouting, "What are you trying to do, kill me?" He stormed around the office in an uncharacteristic way. The therapist explained that she was not trying to kill him, but rather to help him be stronger, more manly, and less dependent on his wife. She praised him for showing that very behavior in the session.

After this session, his behavior was markedly more mature with his wife for two weeks. During the third week the husband became passive and withdrawn again, whereupon his wife left the home. She called the therapist from a local motel to ask for reassurance that she was making the correct move, and the therapist steadied her in her position. The husband also phoned the therapist to tell her that he felt utterly crushed and depressed. The therapist gave him a phone session that evening. They discussed how, even though he felt like he was "dying," in fact he could live without her. The therapist also suggested that the wife was getting too healthy to accept and put up with his being a "nonperson" and that he could be much more of a man with her at this point. Subsequent to these events, the couple were able to reestablish and maintain a much healthier relationship, with great gains for each spouse.

In another case, the fear-of-loss technique was used to both enhance marital relating and satisfy the spouses' individual developmental needs. A couple who were married for 12 years had a strongly homoaffiliative or buddy-type marriage. The husband was very feminine in sexual identification, while the wife was very masculine. Each sought same-sex companionship in the other. Each spouse came from a severely restricted and sheltered background, so that normal homoaffiliative adolescent activities were denied them. The couple's interactions were stale and devitalized.

After forming a strongly bonded reparental relationship with each spouse, the therapist suggested that the spouses go back and recapture their lost adolescence. The spouses wanted to explore other sexual relationships, but to do so secretly. The therapist suggested an open marriage with full disclosure.

With some trepidation and considerable excitement, they proceeded to date other people. They discussed their sexual activities with one another, which seemed to vicariously fulfill their homoaffiliative needs. Each discovered that he or she was attractive to the opposite sex, which enhanced gender-based sexual identification and increased self-esteem. They learned how to flirt with and seduce each other in interesting and exciting ways. They began treating each other with more attention, respect, and care, as well as providing exciting and romantic stimulation for each other. Each spouse reported feeling closer to the other and more fulfilled than ever before. They also discussed how they valued each other more, yet needed each other less. After six months of the open marriage, the couple decided to stop dating other people. They renewed their commitment to each other as lovers.

THE ENDING FOCUS: PROMOTION OF THE INTRAMARITAL THERAPEUTIC COALITION

When the reparental phase of treatment reaches its peak, the mates achieve a deep level of connectedness with the therapist. Actions and behaviors that were formerly performed out of devotion to the therapist as the good parent become spontaneous and are experienced as being congruent with the client's sense of self. Love of self and other has increased, and the spouses are ready to relate maritally out of a more mature regard for each other. The therapist then focuses closely on the promotion of the intramarital therapeutic coalition. The point in treatment when this occurs differs, of course, for each couple and depends on the level of the deficiencies and dysfunctions with which they initially presented. Spouses who are older and have invested heavily in a marriage will show more readiness to provide needed inputs to each other and to collaborate with the therapist as growth agents.

When collaboration seems appropriate, the therapist actively enlists each mate as a growth agent for the other. This program has been embedded from the beginning of treatment in direct and indirect suggestions to the couple. In conjoint sessions, the mates have already seen the therapist at work with each other. They have learned through these observations and from marital discussions about the kinds of inputs each requires in order to grow. The therapist now orients each mate to see the other as a loving, growing, health-seeking being with positive intentions who has pocket areas of dysfunction left over from earlier negative experiences and programming. The therapist dreams with each mate about the other's possible self-actualization, and then charges each one with the responsibility of helping to create a more evolved partner.

The practitioner helps the spouses to identify with each other. The mates are shown how they function together as one psychological organism and how each one's development and success are closely intertwined with the other's. The practitioner discusses the nature of mature love and how it is reflected in the therapeutic relationship. This sets the stage for the creation of a marital contract that is strongly win-win in nature. In this type of contract, a spouse's negative behavior is not viewed as a personal wound or as an attack, but rather as a request or need for corrective input.

The spouses are urged to form a positive homeostasis, a stable relationship, which involves reciprocal growth pressure in regard to both doing and being. They learn to meet many of each other's needs for nurturance, programming, and discipline so that both experience a healthy progressive and regressive maturation. In the progressive trend, each will teach, program, encourage, discipline, and inspire the other to new levels of principled and productive behaviors, so that the couple's marriage, careers, and childrearing are enhanced. In the regressive trend, each will promote new levels of empathy, openness, nurturance, sexuality, and validation so that successful rapprochement occurs between them. Generativity and positive symbiosis become goals for the marriage.

The spouses are encouraged to experience each other in terms of both an I-It and an I-Thou relationship (Buber, 1958). In the I-It relationship, the spouse is to be viewed as a separate and unique being who requires his or her own very specific inputs and has his or her own very special destiny, which is the culmination of the progressive trend. In the I-Thou relationship, the mate is experienced, explored, and adored with full consciousness.

The mates are encouraged to accept, trust, and believe in each other as growth agents. Each is oriented to self-disclose his or her needs, as well as to describe exactly how they can be fulfilled. The therapist stops the spouses from interacting in angry, manipulative, or depressively withdrawn ways to get attention or input. Instead, spouses are pressed to actively ask for what they need in a healthy and forthright manner. Each is encouraged to say, "I need attention and loving," or "I need a kick in the pants," or "Please help me to control this negative thinking or crazy behavior." They are also taught to thank and reward each other for being helpful.

The whole cycle of positive input, growth of the spouse, thankfulness, and reciprocity begins to be functional. The mates are taught to be vigilant with themselves in terms of assuming the proper roles, in order to keep the PAR process going. In individual sessions, the practitioner strengthens and amplifies the PAR process. Working in alliance with each mate vis-à-vis the other, therapist and spouse discuss and plan for the achievement of various goals for the other spouse. Or the focus can be on one mate for a period of a month or two, and then on the other. In the later stages of therapy, the spouse who is the more adept growth agent may not meet with the practitioner for several months at a time, while his or her spouse meets with the practitioner to help shape and guide his or her growth.

In therapeutic coalition meetings, therapist and spouse plan out the triangulation of the other spouse. The mate is helped to adjust his or her style and mode of relating to that required by the partner. Then he or she is aided in developing either a more nurturant or a more disciplinary posture as needed. The therapist may maintain the same type of posture, in a kind of back-up position. Or the therapist may take the opposite stance, in a triangulation model similar to that found in a healthy rearing transaction. The therapeutic mate may be asked to give formal sessions at home, or to work with the partner in the office so that the practitioner can refine the spouse's approach.

For example, a husband who started marital therapy in a meek and rather indulgent role with his wife came to assume a benevolently disciplining role with her in the latter part of treatment. His wife was compulsive in her acquisition of jewelry, clothing, furniture, and other material things. While these tendencies had abated a great deal during the first phase of treatment, they were still operative in the woman's life in the latter stages of treatment. The husband, in collaboration with the therapist, informed the woman in a firm way that he was finally going to help her achieve personal discipline and self-control. Every time she bought something that cost more than $25 without discussing the purchase with him and securing his agreement, he would remove one of her more treasured pieces of jewelry and put it in the safe deposit box for a year.

The wife initially resisted this arrangement, maintaining that she would feel naked without her jewelry. The husband pressed for this agreement. The therapist, in a nurturant and sympathetic position with the woman, allowed her to ventilate her feelings. The wife was angry at both of them because of their alliance and felt that her husband was just like her father and that she would have nothing, just like her mother. The therapist listened to her vivid recollections of her parents. Her father, a very austere and rather controlling man, had not permitted her mother to buy many clothes or household items. As the wife processed these memories and abreacted about the past, she began to admit that her husband was not really her father. She decided that she was, in fact, out of control and did need help. She admitted that material things were not really meeting her needs. Her attitude became more respectful and thankful toward her husband.

The new marital arrangement worked out nicely. The wife lost her great desire for material things, and she became clearer that what she really needed was more affection and attention from her husband. He, in turn, felt more in control and was better able to make contact with and steady his wife.

While spouses at times experience the collusion between therapist and partner as overwhelming and frightening and may offer some resistance, in general they are quite relieved to have such attentive and constant help in achieving their own goals. Spouses become quite thankful to both therapist and mate.

Over time, as the spouses grow, they become more adept than the therapist at assisting each other. Each mate has more information about the other than the therapist can ever have, as they share far more experiences in daily life. The therapist points out to each spouse that now they can be more effective in working with each other than a paid professional. The therapist will work to undo the positive transference at this point, talking honestly about any errors made in the therapeutic process, confusion, or misunderstandings he or she has had about the couple, and generally highlighting his or her own human frailties. The therapist urges spouses simply to turn to one another rather than directly to him or her for input and advice, and becomes the junior collaborator in the growth-promoting alliances.

For instance, a husband collaborated with the therapist to promote his wife's independent transactions. The therapist suggested that the wife, who was quite fearful of success, target the type of job she really wanted and then send out resumés. The husband immediately sharpened the program by insisting that five resumés be sent out each day by 12 noon. This refinement was necessary because he had realized that the wife's addiction to soap operas was a danger to her performance of the task. He then promised to buy his wife a new office outfit for each week in which she sent out 25 resumés. The wife was anxious about her career, but also thrilled to have her husband's support. She sent out the resumés and secured a position that she really wanted within two months. The therapist made a point of telling each spouse how she was not as careful and on top of the situation as the husband was.

When the spouses achieve a firm devotion to one another and are consistently more astute than the therapist as growth agents, the practitioner pushes the couple out of treatment. He or she becomes less and less active in giving direction or advice and meets with the couple less frequently. For example, the practitioner might begin seeing a couple only monthly in conjoint sessions, or might give them a three-month vacation from treatment. The couple learn to become self-sufficient.

At termination the mates are relationally mature and personally competent. Each is grounded in a separate selfhood, but also devoted to the other. Usually, a graceful symmetry of body language appears when the spouses are together. Setting a termination date three to six months in advance can prove quite helpful in putting a final limit on the clients' dependence on the therapist. Fear of loss can be worked through and final adjustments made in the spouses' therapeutic postures with each other.

Case Transcript Segment

An example of the beginning stages of the intramarital therapeutic coalition is illustrated in the following excerpts taken from a conjoint session with Lois and Dave and the senior author. Lois, a successful college professor, was considering a career change after the impending birth of the couple's second child. Dave, on the other hand, had been building up his computer software business so that he could fully support the family.

The couple originally presented with a parent-child relationship in which Lois was the stable, introverted mother figure and Dave, the verbal, outgoing, and irresponsible son. The therapist effected a role rever-

sal in which Dave became more stable and reliable as a husband and
caretaker. This process permitted Lois to reconsider her career goals
and to meet her own dependency needs.

Lois: I need somebody to look up to, someone who is powerful, a male
   father kind of figure. As you continue to maintain that stance, that
   will free me.
Dave: You have it perfect.
Lois: Because what I don't want to get into is another position where
   I can be exploited by another man.
Dave: Like many who have been weak.
Therapist: That's right. Including you. Maritally, you basically started
   out exploiting her.

The husband goes on to take a strong, benevolent position with his wife.
He identifies with the therapist as a model, even though she is, in fact,
female.

Dave: Right, and yet it has been part of a realistic, if not highly attractive, game plan. As we can see, tables are turned. Turned on you.
   You should be happy and you are scared. You never had anybody
   like me before. You deserve somebody like me. I'm like Diana. I
   will teach you how to be outgoing like me. I will tell you how to
   handle that. You would be sacrificing autonomy, but you would
   gain more because you would have me as a real partner. The exact same thing as I had with Diana you would have with me.
Therapist: So, it's clear from what you're saying, Lois, for your real big
   success . . .
Lois: I'm dependent on him.
Therapist: You're dependent on his success. That is, your success is his
   success.
Dave: I'm your leader.
Lois: You will enable me to shine as nobody has enabled me to shine,
   because you've got a lot more farsightedness than any of the other
   key men that have been in my life.
Dave: In terms of you. Not only that, but I also give you more acknowledgment. Farsightedness is wonderful, but acknowledgment is the
   key issue to you and me.

Later in the interview the therapist closes a contract that the wife
had made with the husband to promote his growth. The wife had delineated what her husband needed to do in order to come through for himself
and for her in the ways he had promised. The therapist modeled forceful

contracting for the wife. She then scheduled the next meeting two months in the future to allow the couple to develop more autonomously.

Therapist: (to Dave) Now we have a list here where you're going to put your money where your mouth is. And I want to have a meeting in which we are going to review that list. Why don't we meet on Tuesday, February 19th, two months from now.

Dave: OK, Tuesday the 19th is fine.

Therapist: I will personally examine the proof at that time.

Dave: Let's define the proof up front.

Therapist: OK, I'm writing it in my book. We have agreed that each month you will increase your income by $100. Then the house has to be taken care of. And no traffic tickets. What else did you put on the list?

Dave: Let me get it out. Relatively complete efficiency, no mess-ups at work.

Therapist: So you will demonstrate this proof on the 19th. I like that! And then Lois can proceed to get upset and so forth. Earlier you predicted that she would get upset. But is she going to have another feeling besides feeling strange about you really being a man? Is she going to have other feelings?

Lois: Very, very good.

Therapist: Right. She is going to feel thrilled and relieved and great to have a man, and a benevolent and incredible daddy. And this time around, a daddy who not only takes care of her but will catapult her to the top.

Dave: Acknowledge your smartness, that you married into magic! And acknowledge my smartness, that I married into true love beyond the hope of describing it! And beyond any hope I had of seeing it! In the car, I told you I couldn't imagine having a better wife. And what you and I don't like, I'm going to help change.

Dave and Lois are beginning to relate in a novel and exciting manner. They are forming a win-win relationship in which each spouse is fully behind the other.

SUMMARY

Although marital work is difficult and challenging, the CFT practitioner can work with couples creatively to remediate dysfunction and promote psychosocial health. The next chapter illustrates how the strategies and techniques presented in this chapter are used with various types of marital cases.

CHAPTER 8

Marital Case Examples

O the puzzle, the thrice-tied knot, the deep and dark
pool, all untied and illumin'd!
O to speed where there is space enough and air enough at
last!
To be absolv'd from previous ties and conventions, I
from mine and you from yours!
To find a new unthought of nonchalance with the best of
Nature!
To have the gag remov'd from one's mouth!
To have the feeling today or any day I am sufficient as
I am.

—Walt Whitman (1891, p. 87)

The following three case examples illustrate various aspects of the marital work in CFT. Each couple is at a different stage in the family life cycle.

BOB AND LUANNE

The wife of a young married couple in their late twenties called the junior author to arrange for an appointment. When asked if she would bring her husband, Luanne said that at first she would prefer to meet alone. At the initial interview, Luanne presented as an attractive woman with a rigid and frozen smile on her face. She reported that she had no sexual feelings for her husband, did not respect him, and couldn't talk to him. She had been through a brief affair, of which he had no knowledge. Luanne wanted to make the marriage work but felt the chemistry

176

was wrong. The therapist realized that this couple could be easily fragmented if he supported only the wife's individual needs for self-fulfillment. He discussed Luanne's needs and how they seemed to conflict with loyalty to Bob and her marriage. The therapist told her that she could probably have both if she was willing to work hard.

The therapist then discussed the possibility of leaving the marriage. Luanne was told that if she left the marriage she would probably meet another man with whom she would have to start all over again. The therapist predicted that she would almost definitely end up in the same marital dance in relating to the next man. At the same time, however, the therapist paradoxically suggested that Luanne leave the marriage as an alternative. This therapeutic maneuver allowed the unhappy spouse the freedom to fantasize about leaving the marriage but carried the suggestion that the symptom of marital incompatibility would recur. To a spouse in a new marriage, such a prediction can be just the inducement needed to bring in her mate for therapy.

Bob presented at the second session as a mild-mannered, soft-spoken young man. He spoke in a precise way and explained that he was a patent attorney. Bob said that his wife had never been a happy person and that there was nothing he could do to change her unhappiness. The therapist learned that a typical sequence in the couple's marital transaction was one in which the wife would say that she wanted more self-disclosure and romance, and the husband would try to accommodate her, only to be rejected. The husband would then withdraw into his protective shell, provoking the wife to renew her demands for closeness. The therapist realized that Bob was weak in dealing with Luanne and that he was afraid of her anger. Although married for only five years, this couple had already lost the spark and magic of their courtship period.

The therapist also found out that Bob was still very much involved with his mother, whom Luanne treated as a positive mother figure. Since Bob had still not individuated from his mother, the therapist reasoned that it would be difficult for him to make a deep attachment to Luanne. Luanne, on the other hand, did not discourage Bob's relationship with his mother because she wanted the nurturance that her mother-in-law provided. Luanne was apparently getting more out of the relationship with her mother-in-law than with Bob.

The therapist used the first few conjoint sessions to develop a clearer schema of each spouse's intrapsychic dynamics, and to bond with each of them as a reparental agent. He began to restructure their relationship with Bob's mother. He asked Luanne to stop phoning her mother-in-law directly, but rather to relate to her through Bob for one month. After every contact Bob had with his mother, he was to share any news or information about her with Luanne. Bob resented this and had less contact with his mother, as did Luanne. Meanwhile, both spouses had bonded with the therapist, who continued to directly discourage excessive contact with Bob's mother.

Bob described his role in his family of origin as the oldest of three children who was mother's confidante and advocate. His relationship to father was distant except when he tried to defend his mother during the parents' frequent marital conflicts. He rarely succeeded in this mission and fights would end with father leaving angrily, and Bob and mother comforting each other. This enmeshment had apparently been longstanding, going back as far as Bob could remember. Luanne verified Bob's impression of the triangle. His parents' marriage had become more distant over time and Bob fulfilled his mother's needs for nurturance and love. He became more identified with her than with his father. The weakness and passivity that Bob manifested maritally earned him Luanne's contempt and disdain. Bob said that he hated his parents' fights and remembered being terrified by his father's anger. Bob stated that he avoided fights with Luanne because he valued harmony, contentment, and rationality above all else. The practitioner hypothesized that Bob's basic terrors concerned annihilation.

The therapist formulated the following schematization of the marital transaction in terms of Bob's self-system structures. When Luanne was critical of Bob and withdrawn from him, he experienced her as the critical, rejecting father who was distant from him. He, in turn, would become weak and passive with Luanne, much as his mother had been with his father.

The therapist also asked detailed questions about Luanne's family of origin. She reported that she was an only child and that her mother had been a cold and domineering woman who had berated both her and her father. Luanne's father had been weak and ineffective in relation to his wife, although he, at times, feebly defended her against mother's rage. Luanne had sought her mother's approval unsuccessfully throughout her life. Even as a young adult, she was still attempting to secure her mother's validation. Over time her father had become a shadow figure – there in body but not in spirit.

The therapist hypothesized that Luanne had recreated her parents' marriage, with Luanne playing the role of the dissatisfied, rejecting mother and Bob portraying the weak and passive father. At the same time, she experienced herself on the level of sexual identification as similar to her mother, a woman who was not feminine but more like a rigid man. She felt cold and barren, but also afraid to lose her connection with Bob. On the foundation level, Luanne experienced a profound fear of abandonment, which made it difficult for her to leave Bob. This basic anxiety had a greater influence over her behavior than her feelings of loneliness in the marriage.

The therapist decided to see each spouse individually twice a month to develop the reparental relationship. Individual sessions with Bob focused on changing his identification from a worthless, weak, "maternal" man who was browbeaten by his "husband," Luanne, to that of a strong, competent, and worthwhile man. The therapist began to father Bob through nurturing, disciplining, and programming him. He validated Bob's intelligence and prized his warmth and sensitivity. He encouraged Bob to view his masculinity as a positive attribute rather than to associate it with father's coldness and rigidity. When Bob would withdraw or run away from Luanne, the therapist disciplined Bob. He called Bob a coward, like mother, who never stood up to father and dragged her son inappropriately into the marital disagreements.

At times the therapist paradoxically prescribed this symptom for Bob with statements like, "Keep practicing being like your mother, so that when you have children you can have them fight your battles for you." The therapist showed Bob how to fight constructively with Luanne by having Bob play his wife's part, while the therapist role played the new Bob. In these enactments, the therapist was very playful with Bob, who learned how to relax more during the sessions. The role playing facilitated Bob's formation of an empathic bond with his wife, while simultaneously meeting his own needs for a warm and validating relationship with the therapist. Bob ran away from his wife less and instead pursued her more by initiating dates.

Luanne, meanwhile, was feeling much closer to the therapist, who had confronted her on her bitchiness and successful imitation of her mother. Luanne hated her mother, who had been both cold and domineering. She adored her father who was much kinder. The therapist pointed out that Luanne had a façade of warmth which represented her somewhat superficial identification with the weak father, but that underneath there was a cold and rigid interior much like mother. Luanne sobbed about being like steel inside, and feeling unloved and unlovable. In this case, the therapist had to initially demonstrate his strength and determination to the client. He took a tough, disciplinary stance with Luanne at first, while later he was more nurturant toward her.

Luanne began to respect the therapist because he was as tough as her mother for whom she secretly longed, while at the same time he could be very nurturant. When Luanne would express fears and doubts about herself, he would encourage her to do her best and maintained that he believed in her. Although she had a college degree, Luanne had been working in a woman's clothing store, a job which she did not particularly like. With the therapist's and Bob's support, Luanne enrolled in a graduate program in education to become a special education teacher. As she felt stronger in her independent transactions, she began to experience herself as more relational and feminine in the regressive trend. This process led to greater receptivity to Bob.

Bob, in turn, had also been helped to become more successful. He went out and bought himself a new wardrobe for the new man he felt he was becoming. His practice grew significantly and he was establishing a good reputation.

After one-and-a-half years of treatment, the therapist switched the therapeutic format to conjoint sessions twice a month and one individual session per month with each spouse. He asked the couple to creatively develop a date life. One task was to meet as strangers at a local elegant single's place. They accomplished this task and reported that they had rediscovered each other.

The practitioner then suggested that the couple read erotic literature and view erotic films. The spouses were also to tell each other which scenes aroused them the most and to play out these fantasies with each other. Although both spouses were somewhat reluctant and shy, they agreed to this task as an experiment. After the mates got over the initial discomfort and anxious laughter with each other, they "got into role" and each achieved what they reported as new heights of sexual pleasure.

The practitioner programmed the couple for a healthy intramarital therapeutic coalition but he did not work very actively on it as an immediate goal. Rather, after seeding for health with various images and metaphors, he terminated with the young couple after two years of treatment. Five years later the husband dropped a line to the therapist saying that he and Luanne had two girls and were happily married.

JACK AND LINDA

Marital therapy with Jack and Linda Smithson, who were described in Chapter 6, continued after the presenting problems with their son, John, had abated. This case showed a typical pattern: As the child ceased to function as the identified patient, the marriage emerged as the problem. Jack and Linda had complained about the isolation and conflicts that permeated their marital transaction – the schism that had led to an enmeshed mother-son relationship. The therapist began to see the couple together twice a month and each individually once a month.

Linda was particularly dissatisfied with Jack's lack of attentiveness or affection.

In a typical transaction, Linda would verbally attack Jack for his disinterest. He would then withdraw and drink. She would binge on snacks while watching TV with John. Jack, who had covertly promoted her binging by bringing home candy, ice cream, etc., would then overtly criticize Linda for her indulgence and proceed to sleep on the couch. In order to break this cycle, the therapist started creating positive reciprocal exchanges in the marriage. Jack was to take Linda out on a date each week. He was instructed to treat her as a real "date" by courting her and by finding out all about her. Linda was to prepare a 10-minute hors d'oeuvre reception for Jack when he returned from work each day. After considerable fighting with the therapist, who maintained her insistent and demanding stance, the couple began to fulfill these tasks.

In order to promote greater vitality and romance in the marriage, the therapist had to develop the spouses' sexual identifications. The therapist reframed Jack's drinking as "sucking from the bottle." She suggested that he be a man and talk and work through his frustrations and anxieties instead of turning to alcohol. She programmed him to be assertive in the world instead of withdrawing "to suck" when things didn't go his way.

Jack, who was quite bright, was working in a sales position well below his potential. He was challenged and encouraged to seek a higher level position. Through additional role playing and disciplining and reprogramming interventions, the therapist was able to help Jack achieve the position of sales manager. She helped him relate to each sales person working under him by role playing and modeling positive and motivating inputs tailored to each of his staff. Over time, Jack's success grew significantly. His involvement with the men working under him helped Jack to understand how to deal with his son, John. He became more identified with the practitioner and developed a new internal image as a competent man. His ability to approach and relate to Linda increased dramatically.

Meanwhile, Linda had successfully completed a college business course. She shyly confessed that as a young girl she had wanted to own her own business. The therapist clapped her hands in approval of her dream. Linda went on to say that she really loved fragrances and cosmetics.

The therapist suggested that Linda enter the field by selling nationally known cosmetics to housewives in her neighborhood. Linda refused to do this because she felt unattractive. The therapist nurtured and prized her and Linda became more interested in improving her own appearance. Linda went on a diet and began to lose weight. The therapist taught her how to project a professional and successful image through modeling and direct education. Linda's self-image improved and she set her career sights higher. The therapist role played and taught her how to interview for jobs. Linda then found a management position at a boutique specializing in imported fragrances and soaps.

Linda's growth through the playing out of her masculinity in the progressive trend led to a regressive eruption of her basic terrors. She felt incompetent on the job and believed that she would fail the therapist and then be abandoned by her. In order to avoid the humiliation and abandonment, Linda tried to terminate. She was won back by the therapist, who demonstrated her commitment and resolve by phoning her at home, confronting her with her projections, and validating her fears but not allowing her to terminate. She gave Linda a small perfume bottle necklace as a transitional object to take with her to work. The therapist's reaching out to maintain a deep level of nurturant relatedness was a corrective experience for Linda, and her terrors subsided. Her anxiety on the job decreased. Meanwhile, the couple began discussing means by which Linda could eventually open her own little shop.

The therapist built an entrepreneurial image for Linda, dubbing her Coco the Second, after Coco Chanel. While Linda initially laughed and protested about this name, she nonetheless eventually took it as an iconic image which inspired and organized her vocational progression. Linda's self-esteem grew. She was able to relate to Jack in a more loving and validating manner.

After two years of treatment, the level of both spouses' sexual identifications had grown to a point where they were seriously interested in a romantic and sensual relationship with each other. The therapist began to have frank discussions about their sexual preferences. She then worked with each mate so that he or she could function to fulfill the other's needs.

For instance, Jack divulged that he had a wish to be very passive at times, while Linda massaged, kissed, and licked him all over. The therapist realized that Jack wished to play out his feminine side now that he was more grounded in his masculinity. She challenged Jack to ask Linda to help him bring out his femininity so that he could become a more complete person. The therapist spoke of how she wanted him to be able to be healed and filled up by Linda, to have the kind of loving mothering and fathering he needed available to him right at home. Jack succeeded in having Linda give to him. And he, in turn, began to promote her in her career.

The therapist shared visions of each spouse's possible actualization with the other, which generated intramarital excitement and attraction. She also taught each one about the other's dynamics and the remedial inputs needed to promote such growth. For instance, the therapist told Jack that Linda needed to feel powerful and successful, and yet grounded in a secure, intimate relationship. Working with Jack who played Linda in a dyadic role play, the therapist modeled behaviors that Jack could later use to fulfill Linda's deeper needs. The therapist took Jack's chin in her hand and tilted his face to make eye contact. She said, "You have beautiful eyes! And you are so clever, I can just see you at the top! So successful, gracious, and warm! And I will be with you always."

In couple's sessions the therapist modeled the behavioral inputs each needed, so that the other could learn directly. She disciplined by admonishing them to stop being cowards and to explore new levels of intimacy. And she programmed for a full and gratifying life together. For instance, in one couple's session, she described a scenario in which Jack, the head of Smithson Inc., would take Linda to Paris on the Concorde to romance her and to help her look for new fragrances for her boutique. The couple began to jokingly refer to their big trip as a symbol of their successful future.

After three years of treatment, Jack and Linda's marital transaction achieved new levels of intimacy, mutual fulfillment, and growth promotion. Their sexual life became more varied and exciting. Both Jack and Linda developed themselves professionally. Their parenting teamwork improved dramatically.

In the final phase of treatment, the therapist encouraged the mates to take over more of the therapeutic role with each other. Linda was able to confront and discipline her husband when he behaved inappropriately. She also had learned to nurture Jack deeply by being very attentive to his needs for comfort, touching, holding, and validation. Jack viewed his wife as a competent woman and related to her in an empathic, encouraging, and prizing manner. The therapist then functioned mostly as a supervisor for the spouses and finally terminated with them.

MARC AND GITA

In another marital case, a woman in her late fifties consulted the senior author for advice about whether to divorce her husband. Gita, an attractive brunette, tearfully explained that she had just discovered that her husband Marc, a successful businessman in his mid-sixties, had been having an affair with his beautiful young secretary for the past two years. Gita felt totally humiliated because evidently everyone knew about it before she did. She explained that she had successfully raised three children with relatively little help from her husband. Two years before, the last child had left for college, and at that point she had started writing a novel, which she felt certain would catapult her into the limelight of success.

She reported that her husband, on the other hand, had been considering a leisure-filled and more relaxed retirement. When Gita had confronted her husband about the affair, he maintained that he wanted to terminate it and work on his marriage. Gita had asked him to fire the secretary, which he had refused to do, claiming she was indispensable to his business. Gita felt continually suspicious about Marc and this young woman being together each day, but powerless to do anything about it. She reported that she was totally depressed, demoralized, and worthless as a human being.

The practitioner bonded empathically with the woman and advised her not to leave her husband. She traced the woman's life back to a childhood in which she was the parental child with two younger siblings. Her mother was a passive, hard-working woman who was meek and submissive. Her father was a dominant, hard-working railroad employee. The parents were Russian immigrants who greatly valued upward social mobility.

Gita had married during a time of traditional male/female role division and had followed her prescribed role as the homemaker. However, over time she had matured and gradually become more assertive. As she developed her more masculine side, she dreamed of writing her novel and becoming famous. When the last child had left for college, Gita began her novel. Unbeknownst to her, Marc began his affair. The therapist encouraged her to bring in her husband and she agreed.

At the initial session with both spouses, the practitioner hypothesized that the couple had been threatened and uncomfortable with the impending proximity of the empty nest. The switch in male-female roles had also upset the couple's homeostasis and threatened Marc's sense of himself as a man. This led to Marc's having the affair. The therapist reframed the couple's predicament by explaining that Gita's new strength and vitality and Marc's new passivity were really signs of a mature couple who were advanced in the life cycle.

The therapist went on to say that this role reversal was characteristic of healthy couples, but that at times, especially right after the last child had left home, those couples hit snags in their relationships. She suggested that it would be a tragedy to waste the 36 years of growth that they had shared. Gita and Marc agreed. The therapist offered to step in and help Gita develop some muscle with her husband so that she could even the score. This, in turn, would free up the spouses to get on with their lives and enjoy the many good things ahead. She also offered to work with Marc to help him enlarge his sense of himself as a competent man so that he could handle the marital role reversal. The spouses were much relieved and agreed to work with the therapist.

Marc presented as a depressed and guilt-ridden man who couldn't understand why he had been so cruel to a wife who was quite wonderful and supportive. He explained that he had simply meant to be helpful to his young secretary, but that this had led to the affair. Marc was the only son of hard-working, upwardly mobile immigrants, who were of Polish descent. His parental role model was that of a man who worked 60 hours a week in construction. His father had bought and renovated apartment buildings. His mother was a very religious woman who quietly worked at cleaning and decorating the apartments that they rented out. The parents had a patriarchal family structure and traditional role allocation.

Marc had also been comfortable with the traditional role division he had shared with his wife through most of the marriage. When cultural influences impacted on Gita to expand her role as a woman, and success allowed Marc to consider growing beyond his role, he had no inner programs with which to guide him in the new reality. The prospect of relating to Gita without the children as buffers was anxiety-provoking to Marc. He then turned to a new surrogate wife, his docile and subservient secretary.

The therapist suggested to the couple that she would help each of them to develop a richer and fuller life together. She contracted to help both Marc and Gita feel that they could have it all: love, fun, and success. Targeting an intramarital therapeutic coalition immediately, the therapist insisted that they had to envision new and different goals for each other, and then be behind each other to achieve those goals. But first the large, awful, raw wound resulting from Marc's affair would have to be healed. The couple agreed to this therapeutic contract.

As a punishment for Marc's disloyal and hurtful behavior, Gita was to disappear for an unspecified time and enjoy herself in any way she desired. This fear-of-loss maneuver satisfied Gita's need for revenge, increased her sense of potency in the marriage, and activated strong abandonment fears for the couple to confront and master.

Gita rented a cottage in her favorite locale in the mountains and stayed there for two weeks. Meanwhile, Marc had three sessions with the therapist. He experienced severe chest and stomach pains and felt that he was dying without Gita. Spouses will often report psychosomatic complaints when fear of loss arises. Infantile fears that abandonment will lead to death can become actualized as somatic symptoms. Nonetheless, the therapist sent Marc for a medical exam. The report suggested that the pains were indeed stress-related.

In sessions, Marc examined his own reactions more closely. He found that he had become frightened at Gita's assertiveness and endeavors with her novel. He had refused to participate in helping her with it in any way, and yet he understood how profoundly important the book was to Gita as a measure of her self-worth. He longed to see Gita and talk to her, which he described as a great contrast to the way he usually felt. Marc also worried about Gita's having an affair while she was away with someone better and more attractive than he was. He felt deserving of his pain, and he expressed that it was a cleansing punishment. He also reported that now he really understood the pain he had put Gita through, and his compassion for her grew. Marc spoke of his impending retirement as a great emptiness, which he had tried to forget about in his tryst. All of these insights were experienced as emotionally charged revelations to Marc.

The practitioner educated Marc about the joys of being alive and taking time to "smell the flowers." She talked about androgyny as having the best of both worlds. She described the courage and power it took for a hard-working man his age to explore himself and learn how to relate and to relax.

When Gita returned, Marc professed his love and interest in her. He wept and told her he had been through "Hell." Gita was pleased. She felt that the ledger between them was even. Marc felt that he no longer had to punish himself with depression. The couple had a sexy and romantic interlude for a few days.

Both spouses attended the next session. The therapist asked if Gita felt totally free and clear of the affair. She maintained that she really wanted the secretary to be fired. Marc vacillated between wanting to please his wife and being worried about his business. Finally, the therapist challenged Marc to make the choice between a marriage to his business or a marriage to his wife. The therapist explained that Gita had to feel that she came first in Marc's life, particularly at this time, and that if he met this and other needs the couple could have a wonderful life together. Marc agreed to give the secretary notice and to help her to find another job.

The therapist continued to meet with the spouses individually and conjointly over the course of eight months. She programmed the wife to view herself as a worthwhile and generative woman, and she empowered her to ask for and demand more time, attention, and support from her husband. The therapist validated the husband for his accomplishments, and stretched his definition of masculinity to include self-disclosure, relaxation, and relating. She taught Marc to experience vicarious satisfaction of his residual needs for recognition, power, and success through his wife. The therapist also urged him to promote and support his wife's writing project.

The therapist role played and modeled the inputs that each mate needed to grow and urged the spouses to take over her job. She had them give reparental sessions to each other in her office so that she could refine their interventions. The husband began editing his wife's novel and became her most enthusiastic supporter and coach. At their final session, he was insisting that she appear on a national TV talk show, while she laughed and blushed. Gita, on the other hand, became romantically involved with Marc. She began giving him massages and taking him away to seashore hideaways to relax and to play with her. Gita also became truly validating of Marc as a strong and successful man of many accomplishments.

At termination, Marc planned to sell his business and move into a consulting role. This move would require less of his time and involvement, while providing travel opportunities for the couple. Gita was completing her novel and discussing it on a local TV talk show. Each spouse felt devoted to the other. Three years later Gita's novel was published and Marc had become the consultant to his firm. The couple sent a postcard to the therapist from a vacation trip they were enjoying together.

SUMMARY

CFT can be tailored for use with couples at various stages of the life cycle, from Bob and Luanne's young marriage to Marc and Gita's seasoned relationship. In each case we see clinical goals appropriate to the couple's life-cycle demands. However, there are similarities in the treatment process in these cases. Most notably, the spouse's individual growth is promoted in tandem with changes in their marital transaction. This biphasic approach seems to produce the most comprehensive and long-lasting results.

CHAPTER 9

Treatment of the Single Adult

"Would you please tell which way I ought to go from here?"
"That depends a great deal on where you want to get to," said the Cat.
"I don't much care where . . . " said Alice.
"Then it doesn't matter which way you go," said the Cat.
" . . . so long as I get somewhere," Alice added as an explanation.
"Oh, you're sure to do that," said the Cat. "If you only walk long enough."

— Lewis Carroll, Alice in Wonderland (1978, p. 53)

When a single adult presents for treatment, the CFT therapist will usually tailor a reparental stance, meet the client's needs, and work with the client to evolve and actualize an optimal life plan. The life plan generally involves growth in three critical areas: individuation from the family of origin, career progression, and social relationships.

At times single adults present with minor problems or symptoms. If a young adult is temporarily stuck in the process of individuating from the family of origin, and/or simply confused about issues of sexuality or career development, a few sessions of strategic intervention or encouragement may suffice. Many single adults, however, present with more serious symptomatology and developmental arrests, and the therapist must bond and contract for longer term treatment.

Older single adults follow much the same treatment process as younger clients. Individuation issues that remain must be resolved, although, of course, usually without the option of systemic restructuring of the rearing transaction in the family of origin, since parents may have already died. Independent transactions are still promoted, but often the clients seek to have more fun/play in their lives. With older adults, there may be a mourning process to complete, especially if a previous spouse has died. Most older single adults seek to find a partner with whom to enjoy life, and dating and/or remarriage is often a goal of treatment.

This chapter presents the tripartite CFT approach to working with single adults. The promotion of individuation, career, and social progression is described. This is followed by a transcript in which a single adult discusses her treatment. The chapter closes with a detailed case example.

INDIVIDUATION FROM THE FAMILY OF ORIGIN

As with other adults in CFT treatment, the single adult regresses in relation to the practitioner. The client becomes attached to the therapist and begins to differentiate from the family of origin. Original loyalties begin to dissolve. With the single adult, however, this dissolution of family-of-origin loyalties is even more critical than with couples because single adults are usually much more involved with their families, both intrapsychically and behaviorally. The practitioner, in order to hasten his or her own impact on the client, must accelerate the client's psychological detachment from the family of origin.

The therapist works to individuate the client both intrapsychically and transactionally since psychological individuation facilitates systemic changes while systemic changes, in turn, lead to greater intrapsychic differentiation. Initially, therapist and client explore and delineate the client's historical and contemporary role in the family system, noting how this role has undermined self-actualization. The client may function as a parental child, a scapegoat for marital tensions, or as an incestuous object in the family-of-origin rearing transactions, rather than as a more autonomous individual. In addition to exploring these transactions, the client may be sent into the family system to observe typical phenomena in the rearing and/or marital transactions. This maneuver alone can facilitate a leap toward individuation.

For example, a bright, but depressed 27-year-old man, Stan, entered treatment with the senior author. He had never dated women and was marginally functional in his job. Stan initially reported that his parents, with whom he lived, were quite normal and supportive. As the therapist questioned him, however, she learned that his mother was a depressed and minimally functioning housewife, whose only companions included the 10 horses the family owned and Stan. Stan's father was a physician who was barely involved with the family.

The therapist reframed the situation to Stan as one in which he was "married" to his mother as his father's replacement. Stan was told to go home and observe his parents closely, paying particular attention to the programming with which mother and father had tied him into his role. He was astounded to find that almost every sentence his mother said contained a suggestion regarding his defectiveness or incompetence. She continually programmed him to fail, with statements like, "Too bad you're such a quitter, or you could go back to college!" His father's brief verbalizations concerned Stan's repairing and building things around the house. After a few weeks of studying these sequences of interaction at home, Stan moved out of his parents' home.

In the case of a more disturbed single adult, the family may also be brought into the office so that the therapist can vivify and directly change the rearing transactions in the family of origin. The therapist will use the family session to detriangulate the young adult and help him or her to leave home properly. If the enmeshment is too severe to be remediated in a few sessions, the parent(s) may require a referral for therapy.

For example, an 18-year-old girl, Mary, was enmeshed negatively with her mother with whom she lived. Her mother continually and ineffectively nagged her regarding her appearance, her choice of friends, her lack of a job, and so forth. Mary's father was deceased. The practitioner asked Mary to bring her mother into the office and, over the course of several conjoint and individual sessions, bonded with her as an ally. The therapist sympathized with the mother's difficulties with Mary and offered to give her respite from the heavy load by being a demanding parental figure with Mary. The therapist then insisted that mother and daughter work on being more positive with each other.

The therapist validated Mary and dared her to show her mother that she could be a competent adult. The girl's dream for herself involved modeling. The therapist suggested that Mary find a related job, selling clothing in a fashionable department store. Also, she was to save up her money to move out of her mother's house. The therapist disciplined Mary by asking her to bring in a favorite item of clothing to be confiscated when she did not carry out the agreements relating to her goals.

In the fourth conjoint session, Mary's mother helped to set the date for Mary's move out. The mother was asked to pay for modeling school if Mary demonstrated responsible, mature, and respectful behavior toward her. Mary moved out of her mother's house within the agreed time schedule and completed modeling school. She remained in individual treatment with the practitioner. Her mother requested treatment for herself and was referred to another therapist.

In some instances, of course, single adults who are extremely distantiated in the family system require just the opposite process. These adults are urged to reconcile with those family members who can provide positive relationships. In this manner, they can heal old hurts and receive further economic assistance and/or psychological input. For them, several family sessions are usually held in which negativity is discharged and dispelled, and mutual longings for interaction are uncovered. The practitioner helps the family arrange plans for consistent and normal contact, which include visits and phone calls.

In one case, for example, the therapist asked a "long lost" father to fly into Philadelphia from Alaska for a session with his daughter. In the session, father and daughter confessed their hurts, disappointments, and sense of loss in regard to the other. They agreed to have phone contact on a bimonthly basis. The practitioner maintained phone contact with the father in order to reinforce the father-daughter relationship.

During individual sessions, clients are encouraged to understand their role in their family systems and then to define themselves as separate from the family in order to move "out and up." To this end, the practitioner realistically continues to depict the growth-inhibiting attributes of the family of origin, until the clients are able to differentiate themselves more adequately. The practitioner actively programs the single adult to erase dysfunctional programs and models and enables the client to actualize innate potential. At times, some experiential work, such as gestalt role plays or guided imagery, are used to uncover suppressed or repressed scenes and experiences involving the family of origin. Usually, a great deal of anger and bitterness surfaces. These feelings can then be discharged in the role play.

While the client is in the hypnotic-like condition induced by these exercises, the practitioner enters the role play as the remedial/healthy parental figure. The therapist may then create a story that generates a corrective experience for the client. For example, Jon was a young man who had been infantilized by his mother. Early memories of his mother's infantilizing behavior would surface in session which he was encouraged to describe in detail. As he spoke, his voice would shake with anger. The therapist asked Jon to take a soft pillow, which she kept nearby, and suggested to him that it was really his mother. In the trance state, Jon grabbed the pillow and ripped it to shreds. After this cleansing outburst, the practitioner moved into a reparental position and said, "I'm your mother now. A mother who believes in you!"

As a result of these techniques, which are directed toward intrapsychic change, the single adult usually begins to change behaviorally in the relationship with his or her family of origin. The practitioner can accelerate these morphogenic movements by enabling the client to ventilate some of the anger he or she feels toward his or her parents directly to them, or to deliberately break away from the well-defined role in the rearing transaction. Often this can be accomplished by encouraging the client to assume a role in the family that is diametrically opposed to that role that he or she ordinarily takes. For example, the "good boy" may be instructed to complain or voice disagreement while visiting his family. This maneuver also helps the client to be in touch with latent and unintegrated aspects of the self.

Most single clients are instructed to break away from family-of-origin figures with whom they are enmeshed, and/or contact those with whom they have been distant. The client is helped to complete unfinished business with parents and/or siblings, both by discharging affect in individual sessions and by relating differently to family members. Reluctance to pursue these tasks may be great. Over time, however, the client's willingness to change his or her role increases, as the attachment to the therapist grows. If need be, the therapist may have to discipline the young adult to enable the client to gain the courage necessary to individuate appropriately from the family. And by changing his or her role in the family, the client is free to pursue more self-fulfilling and goal-directed behaviors.

As the single adult differentiates from the family of origin, important self-system changes occur. At the level of sexual identity, there is an expansion of self-definition and enhanced potency. Childlike needs for approval from the family or other transference figures diminish. At the foundation level, primitive terrors of annihilation or abandonment tend to be dispelled after the client dares to behave in typical "forbidden" ways and discovers that he or she does not end up annihilated or completely abandoned by significant others. Even though family-of-origin members may initially reject the client, he or she does not experience the infantile helplessness which had been dreaded.

For example, a few months after Jon (mentioned previously) had left the role of mother's companion and had moved out on his own, he reported that he had never felt better in his life. He experienced himself as having more energy and being more productive than ever. Jon also felt more competent and able interpersonally.

CAREER PROGRESSION

The second focus with single adults in treatment is on the promotion of independent transactions. Long-term goals include sufficient income for an independent lifestyle, as well as the gratification of needs for mastery, creativity, and recognition. The practitioner works in a step-by-step fashion toward these goals, starting at the presenting level and working toward the client's own desires and dreams.

In developing the independent transactions, the practitioner first gives free reign to brainstorming about the client's potential career. The client is invited to join him or her in envisioning an exciting future. If needed, the client is helped to search for clues and ideas about career activities that would be inherently exciting, challenging, or attractive, as well as suited to his or her temperament and unique abilities. Current work involvements, as well as hobbies and leisure activities, often contain the seeds of a potential career goal.

If clients are particularly impoverished in terms of experience in the world, they may be encouraged to experiment, travel, and explore, so that they can make informed choices regarding career plans and goals. The single adult has, of course, much greater range and freedom in the exploration of the world than married clients or clients with children, and the practitioner takes full advantage of this. The therapist may promote travel or study periods abroad, or participation in creative job or business opportunities that involve a great deal of travel or large investments of time and energy.

The practitioner's task is to break through ceiling barriers in the client's thinking about him- or herself. Artful dreaming and programming by the therapist usually strike some chord which engages the client's imagination and interest. The therapist, reacting to the client's assets and talents, envisions him or her in arenas that are more challenging, stimulating, creative, and/or more lucrative. Then the therapist describes these images to the client. One or more of these scenarios will typically be chosen by the client as a goal.

Once the client has a goal in mind, the therapist helps to plan step-by-step movements toward it, and as the good parent/mentor, assists the client along the way. If needed, the therapist plans a strategy with the single adult to develop a social façade which is designed to secure personal goals. He or she may educate or send the client to learn about dress, grooming, bearing, and social skills.

For example, Jon started treatment with a basically unkempt appearance. He wanted to start his own business and had to meet with potential clients. The practitioner referred him to a local hairstylist, and, because he was tall and broad-shouldered, to a men's shop specializing in larger sizes.

Like an involved parent, the therapist might take a client shopping for clothing if he or she cannot find appropriate work apparel. Or the therapist might give the client a work-related gift after a major accomplishment, such as a pen or a briefcase. These activities are also aimed at promoting identification with the practitioner, who generally has already worked on his or her own professional image.

Further education may be encouraged. Starting with goals such as a high school diploma, BA, graduate degree, or advanced trade training, the therapist continues to encourage the single adult to move in the direction of his or her ultimate career goals. The client may be advised to read trade journals and books pertinent to the chosen career and to attend appropriate workshops and lectures. The therapist also promotes networking so that the client can develop helpful contacts, role models, and mentors. For example, a young graduate student was encouraged to develop a collegial relationship with her favorite professor around a research topic in which they shared an interest. Subsequently, they wrote and published a paper together.

All along, the therapist has been programming for eventual fulfillment of the client's dreams, and this serves to fuel the client's day-to-day efforts. Scenarios that involve lofty goals for the client can be proffered and bandied about by therapist and client in playful and interesting ways. The therapist delineates the details of the scene, which helps to anchor it as an embedded suggestion. Usually the client will go on to fulfill at least some aspect of the scenario in reality, even if he or she initially has scoffed at the suggestion. For example, a therapist working with a young man who had just started a computer software business told a story in which he saw the young man sitting at his large rosewood desk in an office at the World Trade Center in New York City. Six years later, the practitioner received a note from the man saying that he had been offered one million dollars for his computer business, an offer he was pondering over while sitting at his rosewood desk!

SOCIAL RELATIONSHIPS

Concurrent with promotion of individuation and career goals, the young adult is encouraged to develop in the third critical area: social relationships and dating. The CFT practitioner uses a strategy for dating, which Stein (personal communication, 1981) called the program of three. This program promotes the intrapsychic and behavioral growth necessary for healthy and successful dating and eventual selection of a spouse. Clients on this program are instructed to date three different men or women. In this way they learn about different types of people, and what they need and want in a marital partner. Clients are advised to abstain at first from sexual intercourse with these dates. The goal is to enter relationships in a mature and measured manner in order to avoid premature infatuation and dependency or a pseudo-intimacy, which reflect the clients' dysfunctional interpersonal trends.

The therapist guides, encourages, and disciplines the client so that he or she chooses healthier and more successful partners and more fulfilling relationships. Less stimulating or enjoyable partners are left behind. Thus, the single adult is able to build success experiences that lead to a solid sense of self-confidence with the opposite sex. As the client progresses, he or she moves into higher level social networks. The therapist assists by programming for a richer, more positive sexual identification, and, if needed, by helping the client with self-presentation and social skills.

The therapist programs, as a good parent would, to find a healthy partner: one who is a "good fit," and who is able to provide a relationship that becomes growth-promoting. The therapist programs for a prospective spouse who is emotionally able to give as well as receive, is intellectually and culturally stimulating, successful, playful, and sexually attractive. The single client is taught, however, that the most critical element to look for in a prospective spouse is commitment to personal growth, because this commitment could potentially remedy any problem area.

This type of programming may be met with great resistance. Clients may protest that such people do not exist. The therapist continues to hold out the visionary program and sends clients out to experience various interpersonal situations in order to dispel their illusions.

In order to assist clients in their search for partners, the therapist encourages those on the program of three to enter a number of different social arenas. At first, the clients may go to singles bars or singles groups, or write/answer singles ads in reputable magazines. In these areas the clients are likely to meet partners who are less psychosocially developed. After mastering those experiences, clients are encouraged to network at more sophisticated levels. The practitioner may suggest joining stimulating professional or business associations, and/or organizations devoted to culture, the arts, or political endeavors; attending specialized lectures or courses; or embarking on educational cruises or tours. For example, one client began taking art classes, another became active in local politics, and a third audited a graduate science course. Out of these activities, all three ended up having dating relationships with partners who were more psychologically developed and shared common interests.

Single adults who are more culturally deprived or impaired in their ability to relate follow the program of three later in the course of treatment. Some clients may require a period of a year or two in which they simply learn to have a relationship with the therapist. With this type of client the promotion of individuation from the family of origin and career goals are targeted first. Dating is put on hold. Only after the therapist first establishes him/herself as the "good mother/father," in whom the client feels grounded, can the client begin to recapitulate the normal developmental stages of childhood. The practitioner then proceeds to work on developing friendships, followed by encouraging the client to have sexualized experiences with several companions. These interactions tend to be more adolescent in character. Finally, the therapist introduces the program of three.

Those clients who have experienced a great deal of failure in sexual encounters are also discouraged from beginning the program of three. They are also usually encouraged to have a series of positive sexual encounters before they enter a period of more measured and mature dating.

As clients move along in the program of three they usually become involved in a single, more serious relationship, and the other dating relationships fragment. At this point, the therapist arranges to meet with the new couple. Usually the therapist already has a good idea of the nature of this relationship, as he or she has been guiding the client's interactions in the process and has already observed its impact on the client. Based on interactions with the couple in the conjoint session, the therapist gives feedback to the client about this prospective partner, much as a parent would.

If appropriate, the therapist will assist directly in the partner's growth by seeing him or her in individual or couple sessions. The practitioner kindles natural growth trends in the couple and educates each member of the couple in regard to inputs that the other needs in order to grow. The therapist charges each with a mutual sense of responsibility for the other's maturation and helps to delineate far-reaching dreams for the couple. Then the practitioner eases into a more distant consultant role, putting one or both members on vacation from treatment.

SYNERGISTIC EFFECTS OF THE APPROACH

At times, single adults will insist that they are not interested in any one, or even two, of the three critical areas just discussed. In most cases treated, this disinterest has proven to be a defensive posture used by clients to deal with deep-seated beliefs that particular achievements are impossible for them. Once the therapist succeeds in embedding the suggestion that they can move forward in the blocked areas, desire for growth becomes strong.

By working with single adults in the three critical areas – individuation, careers, and social relationships – the practitioner can produce synergistic effects that allow for growth to a high level of productivity and fulfillment. Advances in one area are typically quite helpful in the other two areas. As single adults differentiate from their families of origin, they can interact more freely with business associates and members of the opposite sex without the need to play out familial roles that are self-defeating. Clients who become more successful in independent transactions meet prospective partners who are functioning on a more sophisticated and competent level. Reciprocally, meeting more developed partners through the program of three allows clients to network at a higher level in the pursuit of goals in the school/work arena.

CASE EXAMPLE #1

Some excerpts from an interview with a single adult who had completed three years of CFT treatment will illustrate the growth process from the client's point of view. Gloria, an attractive brunette in her mid-thirties, spoke about her treatment with the senior author during an interview at a conference for mental health professionals.

Gloria had previously been in treatment with two insight-oriented therapists for a total of six years. At the time that Gloria presented for treatment with the senior author, she was unable to support herself financially and lived with her mother, a widow in her late sixties. She had an enmeshed relationship with her mother, a retired actress who tended to be rather cold and controlling with her. Her father, a successful wholesale businessman, had been dead for six years. Gloria described him as a domineering and distant figure who was at times somewhat seductive and charming. Her parent's marriage was described as patriarchal and covertly hostile.

Although Gloria had been able to complete college, she had essentially failed at a wide variety of jobs, including sales, social work, and clerical positions. When she presented for treatment, she had begun a crafts business. Gloria had a history of failed relationships with men, who were often abandoning, controlling, or manipulative with her.

Gloria had sought treatment for her problems with both work and relationships. In this first excerpt from the transcript of the interview, Gloria describes her rearing transaction and the remedial input provided by the therapist. We can see that the therapist worked to foster individuation from the family system by providing direct instruction and positive programming.

Gloria: When I first started seeing Diana, I was overinvolved with my mother in a negative way, and I think Diana really insisted at the beginning that I not even discuss with my mother that I had this situation (*therapy*), just to kind of separate my life a little bit more.

It was getting less and less bearable being in my mother's house, and the setup was not good for me to do the work that I wanted to do there. I mean, she was definitely undermining my efforts. There was an extra bedroom at home that I could use as a studio, but somehow or other she just didn't want to disrupt this room, you know. So we battled about that for a long time, until my mother agreed that I could use it as an office. And then suddenly, (*she said*), "I don't want to pay too much on the heating bill, so you can't have this room as warm as you need it to be." Or, if I would buy $20 worth of materials, she'd say, "You'd better not spend any money until you see if you can sell that stuff!"

So, the more draining it got, the more Diana urged a quick move into an apartment. And I was really scared. And Diana just very matter of factly said, "You know, you'll produce. Once you're there, you'll produce." And I did.

Note the contrast in the programming provided by the two maternal figures. The programming provided by the therapist in reference to Gloria's work was based on a working hypothesis that seemed reasonable and realistic. Before she started therapy, Gloria had exhibited her crafts successfully at a number of shows. She had also sold her work to a number of stores and thus had demonstrated some capacity to perform. She was open to the therapist's suggestions in regard to marketing and developing her work.

In the next excerpt, Gloria continues to describe how the movement "up and out" from her mother changed their relationship.

Gloria: I think the landmark began when I moved into my own apartment and set up my studio there. There was the beginning of a more civil relationship. Suddenly, I was starting to do something that I enjoyed successfully, so when my mother came to my home or I went to hers, there was less defensiveness about things, and I was less territorial. We could just be two adult women. And I didn't need to be thinking what I could do to take something from her. And she didn't need to be carping about things in her life.

It is clear that progressive movements in the different life areas overlap. Behavioral/emotional separation from this client's mother depended on the achievement of economic independence and vice versa.

The next excerpt describes how the client regressed in relationship to the therapist, as she individuated from the family of origin. In the remedial stance, the therapist provided a warm, positive, validating, and physically nurturant, yet powerful maternal figure. The positive transference and identification with the therapist are evident.

Gloria: We (*Diana and I*) were getting closer. At first I thought this was a little strange, 'cause, you know, we'd hug, and I always thought that that was really inappropriate from everyting I'd heard about. And yet, I know now that it's absolutely the best possible thing that you could do to establish a real contact with anyone.

She gave me a lot of physical contact, a lot of looking in my eyes, names she might call me. Just really being like a mother. I mean, not to the extent of cooking my meals and feeding me, but just that component of closeness.

She is the best Mom you could ever have! She can also be a Dad, too. But to have someone just be absolutely adoring and supportive, and love me, and encourage me, and totally want to validate that I was great and my life was worthwhile, and whatever I wanted was worth going after! It was just totally different than all this carping, negative, critical miserable stuff that I'd grown up with. You know, I mean she's warm. She's real flesh and blood. And my own mother, just . . . somehow, there was a coolness to her. There was not a real, rich, earthy physicality to our relating.

Gloria clearly recognizes the nature of the growth process in the therapeutic relationship: dependence, identification, and introjection, followed by independence. She continues:

Gloria: I just felt really a part of her (*Diana*) and I do now. I feel like everything that I think is wonderful about her is true of me. I just feel that identification with some really wonderful qualities. Not like, "Oh, she's the therapist and I'm just someone seeing her." And I also feel that I've learned from her how to offer that to other people. I know how to somehow or other give them so much of myself in a way that makes them aware of themselves and positive about themselves.

You know, somehow or other I could feel very, very little with Diana and, somehow or other, being real little let me get big. If you get real little, then you get to move out. That's just it. It freed everything up for me.

The client describes how her introjection of the therapist further changed her relationship with her biological mother.

Gloria: As I've grown more, I'm just naturally more responsible in the way I relate to my mother. It's almost like I'm in a miniature way doing for her and encouraging her growth.

In the next excerpt, Gloria describes the nature of the introjection as she experiences it within her own self-system.

Gloria: OK, the question (*from the audience*) is, do I feel like I carry Diana inside of me? Do I have (*internal*) dialogues? I don't know if it's specifically that way, but rather what I said before – the identification with the "good mother" is so deep. I feel like her. I kind of do feel that there's something there for me inside, like the feeling, "Mother is at home," you know, almost all the time.

In working on the independent transactions, the client is guided, disciplined, advised, encouraged, and programmed in order to achieve success. In the following segment, Gloria describes part of this process, as it occurred with her.

Gloria: I moved out of my mother's not much less than six months after I started with Diana. It was just like there was a guardian angel that, you know, showed me the perfect place to be, and I was starting to get busier. Diana gave me an assignment to promote myself – 20 hours each week, doing something to make myself known to people. To get the word out, or put business cards out, or talk to a buyer in a department store or specialty shop – wherever it was that I was going to go.

When a client is in a strong positive transference, the trust and belief in the therapist is very childlike. Gloria generalized this into a sense of a "guardian angel," which helped her to feel secure while she took difficult steps toward individuation and career goals.

In the next segment, Gloria describes how she was able to change her dating behavior in order to find a partner who was more fulfilling.

Gloria: Diana told me not to sleep with men just to avoid going into a relationship too quickly. Because if I was too intimate with someone too quickly, all my neediness and insecurity and crazy stuff would come up. I'm certain that I just repeatedly was driving people away and picking the wrong person. Diana would say things like, "I want you to have three casual boyfriends at all times." And I said, "Yeah, I'd like to have even one these days. I'm not meeting them!" That kind of stuff.

There was an incident pretty early where someone didn't pay for me when we went out one time and she said, "What! He didn't pay for you at dinner! He made you pay for your dinner! I want men to pay for you when you go out!" She was really just teaching me about valuing myself and having men treat me properly. And not to sound like real old-fashioned sexist ideas about what's appropriate, but just not to create situations for myself where I was being used in one way or another.

And somewhere along the line we were discussing what would be the good things or traits, or the good qualities to look for in someone, and I said, "Well, what does he have to do? Seven tasks? Are there 12 tasks or something?" And she said, "Yes, Yes!" And actually, the next week she had the list, but it was 13. Now I'm not certain if I could repeat all 13, but there were some pretty good guidelines for me for weeding out the rogues and the insincere people from the ones who were afraid of really being close to someone. Just some very good general principles of what would be healthy in a relationship. The first one was the funniest. It was: "He must initiate contact 80% of the time." That way I couldn't be chasing someone around. And I would find out who was really interested in being with me and who would play with me if I happened to drop myself in his lap. And Diana said that this person should arrange for interesting and pleasant dates; that they should be eager to see me, reluctant to leave me; that they should be very intelligent and successful; and the list went on. And then, the most really profound and important one was the last one. And it was that the person had to be as totally committed as I was overall to growth and fulfillment in all areas of life. Just really high ethical standards, and, you know, everything: material life, intellectual life, business life, spiritual life, and every way. There had to be that depth of communication and commitment in the relationship. And the idea was that the relationship was two people really prizing and elevating each other all the time, and helping each other to achieve separately and together all their goals.

We just kept working up the ladder, you know, meeting people, working toward those better qualities. I would complain, "They're all ugh. There's nothing good out there. I just can't meet anyone good." Diana said something like, "Well, you get a basically good man, and you just grow him up." And I did.

About one-and-a-half years after treatment began, Gloria met a man who, in large part, fulfilled the criteria on her list. In the final segment of the interview, the client gives her view of termination. The seeds that the therapist planted regarding the development of an intramarital growth coalition have sprouted.

Gloria: I feel that what I've gained here are tools for living. And while there's an incredible relationship, the mommy bird knows how to kick the babies out of the nest. And there have been real specific times when I've sought an answer from Diana about certain things, and she says, "You know, you know, and I'm not going to say any more about it." Or, "I've said everything, and now you have enough input, and you have to go, at this point, on your own." So, I don't have a fear about that particularly. And I also think that when we (*Gloria and her fiancé*) are working as a couple together and we're starting to do for each other what Diana would do for us separately, it will be time to leave. The other day we were talking about it in her office and I realized that when you leave Mommy is when you get married, right?

Gloria's fiancé, a successful and personable businessman in his midforties, completed two and a half years of treatment with the senior author, which included individual and couple sessions. Four-and-a-half years after Gloria started treatment, the couple married. With mutual support, both pursued midlife career changes. Gloria, after achieving success in her crafts business, decided to pursue an advanced degree in the social sciences. Her husband entered a new field of endeavor based on one of his old childhood dreams. They were also planning to have children.

CASE EXAMPLE #2

Joanne, a single adult, presented as a plain, overweight woman of 31, whose dark hair and features emphasized her semitic heritage. With a halting and uncomfortable manner, she asked the senior author for help in dealing with "a horrible weight – a depression I've had as long as I can remember." She also wanted to work on issues with men which she felt had precluded the success of any long-term relationships.

Joanne lived in a small apartment with a female roommate. She was employed as a secretary in a local real estate office. Joanne described herself as a terribly serious, quiet, and shy person. Her childhood and adolescence were spent with few friends and many books. She did not date during adolescence. She had started college, but had dropped out after two years. During college Joanne had become briefly involved with many men and had been highly promiscuous. After college Joanne worked at a few clerical/secretarial jobs and dated less frequently. She had one long-term, on-again, off-again relationship with a young man who showed up sporadically, mainly for sex.

Joanne reported that her mother was a beautiful and quiet woman, a housewife who was meek, unassertive, and quite concerned with appearances. The family was Jewish, but had always lived in a non-Jewish neighborhood, in the midst of which Joanne felt "ugly and different." Joanne's mother was very concerned with denying their heritage and had often expressed disappointment about Joanne's strongly semitic appearance. When Joanne was three years old, her mother gave birth to her only other sibling, a blond-haired, blue-eyed girl, Carol, who, Joanne claimed, became the center of mother's attention. Joanne tried to be the good little girl to gain mother's approval, but felt quite unsuccessful. Carol, the star of the family, became an elementary school teacher. She had married a fellow teacher and was now expecting her first child. Joanne felt that she would never be as successful as Carol.

Joanne described her father, who owned a small grocery store, as a self-absorbed man who was fairly disengaged from the family. When he related to Joanne, he could at times be warm, but occasionally he would be inappropriately seductive. Joanne reported that these episodes, in which he would be overly affectionate and call her "lover," made her feel sick to her stomach. Much of the time he was distant and preoccupied. During these periods, he could become explosively angry. While he never struck Joanne, he did occasionally strike her mother. Joanne described her parents' marriage as angry and distant. Her father worked long hours in their store, and her mother resented this bitterly.

After gathering this information in the first three sessions, the therapist formulated a map (Figure 9) illustrating the marital and rearing transactions in Joanne's family of origin and Joanne's self-system structures. The marital transaction manifested unresolved anger and conflict in which each child would eventually be drawn into the fray. In one typical sequence, the parents would fight bitterly, and father would hit mother or retreat to the store. Mother would then turn to Carol with whom she was enmeshed in the rearing transaction and seek comfort and consolation. Father, in turn, would at times seek out Joanne and

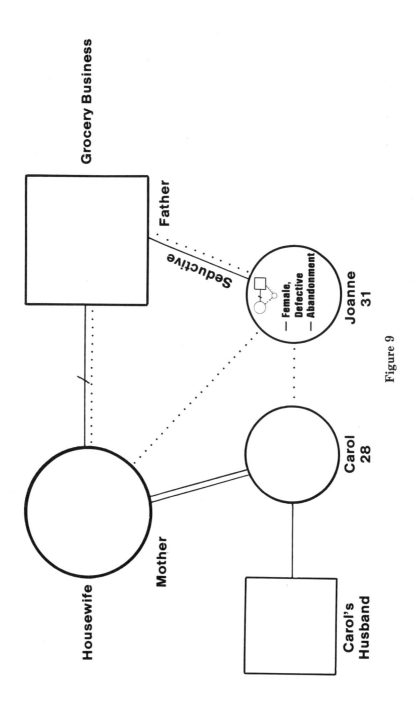

Figure 9

form an incestuous coalition. Joanne's relationship with her father was a very precarious one, however, and she would often find herself being replaced as the parents sought each other out once again. Hostilities between the parents would then emerge anew.

The therapist formulated the following hypotheses about Joanne's self-system structures: At the foundation level, Joanne experienced a diffuse emptiness and fear of abandonment based on early failure experiences and disappointments with mother. At the level of sexual identification, Joanne experienced herself as a defective version of her mother — feminine, quiet, meek, ugly, different/Jewish. This identification was based on the close relationship which she had shared with mother for the first three years of her life. At the triangulation level, Joanne's experience was that mother had abandoned her to father for comfort or sexualized contact. Father, in turn, would then abandon her when mother was available.

The following excerpts from the transcript of the third session illustrate the bonding and contracting techniques used with Joanne. The therapist used a metaphor to describe and vivify Joanne's deficits as part of the bonding process.

Therapist: Joanne, you are the lost, ugly duckling in the family. You deserved to be discovered, enjoyed, and adored by your mother and father! Instead you were dumped. Your mother saw you as the ugly, dark side of herself. And your father taught you that you were only occasionally interesting to men, and then only as a sexual object. So you never were able to turn into the swan you could be!

Joanne wept in response to these words. The therapist went on to propose the therapeutic contract.

Therapist: I want to find that swan in there and help her get attached to the right fellow. But in order to get there, I'd have to give a lot. You have to have the right inputs, the kind of nurturance, programming, and discipline you should have gotten in the first place. Someone who values you for who you are, who believes in you, who can find the beauty in you!

Joanne: This is impossible.

Therapist: (moving closer to Joanne and holding her head so that their faces were a few inches apart) That's nothing but your mother's program for you! You're very bright and, I have a hunch, special in a lot of other ways I don't know of yet. You were never discovered and developed by a delighted mother or a delighted father.

Joanne: Well, I can't change that.

Therapist: Well, you can change that somewhat. You could receive some of those inputs from me. But, of course, you'd have to merit them.

Joanne: (still crying): How?

Therapist: By turning yourself inside out and really playing ball with me. You'd have to leave that family and really be like my kid and let me raise you. Really be in touch with me, following my advice and ready to hear it from me if you don't.

Joanne: Would you really do that for me?

Therapist: Maybe, if you agree to really open up to me the way I said.

Joanne: Why should I open up to you?

Therapist: Because I can most probably help you get ahead in life — move out of that ugly duckling position in that family to find a man and a fulfilling career.

Joanne: (quietly) I want that. I can barely believe you, but I want to do it.

The therapist contracted with Joanne to give her the nurturing, disciplining, and programming that she needed. She was seen for one hour per week, with telephone backup.

After contracting with Joanne, the therapist targeted each self-system level for growth. In order to fill foundation deficits, Joanne required a great deal of prizing and unconditional positive regard. She needed to experience herself as the center of attention, as special and favored over others. In order to build Joanne's sense of a positive, feminine sexual identity, the therapist modeled as a strong woman who cared less about appearances and more about integrity, caring, and generativity. She programmed Joanne to be a successful woman who had real inner substance. At the triangulation level, Joanne needed to learn to view men as potentially fulfilling and adoring companions, while being grounded in her own femininity.

In a typical therapeutic intervention, the therapist would take Joanne for a walk in the conservative residential area in which the therapist worked and lived. She would put her arm around Joanne and tell her how she believed that a woman should enjoy the pleasures of life, power and success in her own job, a loving relationship with a man, and the enjoyment of having and raising children. Joanne would laugh self-consciously and ask the therapist how she could be so uninhibited as to have her arm around her in this neighborhood. The therapist would reply that she didn't care about the neighbors' perceptions, but only about Joanne's needs. On one such outing, Joanne wept at these remarks and said, "That is what I always wanted my mother to say to me!"

In another session, the therapist said, "Your mother didn't realize how wonderful you are. I know you think I'm crazy when I say this, because you've been so programmed to think of yourself as a piece of crap, but I'm not crazy. I know you are special." Thus, the therapist both reprogrammed Joanne and worked to build positive transference. The building up of the therapist in Joanne's eyes served to heighten her bond with the therapist and provided a positive model of self-love and appreciation.

At the same time as the therapist worked intrapsychically, she enabled Joanne to disengage from her role in the family system. In family interactions, Joanne would try to please her mother with car rides and small gifts. She rarely attempted to interact with her father. Usually she would be hurt by her mother's continual praise of Carol and her endeavors. Joanne was instructed to set up a lunch date with her father to begin a warm and closer relationship with him. She was told to limit his inappropriate interactions with her by asking him to not call her "lover." Instead, she was to ask him for ideas regarding the possibility of starting her own small business, a move designed to structure a normal father/daughter relationship. She was also instructed to stop trying to buy mother's approval. Joanne stopped initiating contact with her mother, whereupon her mother began pursuing her. Joanne began to feel much more powerful and valuable in the family system.

Along with these maneuvers, the therapist also programmed Joanne to be tougher and more assertive with others. The therapist modeled this for Joanne by being strong and assertive with her. For example, when Joanne would break her agreement regarding not contacting her mother, the therapist would become angry and demand that the breach of her word be "made up" by the payment of a fine. The chaining effect was immediate. When a co-worker neglected to repay Joanne money which she had borrowed, Joanne triumphantly reported that she had demanded payment from the woman by a certain date. The debt was repaid.

By the midphase of treatment, Joanne's dependency was at its height. The therapist became even more demanding. Joanne then developed a transference reaction and began experiencing the therapist as cold to her and more devoted to another client whom Joanne knew. She became quiet and withdrawn during sessions. The therapist viewed this reaction as an opportunity to break through another piece of Joanne's negative programming – a chance to pass a demanding test of the potency of the therapist's programming versus the family's. In a semi-controlled rage reaction, she paced the floor and forcefully demanded that Joanne tell her what was bothering her. Moving in face to face she said, "I must know *now* what is taking you away from me. You are very important to me and I care deeply about you!" Joanne then confessed that she felt that the therapy was an "act" designed to fool her and that the therapist really cared only about her friend, the other client. She had become obsessed with this idea.

In fact, this was not the case, as the therapist was really quite fond of Joanne. At this point in the session, the therapist actually wept. Joanne wiped away the therapist's tears. The therapist said, "I don't lie. If I say I care and you are special, I mean it. I'm giving you this (a necklace). It's a real piece of me." This session, which occurred 18 months after treatment began, was the turning point in Joanne's treatment. Joanne's attachment to the therapist as a model leapt forward and she let go of her dysfunctional programs more easily. Joanne cut and styled her hair, and began to lose weight.

The therapist continued to generate corrective emotional and transactional experiences designed to restructure Joanne's sexual identification model. She often talked about the swan emerging from the ugly duckling. The therapist carefully discovered Joanne's assets and worked to develop them. Noting that Joanne had considerable grace, she had her take various kinds of dance lessons. Then she instructed her to dance the night away like a "star" at a local disco. Joanne reported that she had a peak experience as the center of attention at the club. The therapist responded by saying that she felt like a "star therapist," thus structuring the win-win relationship necessary for successful parenting.

Typically, when the therapist is in the proper remedial parental stance, the client will perceive the historic parental inputs in sharp and contrasting relief. As Joanne's treatment progressed, her rage intensified at the way her parents had failed her. Gestalt techniques were used to facilitate Joanne's abreaction and working through of these feelings. Joanne was encouraged to scream, cry, and pound "father" or "mother" through use of the pillow and empty chair techniques. These procedures also deprogrammed Joanne's fixation on being controlled and socially appropriate at all times. The therapist/mother orchestrated and approved this freely expressed affect.

As Joanne let go of her attachment to her family, positive transference to the therapist grew. Joanne questioned the therapist about various aspects of her life. Joanne wanted to know if the therapist had had treatment, how she met her husband, what she did for recreation, and so forth. In CFT, such questions are answered truthfully and briefly with an eye to positive modeling, and this was the case with Joanne. The therapist shared a few of her life experiences in an honest and authentic way.

Joanne had never been very successful in her independent transactions. She had dropped out of college after two years and then held down low-level sales or clerical jobs, generally at a poor salary. In this area,

Joanne had received little encouragement or positive programming from either parent. She was actually very intelligent, with an extensive vocabulary developed while reading "every book in the library" as a child. The therapist's remedial position on this issue was that Joanne was too bright to waste and that she must find a career in which she could showcase and develop herself. The therapist again used the iconic image of the swan. She suggested that Joanne was the elegant one, white and graceful, and yet magically strong and productive. Joanne discovered that she felt this image as her own identity most strongly when she was trying to be helpful and nurturant to other people. She decided that she wanted to become a midwife.

The therapist helped Joanne plan and organize her return to the local university to complete an undergraduate degree in nursing. Joanne took out student loans and got a part-time job with flexible hours. She was quite frightened that she would repeat her earlier failures. Joanne had simply not completed final projects in various courses and had left school with incompletes on her record. Her parents had made little comment at that time. The therapist informed Joanne that failure was not allowed and to ensure this she wished to be informed regarding all papers and tests. She then checked on Joanne's progress in school. For example, the therapist would phone Joanne at strategic times or have Joanne phone her to report on her progress, in a very structured manner. At one point Joanne left messages on the therapist's answering machine reporting the studying she had accomplished each day.

With caring and involvement from the therapist, Joanne's anxiety diminished. However, as she began to succeed at school, she did continue to experience periods of intense anxiety and regression. At these times, Joanne reported that she felt out of her mind and lost and would amble aimlessly around rather than do her work. The therapist disciplined her and informed her that if she was going to waste time, she might as well do something useful like yard work at the therapist's house. Joanne hated gardening, and this threat was particularly useful in helping her get her work done.

As long as Joanne completed her schoolwork, the therapist was sympathetic about her anxiety and inner turmoil. She would reframe these tensions simply as signals of Joanne's progress at school. They explored and analyzed her feelings of dread. Joanne felt as if she were dying. The therapist pointed out that Joanne's old self, the self generated by the original family, was in fact dying. In the face of this, the old loyalties and programs were emerging to pull her back into line as the worthless little girl. The therapist countered the regression by calling her E.S., the abbreviated suggestion used for Elegant Swan, her new identity.

As Joanne continued to be successful at school, the old anxieties and fears diminished and she began to enjoy herself and be proud of her performance. When Joanne graduated with a BS in nursing, the therapist gave her a small gold necklace as a gift. The gift carried a remedial/ healthy program, as the necklace depicted a mother-child scene.

The therapist then helped Joanne to apply for a master's program in nursing with a specialty in midwifery. Like a good parent, she helped Joanne write an autobiographical statement and fill out application forms. Shortly thereafter, Joanne was accepted into a highly rated master's program. This progressive movement led to a new siege of anxiety and self-doubt. Joanne had a series of nightmares in which she found herself anxious, alone, and lost while trying to hurry to an exam or class at school. The therapist had her role play parts of the dreams in various Gestalt exercises in order to promote integration and to develop the repertoire of responses available to E.S., the competent ego. The therapist began to be included in Joanne's dreams.

At the time that Joanne had started treatment, she was not dating at all and claimed that there were no good men available. The therapist laughed and dismissed such a notion as rubbish. She programmed Joanne with the reality that high-level men were available but they were rather rare, and she would have to develop herself in order to meet them. The therapist forcefully repeated that Joanne was really E.S. and that as she differentiated herself from the family and actualized her potential, she would discover that she was a woman with beauty, brains, and considerable ability, who deserved a quality man – a man who was crazy about her just like the therapist was.

Through giving Joanne a corrective maternal experience, the practitioner was changing one of the primary models upon which Joanne's relationships were based: the mother/child interaction. The therapist actively programmed for Joanne to go out and find a man who was like the therapist: successful, interested, warm, prizing, and giving. Joanne would laugh at this program and claim that no men were loving in that way and that this was an impossible task. The therapist would sharply scold Joanne for maintaining her old programming. She insisted on her reality that there were a few loving men in the world who would absolutely adore Joanne.

In order to find these men, Joanne was asked to follow the program of three. Abstaining from sex forced her to be assertive and define boundaries. It also minimized the possibility of Joanne's recreating the pattern she tended to follow in which infatuation was followed by rejection. The therapist asked Joanne to explore different types of men and their worlds, and to see how she felt about herself as she became involved with each man. The goal was a man who made her feel special, intelligent, loving, and beautiful.

For months Joanne attended various local singles functions but did not meet anyone of interest. During this time, the therapist coached her on making contact with men and role played the projection of a warm, inviting stance by smiling and making eye contact – but to no avail. Finally, the therapist promised Joanne a special treat if she was successful in arranging three dates with three different men. The therapist said that she would take her on a shopping trip and buy her a couple of special outfits for dating. This reward was particularly exciting to Joanne. In her childhood, her mother and favored sister, Carol, frequently went out on shopping expeditions from which Joanne was excluded. Joanne rather quickly met three men. Of course, she reported that these dates were with men whom she labeled boring and unstimulating. The therapist instructed Joanne to keep progressing forward in terms of finding men who were more integrated and exciting. She also fulfilled her promise by taking Joanne shopping and buying her two outfits.

After testing the waters further and finding some success with men even though she did not offer sex, Joanne became more sure of herself in the dating arena. The therapist suggested to Joanne that she attend professional workshops related to her career in order to develop professionally, as well as to meet more successful and stimulating men. She then began dating men who were more introspective, sharing, and sophisticated. Whenever she went out with a man who was rejecting or inattentive, or one who was simply interested in sex, the therapist disciplined her. Joanne began to feel attractive to men. She worked to enhance her appearance even more, and this, plus her new self-confidence, gave her a completely different social image.

After two-and-a-half years in treatment, Joanne met a young man at a party who became quite infatuated with her. Jerry was an attractive, intelligent man in his mid-thirties who was five years out of a divorce. He was a successful real estate agent. Joanne was particularly smitten with him because of his waspish looks, which reflected her mother's old programming regarding worth and appearance. As she became involved with Jerry, Joanne fell into a regressed state and complained that she felt ugly and inadequate in his world. She reported to the therapist that Jerry was too good for her and that she wanted to break up with him before he broke her heart. The therapist then moved in on Joanne physically and psychologically. She grabbed Joanne by the shoulders and said, "I will not permit you to destroy this relationship, damn it! Now you swear to do exactly as I instruct you, or there will be Hell to pay!" Joanne visibly relaxed upon hearing this and agreed to the contract.

The therapist limited their dates to twice a week to slow down the relationship. Joanne followed this and a few other rules as well. However, after several weeks she did have sex with Jerry. This sexual experience was rather awkward and anxiety-provoking for Joanne, who reported that she felt herself withdrawing, according to her usual pattern. The therapist disciplined Joanne by having her complete two hours of yard work to make up for breaking her promise. The ordeal was experienced as being worse than her anxiety about maintaining the relationship. Joanne stopped having sex with Jerry. Joanne also continued to see a couple of other men.

The relationship with Jerry improved. He was nurturant, physically affectionate, and very devoted to Joanne in a rather caretaking and maternal manner. This made him a highly suitable partner. The therapist discussed this with Joanne and suggested that she enjoy and absorb this man's caring as she had done the therapist's. Six months later, Joanne announced that she loved Jerry. At that point, the therapist asked Joanne to bring Jerry to a session.

Jerry presented as an attractive man who related well with the therapist. She bonded with Jerry as a benevolent parental figure, congratulating him on his good taste in choosing Joanne. She also asked him some questions about himself, his past, and his future plans. His answers essentially confirmed the impressions the therapist had derived from Joanne's reports. Then, in front of Jerry, the therapist informed Joanne that she approved of her choice.

Two months later, the couple's honeymoon phase ended, and Joanne's relationship with Jerry deteriorated. They had begun to spend each night together, and Jerry began to court Joanne less. As this occurred, Joanne began to experience Jerry as if he were her abandoning father. She became anxious and started to withdraw from him. He then began to experience her as similar to the cold, rejecting side of his own mother.

In repetitive sequences of interaction, Jerry would inform Joanne that he had to work late. Joanne would then become sullen and withdrawn on the phone, and then he would spend extra amounts of time out with his buddies. Finally, Joanne would quietly goad Jerry into a loud explosion, after which he would court her out of his own guilt. They then would have intimate contact. These interactions exacerbated old anxieties, which Joanne and Jerry both harbored, and tended to reinforce dysfunctional models and programs. The therapist had sessions with the couple in which these sequences were vivified and restructured. As Jerry's own developmental arrests became apparent, the practitioner worked with him in a more tailored remedial stance as a completely validating and prizing maternal figure. He then asked to meet in individual sessions with the therapist.

The case proceeded from this point with both conjoint and concurrent sessions. The practitioner provided remedial/healthy reparental inputs to both Jerry and Joanne, as well as direct and paradoxical interventions directed at their relationship. Two years later, they resolved much of their conflict and were married. Treatment was then terminated.

SUMMARY

In sum, in working with the single adult, the CFT approach seems quite promising. Single adults who are lonely, alienated, unsuccessful, or mired in the family of origin can be helped to move forward and find greater satisfaction in life.

CHAPTER 10

Treatment of Alternative Family Constellations

Everything in the universe is made by union and generation – by the coming together of elements that seek out one another, melt together two by two, and are born again in a third.

– Pierre Teilhard de Chardin (1973, p. 143)

The most recent census taken in the U.S. (1980) showed that approximately 50 percent of all households are single-parent or stepfamily households. When single-parent and blended families present for treatment, they manifest special needs. Goals for these families are also somewhat different than goals for intact families. This chapter describes the CFT approach with single-parent and stepfamilies, and presents a transcript of a consultation with a stepfamily.

SINGLE-PARENT FAMILIES

Regardless of the presenting problem, single-parent families generally present for treatment with members in an economically overloaded and psychologically stressed condition. Providing economic security for the family, together with the parenting of children, is a heavy burden for one person. In addition, there is often a less than healthy entanglement with an ex-spouse. In CFT work with such families, the presenting problems are a focus for remediation, along with the development of underlying potentials for psychosocial health, as with other families. But treatment also takes into account the specialized needs of the single-parent family.

Single parents often require more direct assistance with the rearing transaction than do intact families. The children will usually be seen more often in conjoint sessions with the parent, and the practitioner will bond, nurture, and discipline them directly by teaming with the parent. For example, when a fatigued single-parent mother of rambunctious 10-year-old twins presented for treatment, the therapist took on a direct disciplinary role with the twins in the session. She instructed the mother to relax and simply have more fun with the boys. Meanwhile, the therapist and the mother prepared a chore list in front of the boys. Then the therapist instructed the mother to go home and remove five of the twins' favorite playthings and to drop them back at the office. The boys were told that upon satisfactory completion of their chores each week, one item would be returned in the session.

The single parent is also taught to directly program, nurture, and discipline the children in a competent and effective way. As treatment progresses, the single parent incorporates the therapist as a role model and becomes more competent. In addition to direct interventions with the children and the parent, the therapist may also use the decentering technique in which the single parent role plays the children while the therapist plays the parent.

Ideally, the single parent has to take on two roles with his or her children – one nurturing and understanding, the other disciplining. The key to the success of this process is flexibility in taking one role and then another. The single parent must discipline the children, then later reassure them with unconditional positive regard and also allow them to ventilate feelings. The parent must then examine the disciplinary actions and be ready to modify them if this is reasonable. The provision of a steady unconditional love and relatedness, even when discipline must be strong, is very important to children of single parents. They have already suffered the trauma of loss through death or divorce, and their abandonment anxiety is usually strong. Ongoing availability of emotional rapport and contact with the custodial parent assuages these fears. The nurturant and empathic role is also needed to help children express and dispel any residual guilt and/or self-hate they might feel in connection with the death or divorce.

In working with single parents, Stein developed a technique in which the single parent makes verbal reference to the other partner, so as to suggest the presence of two healthy parents. This is especially effective when the other parent is deceased or out of contact with the children, and if it is congruent with what the absent parent might say to the child. A single father might talk with his daughter about what her competent, loving mother might say to her, and with his son about what his nurturant yet strong mother might say or do. In one situation, when his son hit a home run, a single father said, "If your mother were alive today, she would have laughed and jumped for joy, she would have been so proud of you!" If such statements are not congruent, other healthy models or members of the opposite sex from the single parent can be used. This process enables the child to develop a fuller triangulation blueprint.

For example, 12-year-old Jean confessed to her mother, Betty, that she had been smoking. Her mother became furious and punished her by grounding her for three months. The therapist asked the mother to come to Jean in an empathic mode and ask her why she had been smoking and how she was feeling. She instructed the mother to listen, and then say, "Your father would have said that smoking is stupid and makes you look ugly. He would want you to be healthy and happy." As Betty listened to her daughter, she began to realize that Jean's smoking reflected a need for peer approval and that these needs had grown out of her daughter's sense of loneliness. Betty discussed this insight with the therapist, and they decided to modify Betty's work schedule so that she could spend more time with Jean.

Other Resources

In addition to helping the single parent to parent more effectively, the practitioner looks to other resources for direct support and help in the rearing transaction. The practitioner examines the extended family network with the client and then works to include some of them in the rearing of the child. A grandfather might be organized to father a single mother's son by taking him to football games or teaching him math. Or an aunt might watch prepubescent girls after school, so that she can mother the children while the single father works. If the extended family is too distantiated to provide assistance, the therapist may have them come into the office to iron out difficulties and to reconnect them as a loving and supportive family.

If a paramour is involved with the family, he or she can be encouraged to provide attention and nurturance to the child as well, in order to give the single parent relief time. He or she may also be involved in treatment to improve the quality of the couple's relationship.

Outside agencies or clubs, such as Big Brothers or Big Sisters, can also serve as supportive adjuncts. They can be quite valuable in providing specialized parentlike inputs to the children. Having others help in the rearing transaction not only lessens the single parent's burden, but also helps to prevent parentification of children or enmeshments with them.

Of course, a single parent may have to be individuated from an enmeshed family of origin and this must be taken into account. The extended family can provide help, but should not be allowed to undermine the parent or usurp the parent's role with the child. If this is in fact the case, the single parent may be helped to sever contact for a time, or to otherwise discipline intrusive or undermining grandparents. At times, intrusive grandparents will be seen in sessions along with the single parent in order for the therapist to promote individuation. Generally, these grandparents have impoverished lives or marriages themselves and are overinvolved with the children and grandchildren in order to compensate. They may be referred out for their own individual or marital therapy.

The treatment approach with single parents is similar to that with single adults in regard to social relationships and career progression. They are encouraged to follow the dating program of three, as described in Chapter 9. They are also assisted to move forward in their careers.

Usually, the single parents' independent transactions must be promoted at the same time as the rearing transaction is being elevated. Financial pressures are generally high, and time is more constricted and precious. Higher pay and more flexible hours are often the first goals with single parents. The therapist may help to plot out the next strategic moves on the job, role play how to handle them, and then encourage the clients to make the moves. Or the therapist may help clients to develop their own businesses, so that there is greater availability for childcare when needed.

The Noncustodial Parent

The noncustodial parent is an important member of the family holon. If he or she is available, the therapist should assess the possibility of a reconciliation. Often the single parent may not be aware of unconscious longings for and attachments to the ex-spouse. Passionate and violent hatred for the ex-spouse often masks deep feelings of love. Even if there is no hope of reconciliation, the unfinished business from the past must be completed in order for the client to move forward in life, as well as for the two parents to team up to parent their children. The practitioner guides the single parent client, and where possible the ex-spouse, in accomplishing these tasks.

If there is considerable anger or unfinished business, or if the parents are unable to team cooperatively, the practitioner may, with the client's permission, become directly involved with the ex-spouse. The practitioner may phone him or her, and/or arrange for conjoint or individual sessions. The ex-spouses are helped to ventilate angers and hurts from the past, own responsibility for the past failures, and forgive each other. If one parent is extremely distant or uninvolved, he or she can be brought back in as a parenting partner. In this way, children can be freed of any entanglement in the old marital battle. The therapist helps the ex-spouse move toward a more mature individuation, so that he or she can forge a new and healthy contract to follow in parenting the children.

For example, in one case, where an uninvolved noncustodial mother lived out of town, the practitioner, after securing the father's permission, developed a phone relationship with her. He asked her to fly in for three sessions with the custodial parent, which she did. He was able in this manner to draw in the noncustodial parent as a joint decision maker and active parental figure.

In most cases, it is relatively easy to involve ex-spouses in treatment. Because the practitioner typically is taking a directive and confrontational stance with the single parent, and graphically describing and working with his or her areas of deficit, he or she can, with the client's permission, report this to the ex-spouse. Generally, the ex-spouse is relieved to hear that the single-parent client is being "called on the carpet" and made to face immaturities and pathologies with which the ex-spouse has personally struggled.

Ideally the new contract for parenting between the custodial and noncustodial parents should involve the following: 1) There is to be no downgrading of each other in front of the children; 2) the child will be allowed clear access to both parents and will be programmed to love both parents by the two ex-spouses, so that loyalty binds are minimized; and 3) all major goals for the children will be agreed upon and promoted by both parents. To this end, the therapist works to open communication lines on a regular basis. The visitation schedule is made clear, and both parents are helped to implement it properly. The therapist also facilitates teamwork such that disciplinary action on the part of one parent will be backed up by the other. The implementation of this contract over time between the ex-spouses can have a tremendously freeing and positive effect on the children. Often, children will feel psychologically grounded when both parents are involved properly. And symptomatology they may have been manifesting tends to disappear.

The therapist attempts to implement this type of contract in most cases. He or she often meets for several sessions with the parents to solidify them as a team. The therapist helps them hammer out agreements and assists them in holding to these agreements.

If the ex-spouse has remarried, the practitioner may work with this stepparent as well. The goal here is to diminish jealous or negative feelings toward the "old family" and to encourage the stepparent to support the executive team of the previous marriage. Competition with the ex-spouse often prompts a stepparent to go along with the therapist's program. He or she may try to be more gracious and supportive of the spouse's proper involvement with the biological children. The therapist's contract with this family must be brief to avoid disturbing the therapeutic relationship with the original client family.

If the noncustodial parent is extremely disturbed, i.e., hospitalized for mental illness, in prison, or is a destructive influence, it may not be possible to forge a contract between the parents. At that point, the practitioner will have to evaluate if the noncustodial parent can be a resource to the children in the future.

STEPFAMILIES

Stepfamilies also have unique issues and goals. Loyalty conflicts can abound in these families, especially in the early stages of their formation. Spouses have to resolve loyalty issues regarding ex-spouses and their children. Children have to deal with conflicts of allegiance to biological parents and stepparents. Guilt and lowered self-esteem can be problems for many family members. A stepparent often feels guilty for disrupting the children's family unit, and at times, for abandoning the ex-spouse. Children often feel responsible for fragmenting the family, as well as ambivalence for resenting or not loving the stepparent. Children must also deal with the sense of abandonment, loss, and mourning they experience with the breakup of their primary families, as well as with the anxiety and confusion of adapting to the new family system.

Stepfamilies are also fraught with tensions at the core of the system, i.e., the remarriage. As in other constellations, the marriage is the hub of the stepfamily. Thus, the formation of positive stepparenting relationships depends upon the success of the remarriage. If the new husband or wife is made to feel insecure about the ex-spouse, the new marital relationship will suffer. As a result, the stepparent's relationship with the spouse's children may not form properly. In this configuration, the children may then be viewed with resentment and suspicion as manipulative rivals for love and affection.

Quite often, if the stepparent is a woman, the burden of childcare is placed on her before there has been a period of bonding and growing love between her and the children. Then her authority may be unsupported or undermined by the children's father. The stepchildren are experienced as a drain instead of a delight.

Another frequently occurring dysfunctional configuration in stepfamilies is created when the stepparent is the new father who is precipitously set up as the disciplinarian for the children. With little or no bonding period, both children and spouse tend to perceive him as the antagonistic and overly reactive "heavy." In these configurations, resentments and tensions reverberate throughout the marital and rearing transactions. With so many conflicting pulls and problems, these families require active clinical leadership and clear treatment goals.

Creating Boundaries Around the New Marriage

An important priority in the treatment of stepfamilies is to create clear psychological boundaries around the marriage. Primary loyalties need to be cultivated in the direction of the current spouse and away from the former spouse. The practitioner guides the couple toward a strong and united relationship.

The spouses must also be strong and united in the rearing transaction. The children are in need of secure and stable parenting in sorting out all of their relationship issues. In the periods during and after the fragmentation of their parents' marriage, oedipal win fantasies may have blossomed. Also, there is usually at least some resentment toward the "outsider" stepparent, who is often seen as having closed off any hope that the biological parents would reconcile. These factors lead to children becoming a potential divisionary force, prying the new couple apart. Children must be shown that they cannot achieve an oedipal win and become the biological parent's preferred partner. Also they must be taught to relate to and respect the stepparent.

Using the Optimal Stepfamily Rearing Model

Using the optimal stepfamily model (see Chapter 2) as a guide in treatment can be very helpful in facilitating the stepparent-child relationship. The stepparent is encouraged to take the role of nurturer and facilitator, regardless of the gender of the child. This allows the child to begin to deal with the feelings of resentment and loss and to bond with the new parent.

A sympathetic and empathic stepparent who openly acknowledges the difficulties inherent in the child's position can pull the whole stepfamily into positive alignment. The stepparent can help a child sort out his or her feelings and heal some of the abandonment pain. Meanwhile, the biological parent's facilitation of the nurturant/empathic bond between stepparent and stepchild helps to lessen his or her guilt over failing the child. With less guilt operating, the biological parent is less apt to indulge and spoil the child to compensate for destroying the child's home base.

When the stepparent takes the nurturant role in the stepfamily, the new couple's relationship is enhanced. The stepparent is, in a profound way, nurturing the spouse vicariously in giving to his or her children. Consequently, the spouse feels appreciation and thankfulness toward the stepparent, which draws them together.

The biological parent's assumption of a disciplinary role also helps to align the family in a healthy way. The children may then open up to the stepparent for an emotional outlet. And they can also receive discipline more easily from a biological parent because this person has usually established him- or herself, at least in part, as a benevolent figure, who is acting out of love and for the children's own good.

The Noncustodial Parent

The ex-spouse of a stepfamily constellation is viewed as an important member in the family holon. An ex-spouse is handled in a manner similar to that used with the ex-spouses of single parents, although there is no exploration of reconciliation. This parent should be able to have a healthy access to the child, and should have status as an executive team member in parenting the child. Accordingly, the practitioner aims at forging a contract between the biological parents according to which they can function as a team, with agreements similar to those delineated for the single parent's ex-spouse. In the stepfamily, then, a semipermeable boundary is developed between the new family and the ex-spouse, as well as a strong and clear boundary around the new marriage.

The stepparent is urged to be supportive of this team, as part of a healthy intramarital therapeutic stance. The practitioner assists the stepparent to transcend jealousies in order to promote this team so that the stepchildren can have stability and mature properly. However, boundaries around the new couple must be secure before this move can be implemented. The stepparent must feel extremely certain that he or she is in the number one loyalty position in order to be able to have his or her spouse interact with an ex-spouse. Often stepparents are highly competitive with ex-spouses and are eager to outdo them as parents and spouses. The competitiveness often helps stepparents to move into the growth-promoting position with both spouse and children.

CASE EXAMPLE

In the case of Anne and Clark, the new stepmother, Anne, was initially rather cold and rejecting toward her husband whenever he even mentioned his ex-wife Bea. In individual sessions, she confessed to the practitioner that she felt sure that her husband still loved Bea, and this left her feeling terribly insecure. Bea and Clark had two sons, who were in Clark's custody. Both were problematic. One was withdrawn and depressed, the other out of control. Anne resented the children, seeing them as symbols of Bea and Clark's former life together.

The practitioner helped Clark to detach from Bea. She explained to Clark that if he wanted real love in his life, he'd have to show Anne that she was his "one and only." Bea often played the helpless role to manipulate and gain attention, money, and assistance from Clark. She called him almost daily. Clark was instructed to use a telephone answering device as a buffer between himself and Bea. Bea then began to come to Clark's office. The therapist asked Clark to refuse to have any interaction with Bea. Although this was hard on the sons in the short term, it proved to be beneficial to them in the long term. Bea was not to be admitted to Clark's office, and, if Clark saw her on the street, he was to completely ignore her. He was not even to be present when the boys were picked up or returned for visitation. This state of affairs lasted for two months.

At that point, the practitioner secured permission from Clark to call Bea and ask her to meet with Clark and her. Bea attended six conjoint meetings over the course of three months. The practitioner helped her ventilate her feelings about Clark and helped Clark finally accept that he would never return to her. The therapist repeatedly underscored the critical nature of their relationship in terms of its effect on their sons' futures.

Clark and Bea were initially wary and mistrustful of each other. The practitioner agreed to hold them to agreements about their children, but only if they were prepared to face consequences of not living up to them. The couple agreed that if either partner broke an agreement, he or she would be fined $25 by the therapist. With this "insurance" of the other's performance, the partners were able to make agreements and follow through on them. The boys proceeded to improve significantly in their behavior.

Meanwhile, the practitioner urged Anne to play a supporting role toward Bea and Clark's parenting team. Anne had relaxed considerably and had become more accepting of Bea and the boys since Clark had disengaged from Bea. Anne still felt competitive with Bea, but felt empowered to be the "winner." Anne began to assume the role of supportive collaborator in regard to the parenting team. She received copies of the agreements made between Bea and Clark and helped to hold Clark to his side of the contracts. She also became much more nurturant with the boys, as encouraged by the practitioner. The boys proceeded to do extremely well in school, as per all three parents' programming. The younger one, who had been withdrawn, developed normal peer relationships. Clark, in his gratitude to Anne for her self-transcendent and devoted behavior, proceeded to help her actualize an old career dream.

STEPFAMILY INTERVIEW

The following transcript is taken from a second consultation session with a stepfamily conducted in front of an audience of mental health professionals. The junior author met with Brian and Gail, an attractive couple in their mid-thirties who had been married for five years. Brian and Gail's presenting complaint revolved around Brian's daughters, ages 12 and 14, who had been living with them for the past one-and-a-half years. They were disrespectful, defiant, and out of control both at school and at home. Brian's ex-wife had had custody of the girls since the divorce. According to Brian and Gail, she had not been able to settle down and live in any one place and had been neglectful of the girls. The girls had been moved through six states in a nine-month period.

The stepfamily had been referred by the school to a CFT therapist, Molly Layton, Ph.D. Layton arranged for a series of consultations with the junior author. In the first consultation session, Sam Kirschner met with Gail, Brian, and Layton. The consultant realized that the problems in the rearing transaction were interconnected with unresolved issues in the marriage. Gail had been ineffective in helping her husband deal appropriately with his daughters. In this sense, she had failed him as a wife and the girls as a stepmother. Brian, on the other hand, had simply put Gail in charge of the girls without promoting a relationship between them. Gail was drained emotionally and physically by the girls. Thus, he had also failed as a husband and as a father. The therapist programmed the couple to put Brian in charge of his daughters, since he was the biological parent. He asked Gail to be nurturing and facilitating with the girls. The couple made a tentative commitment to the plan.

In this transcript of the second consultation session, the consultant firms up the prior agreement of the role allocation in the stepfamily. Father is to discipline and stepmother is to nurture. Also, the consultant asks the wife to discipline her husband to ensure that there is follow-through on the contract.

Consultant: You're here because I promised you that I would help you with the girls, and help you with Brian, and help you with yourself. And Molly *(the therapist)* is watching this, because she can help you later.

Gail: She's going to help me later?

Consultant: She's going to help you later. That's right. I like to work very economically, because if I can help a broader number of people, there's a ripple effect, right? So, if I help you with the girls, then what'll happen? Then those girls will go on to do bigger and better things in the world! They can contribute to mankind! Right? If I help you with Brian, then he can go out and be productive, right?

The consultant describes the comprehensive growth contract and programs for optimal goals in the rearing and marital transactions. In the interview, he frequently uses the word "right" following a program or suggestion. He also nods his head and makes eye contact at these critical moments, to induce a "yes" set.

Gail: Right.

Brian: (to Gail) So can you.

Consultant: And then he can help you better, right?

He completes his outline of more optimal functioning.

Brian: You made us realize the things that we didn't see the other night, when we only met you one time.

Consultant: That's right. But the thing is that I have certain knowledge that you may also have, but you're not aware of it. For example, your wife knew all along what had to happen with these girls. But . . .

Gail: . . . but I wimped out.

The stepmother's sexual identification seems to be rather male and weak, as suggested by her choice of the term wimped.

Consultant: But you wimped out. That's right.

Gail: (to Brian) I knew that's what he was going to tell me.

Consultant: That's right. You wimped out. You beat me to the punch. That's right.

Gail: I knew it was coming.

Consultant: You knew what had to be done with these girls. They were running out of control, right?

Gail: Uh huh.

Consultant: There were problems at school, right? Problems at home. They don't listen. You knew what had to be done, but you wimped out. But, of course, it's true, nobody ever really showed you how to be a mother.

Brian: It just came about.

Consultant: What do you mean "It just came about?" It, it just . . .

Brian: One day it was there. It was just like they fell out of the sky.

Consultant: You're walking out on the street, and two children fell on your head.

Brian: Yeah. They were dropped off, and then there was a big fight, and they were there.

Brian suggests that he feels rather passive and impotent in his sexual identification.

Consultant: Wait a minute, wait a minute! There was a big fight . . .

Brian: Yeah.

Consultant: And then *you* decided that *you* were going to keep them.

Brian: Right.

Consultant: So you chose to keep them.

The consultant works to have Brian feel more potent and in control, and to take greater responsibility for his family life.

Consultant: (to Gail) Will you help me out here, would you? Go ahead.

The consultant empowers and enlists the stepmother as an allied growth agent.

Gail: (to Brian) That's the way you think of it but . . .

Brian: It's not that way?

Gail: No. You chose to keep them, too!

Consultant: (nods his head)

Brian: I know, I know that. Yeah.

Consultant: You know that. You just got through saying that they fell from the sky.

Brian: That's what it seemed like to me.

Gail: What, that they were just dropped?

Brian: Yeah.

Consultant: What are we going to do with this guy?
Gail: I told you, load the gun.

The wife indicates that she feels anger in the marital transaction. This remark also suggests that she feels her husband needs discipline.

Consultant: (to Gail) They just fell from the sky – can we get this guy to say that he chose to do it?
Brian: I did it, OK? Yes, I did. I said, "I don't want them in the environment they were in! I'll keep them."
Consultant: Yeah. So you did the right thing. You were a good father. You didn't want them trampling around six different states. How many states were . . .
Brian: Six, in about nine months.
Consultant: Six states in nine months! Without a home, right?
Brian: No school.
Consultant: No school! You acted in good faith as a father and as a man. That's what a man does. And, then, once you got them, then you decided they – "it" – fell on you.

Here the consultant programs for a strong masculine identification, tying it in with Brian's actions and then contrasting it with his more weak and helpless sense of himself.

Consultant: (to Gail) You tried to help him by opening your heart to these girls who are not yours, right? By making a home for them. Right?
Gail: Right.
Consultant: By taking them in good faith and then what did he do?
Gail: He wimped out.
Consultant: He wimped out.
Gail: He tries.
Consultant: He tries?
Gail: Sometimes.
Consultant: He tries *(touching Brian on his arm)*.
Brian: (laughing) I do, sometimes.
Consultant: You do. You do. You try.
Brian: But I get away with a lot, too.

Brian's statement is a releaser for disciplinary input.

Consultant: You get away with a lot. *(to Gail)* He doesn't want to get away with things.

Brian: I do.

Gail: Yes, he does.

Consultant: No, a real man does not want to get away with things. He works to be straightened out. Now, I believe that.

The consultant reprograms Brian at the sexual identification level.

Brian: OK.

Consultant: Right? A real man wants to do right in the world.

Brian: Right. Yeah, that's right.

Consultant: So he can wake up in the morning, look in the mirror and say, "Hey, I'm OK."

Brian: (nods his head)

Again, Brian gives out releasers for disciplinary input.

Consultant: Right?

Gail: (to Brian) Do you do that?

Brian: Not yet.

Consultant: (to Gail) No, of course he doesn't do that, how can he do that when he dumped the responsibility for the girls on you! And you're the one who has to discipline them and change them around and run after them. And then you're trying to be nice to them. We were talking . . . you were telling me the other day that you take them to the mall shopping, even though they've acted like complete creeps, right?

Brian: No respect.

Consultant: No respect. And then you take them out to lunch. I mean, the woman opens her heart to these girls and so forth, and you don't ensure that they are respectful and loving. They should be kissing her feet!

Brian: That's right.

Consultant: Considering the kind of home that she's providing for them. So why aren't they?

Brian: Because I let them get away with it.

Consultant: Because you're dumping, you're dumping . . .

Gail: Here we go again. I'm getting covered with it, right?

Consultant: Your crap . . . that's right. You're covering her with . . . a four-letter word. *(to Gail)* Should I say it?

Brian: Shit.

Gail: Why not?

Consultant: Shit. You're covering her with shit.

The consultant allies with the wife, which serves to empower her. He has tied the rearing and marital transactions together. Optimally, a husband would be structuring the situation so as to protect his wife. In this case, just the opposite is happening.

Gail: (to Brian) Please, I don't like it.
Consultant: First of all, if you say it to him that way, it doesn't register. *(grabbing Brian's tie at his neck)* "I don't like it!" Right, that's better. *(to Brian)* She doesn't like it.
Brian: Well, we'll have to change it.

The consultant role plays disciplinary behavior with the husband, which simultaneously disciplines him and provides a model for the wife to follow. The husband's reaction confirms that the disciplinary stance is correct.

Consultant: How are you going to change it? You don't even know how to raise girls.
Brian: I'll have to learn.
Consultant: First of all, here you have a problem. In a normal family, a woman is supposed to raise her daughters, right? She's supposed to run her daughters. But in a stepfamily, like we have here, we have to do some things a little differently.
Gail: Like?
Consultant: Like you have to form a positive relationship with these girls instead of having to be a policeman. *(to Brian)* I mean, should she have to be the policeman?
Brian: No. Definitely not.
Consultant: Yeah, Brian. Who should be the policeman?
Brian: Me.

The consultant, in a strong and fatherly way, programs Brian and his wife so that they move into healthy stepfamily roles.

Consultant: Now, can you be around your daughters 24 hours a day?
Brian: No, but I should be. Not physically. But they should know I'm there.
Consultant: Yeah, that's right, they should know. *(to Gail)* See?
Gail: That's what I tried to tell him the other night.
Consultant: They should know that. How can a father be there and not be there?
Brian: The spirit, like you were saying the other night.

Consultant: I was saying that your spirit should be in them. Now how do you get your spirit into these girls?

Brian: I don't know yet.

Consultant: Into their conscience, into their hearts, so that whenever they are in school and they're out in the world or they're with Gail, before they act like complete idiots . . .

Brian: Right.

Consultant: . . . they should be able to look inside their own hearts and say, "This is wrong." "This is right." "This is moral, this is not." "This is what Dad wants me to do." "This is what Dad doesn't want me to do." Did anybody ever do that with you?

The consultant educates Brian about the nature of healthy internalized discipline which serves as a guide for living. He then explores Brian's family-of-origin deficits.

Brian: No.

Consultant: Did anybody sit you down when you were growing up and teach you right from wrong?

Brian: No *(laughing)*.

Consultant: Where did you grow up?

Brian: In the streets.

Consultant: You grew up in the streets. So you want your daughters to grow up in the streets.

Brian: I wouldn't be here if I wanted that.

The consultant moves on to give a symptom amplification suggestion, which seems to mobilize the parents' anxieties and commitment to change the rearing transaction.

Consultant: (to Gail) Is the older one going to get knocked up by the time she's 15, 16?

Gail: If she wants her legs broke, she will.

Consultant: Who's going to break her legs.

Gail: (emphatically) Me. She keeps asking me, "What would you do if I came home pregnant?"

Consultant: Here we go again. She's asking you?

Brian: She won't ask me.

Consultant: If she's going to get . . . she won't ask you. She wants a relationship with a woman. *(to Gail)* So what are you going to say to her? That you're going to break her legs?

Gail: No, I only said that jokingly. I told her, "Cheryl, you're not going to be involved in that stuff right now. Why do you think about that?" "Well, just in case," she tells me.

The older girl seems to be testing the stepmother for limits.

Consultant: Just in case.
Gail: I never thought of that stuff at 13.
Consultant: Yeah, well, so kids are faster today, especially his daughters.
Brian: I don't think I'd be able to accept it.
Consultant: He's training them for the streets! You don't think you'd be able to accept it!

Here the consultant reframes the father's role metaphorically in a highly negative way to mobilize further commitment to change.

Brian: I explained *(to Cheryl)* about how I feel about a kid having a kid. I'm not going to raise her kid, and she knows all about it. She learned about it in school. Now she learned my way. I have my own little rules that I believe in.
Consultant: Yeah. So how are you going to follow up on these rules, when you come home and Gail tells you they've been climbing all over the walls?

The consultant zeroes in on the father's problem in disciplining—his lack of follow-through.

Brian: Things will have to change.
Consultant: What does that mean? That sounds like, "It fell from the sky."
Brian: Well, I'll have to get harder.
Consultant: How?
Brian: Well, like now, I can say one thing to them, and tell them, "OK, go to your room for the day!" And three hours later I go up to the room and say, "I'm going somewhere, do you want to come!" I won't do it.
Consultant: Right. But we're talking about when you're not there. We're talking about when Gail has to deal with these people.
Brian: I feel the girls should do it out of respect for Gail.
Consultant: Yeah, but they don't. So how are you going to ensure it?
Brian: How am I going to ensure it?
Consultant: Yes, how are you, you, you?

The consultant emphasizes the father's responsibility in the matter.

Brian: I'm going to try. I'm going to do my best, do everything I can do.
Consultant: No, no. You're going to ask me what you're going to do. You're going to ask me how to do it, because you don't know.

The consultant programs the father to come to him.

Brian: Well, you're going to help me.
Consultant: That's right.
Brian: OK.
Consultant: I'm only going to help you, though, if you're cooperative.
Brian: I'll try to be.
Consultant: No, no, that's not good enough.
Brian: Then I will be.
Consultant: You will be cooperative.

The consultant assumes the kind of strong demanding role with Brian that Brian will have to assume with his daughters.

Consultant: (to Gail) So, if I tell him what to do and he doesn't do it, what are you going to do about it?
Gail: Rap him one.
Brian: Kick me in my ass.
Consultant: That's right. You're going to make his life miserable.

Here the consultant shapes a contract by which the wife will discipline her husband so that he assumes and maintains his stance with the girls.

Gail: OK. *(to Brian)* You're in for it now. Prepare yourself.
Consultant: They are your kids, your responsibility. You're going to do it or else! You're going to be a happy man 'cause you'll be able to wake up in the morning feeling good about your kids, knowing that she cares enough about you to really take you by the horns!

Again, the consultant takes charge with Brian in a powerful way. And he empowers the wife to do the same.

Consultant: It'll stop the dumping of shit on her. And she's going to teach you once and for all, and maybe it'll take you a few lessons, to figure out that she's not going to stand around while you destroy her and you destroy the girls too. You're not helping the girls. *(pause)* So you're going to cooperate.

Brian: (nodding) Very much.

Consultant: (to Gail) Aren't you happy?

Gail: Oh, I'm very happy.

The consultant has sewn up the contract for rearing and marital growth.

Consultant: Yes, that's right.

Gail: I'm so happy!

Consultant: Yeah, that's right.

Brian: It'll make it easier for you.

Consultant: Your marriage is screwed up. Your marriage. He's dumping shit all over you by abusing you with the girls, right?

Again, the consultant spreads the problem to the heart of the family holon, the marriage.

Gail: Right.

Consultant: And without a marriage, I mean, what kind of family are you going to have? That's why you'll have to walk out on him unless he shapes up. The marriage. Here you were living together for three-and-a-half years, right? And then the girls appear on the scene, and what's happened to your marriage during that time?

Gail: It's put a strain on it.

Consultant: Put a tremendous strain on it! You've gotten sick, physically ill.

Brian: Uh-huh.

Consultant: So the kids have driven a wedge in between the two of you, and you sit back and enjoy the scene. And it's destroying the marriage.

Brian: That's how we got here. But we didn't know it was destroying the marriage.

Consultant: Yeah, you didn't know.

Gail: We didn't think of it like that.

Consultant: Well, but you always think in terms of something falling from the sky. You don't think about what's going on in the real world. You only think about, "Well it happens, you know. You win the lottery, you know." "Chance." "Get hit by a truck." Right?

Gail: (to Brian) Diesel *(truck)*.

Consultant: People make marriages work or they make them fail. They make children grow up to be successful or they make them less successful.

The consultant reiterates that the spouses have to assume greater responsibility for shaping the whole family. With the consultant's positive modeling and impact, the father has assumed a stronger position already.

Brian: We're going to make it work.
Gail: With a little bit of help from Sam.
Consultant: You've got to get their attention. That's precisely the point, you have to get the child's attention. Something you've never done.

The consultant is clarifying and refining his role prescription for Brian.

Brian: Don't know how to do . . .
Consultant: And then you sit down with them, you know how to do it. You say, "Hey look! Sit down! Now, how come I have to come home, and you kids are, you're asleep and no chores have been done? You're almost 14, you're almost 13, and nothing's done here. Now get out of bed and go do what you have to do." *(imitates the girls)* "But I'm sleeping! I'm tired, I'm this, I'm that." Right?
Gail: (to Brian) You thought Cheryl was going to do . . .
Consultant: Yeah, right. "I don't care, you get downstairs!" *(to Brian)* And you supervise it. And then Gail does what? She takes a bath.
Brian: Yeah, she won't have to do anything.
Consultant: Yeah, she relaxes. So now, the next day comes, you're at the store, right?
Brian Uh-huh.
Consultant: It's 7 o'clock. *(to Gail)* You get home, you've been working overtime. The girls are not helping you clean up. They're not doing this. They're not doing that. What do you do? He's not there.
Gail: I yell and I scream.
Consultant: No.
Gail: Oh. "Dad's coming home and he's going to get you."
Consultant: No, it's very simple. You're going to call the store.
Gail: Uh-huh.
Consultant: You say, "Excuse me, girls." You call the store and you put him on the phone. *(to Brian)* You're going to ask to speak to your daughters. And what are you going to tell them?
Gail: Do it.

Brian: That's usually what I tell them.

Consultant: You're going to tell them, "Do it."

Brian: And I'll be home.

Consultant: (to Gail) And, then, if they don't do it, what are you going to do?

Gail: Me? I'm going to go out.

Consultant: You're going to go out.

Gail: I'm going to leave them there.

Consultant: That's right. But I want you to tell him, when he's on the phone, that if the girls don't shape up, you'll be leaving. But you put in a call first to let him know.

Gail: All right.

Brian: (to Gail) That seemed pretty simple.

Consultant: (to Gail) There are lots of great men out there, you know.

Here the consultant again introduces a fear-of-loss maneuver. His main goal is to use this maneuver to empower the wife, who has been weak in her efforts to work with her husband.

Consultant: I mean, if he doesn't want to take care of you and love you the way you want to be loved. . . . *(shrugging his shoulders and speaking to Brian)* Hey, you could replace her with two girls.

Brian: (laughing) I know.

Consultant: Instead of having a woman who adores you and is crazy about you.

Gail: I do something, too.

Brian: Yeah.

Consultant: Sounds like a good deal to me.

Brian: Not bad.

Consultant: Yeah, you'll have two girls who don't do a thing, and who drive you crazy instead of this lovely woman.

Brian: We're not trading Gail *(in)*.

Consultant: What's that?

Brian: We're not trading Gail.

Consultant: We're not? What, are you speaking in majestic plurals?

Brian: I'm not.

Consultant: I mean, you're not . . . I . . . I . . . right?

Again, the consultant programs for an individuated and strong identity for Brian.

Brian: I'd like to keep her, you know.

Consultant: You'd like to, you'll try to keep her.
Brian: No, I'm going to.
Consultant: You're going to keep her. So then you have to come home from the store, and you have to straighten out these girls. So now, the next day they do it again. What are you going to do then?
Brian: I don't know.

Repetition of the desired behavioral sequences in the roles is extremely helpful in ensuring that they will be internalized by the couple.

Gail: Pick up the phone again.
Consultant: You're going to pick up the phone, good.
Brian: Call Dad.
Gail: Dad, handle it.
Brian: OK.
Consultant: So he's going to be having to run back from the store all the time.
Gail: He's going to get pretty pissed.
Brian: And the girls will get pretty pissed.
Consultant: Yes. And? So what's going to happen then? You're going to be pissed and they're going to be pissed, so now what happens? She's not in the middle.
Gail: Me, I'm going to be out shopping.

Consultant: Who washes the dishes?
Gail: The girls do. Yeah, I don't do dishes. I don't do babies and I don't do dishes.
Consultant: What do you mean you don't do babies? You're doing babies right now!
Gail: Well, not anymore. I'm goin' out.

The stepmother, empowered by the consultant's inputs, assumes the prescribed stance.

Consultant: You're going out. OK.
Brian: I'm going to take charge.

The husband moves into his prescribed role.

Consultant: That's right.
Brian: And the whole thing will come together.
Consultant: *(to Gail)* If he doesn't take charge, what're you going to do?

Gail: (waving) Happy trails.
Consultant: No, no. You don't have to go happy trails right away.
Gail: OK.
Consultant: No sex.

A fear-of-loss task is prescribed for the wife to use in disciplining the husband.

Gail: Oh, forget it.
Brian: No, that won't work.
Consultant: (to Gail) That won't work?
Gail: No.
Brian: No.
Gail: That's punishing myself.
Consultant: Yeah, well listen you'll have to use. . . . You've got to get used to not being with him.
Brian (laughing) No, no, no.
Consultant: Wait a minute. How are you going to get used to not being with this guy?

The consultant ties in the withholding sex threat to the overall fear-of-loss maneuver.

Gail: I'll have to figure that out if it's going to happen.
Consultant: What do you mean, "If it's going to happen?" You think he's going to get cracking on these girls right away?
Gail: Yes, he is.
Consultant: Why's that?
Gail: Because I'm not going to let up on him.
Consultant: (nods his head)
Gail: (to Brian) Right? Haven't I been harping on you all week now?
Brian: Uh-huh.
Gail: (to Sam) See that?
Consultant: Boy, ever since Monday *(the first consult)*, things have really been cooking here.
Brian: I would say so.
Consultant: Are you going to talk with those daughters of yours about the importance of treating Gail with respect?
Brian: I already did.
Consultant: Yeah. What did you say to them?
Brian: Well, I told them why I think they're unfair to Gail, and if they think that we're doing something wrong or we're being unfair, to

let me know. Tell me. If not, just shut up and listen. What they do for Gail or to Gail isn't right. Now, if they were living with their mother, they would do it. They would just do it because they had to.

Consultant: Right.

Brian: If they like their environment, and they like us so much, and love us, they can do it. They can do it with me there or without me there. And I explained it to both the girls the same way at the same time.

Consultant: Yeah. But why should they treat her with respect? You're just telling them what not to do.

Brian: No, no. They should. Why shouldn't they?

Consultant: She's not their mother.

Brian: They're getting everything from Gail now. They can't get anymore.

Consultant: Uh-huh.

Brian: If they do, Gail's going to go in the hospital, or we're not going to have her. And I put that thought in their heads. "What're you going to do if Gail isn't around? It is you, you and me."

Brian has already been able to incorporate from the first consultation session, the consultant's use of a fear-of-loss technique as a disciplinary tool with the girls.

Consultant: When did you do this?

Brian: Wednesday, Thursday.

Consultant: After our first session?

Brian: Yeah. I said I met this man one night.

Consultant: (to Gail) You may not have to leave him yet.

Brian: No. I met you one night and you made me see things that maybe just passed my head that I didn't realize.

Consultant: Passed your head. You had your head, you know, up your . . .

Brian: Ass.

Consultant: That's right.

Brian: And let the girls do it. It's not fair to Gail! It's not fair to me! It's not fair to them!

Consultant: Hey, I'm impressed, I'm impressed! *(slapping Brian on the knee)*

Fatherly approval is given for Brian's follow-through behavior.

Brian: (grins from ear to ear)

Brian gives indication that nurturing approval is a correct input for
him.

Consultant: (to Gail) He needed a little pep talk from a dad, I think.

All along the consultant has been regressing Brian in relation to himself
transactionally. Now he furthers the regression by making a clear suggestion about his role as a father.

Brian: I never had that.
Consultant: (to Gail) Do you have an extra bedroom in the house?
Gail: Uh-huh.
Consultant: Oh, great. Make plans. That'll be like your escape valve.

The consultant adds an additional fear-of-loss maneuver to the stepmother's disciplinary armamentarium.

Brian: That's my workroom.
Gail: Yeah.
Consultant: Well, you'll throw him in there then.
Gail: Oh, all right.
Brian: That's my workroom.
Consultant: That's OK. You'll live in your workroom. That's OK. No
    problem. You know doctors, when they're doing internships and
    residencies and so forth, they live in the hospital. They sleep in the
    hospital, right?
Brian: Yeah.
Consultant: They don't get much sex either.
Brian: (laughs)
Consultant: (whispers to Gail) You have to get him where it hurts.
Gail: Oh.
Gail: (whispers to Sam)
Consultant: I understand. Listen, if he doesn't come through for you,
    right? *(moves his index finger across his throat, and then reaches
    over and puts his hand on Gail's hand).* You said you weren't go-
    ing to let up, right?
Gail: Right.
Consultant: Well, what does that mean? It means you have to take
    away. . . .
Gail: Don't I have any other choices?
Consultant: What other choices do you have, other than simply leaving
    him and just packing your bags? You don't want to do that.

Brian: No.
Consultant: Not yet.
Gail: So, I have to get tough on him so he gets tough on them.

This is an optimal triangulation. The consultant goes on to further refine the role prescription for Gail. He programs her to also mediate between Brian and the girls.

Consultant: Yeah. And then they *(the girls)* will be sweet to you again.
Brian: Yeah. He told us it was simple.
Consultant: They're going to come running to you. "Dad is awful, he
    grounded us for three months." And then you'll say, "There, there.
    I understand. But, you did promise you were going to do certain
    things, right?"
Gail: Uh-huh.
Consultant: "And you didn't. So what choice did he have? If you really
    start doing things around the house, like for the next month or so,
    I'll talk to him and see whether or not I can reduce your sentence."
    Right?
Gail: All right.
Consultant: But they would have to, like, scrub the floors for a month.
    You have to make a list of things. They get checked off. That's
    right. And after a month of doing that, and they really do it well,
    you know, they vacuum well, and they do everything well, right?
    (to Gail) And you're going to go to him and you're going to say,
    "Now look, let's let off a little bit and so forth." *(to Brian)* And you're
    going to go to the girls and you're going to say, "Well, Gail talked
    me into letting you girls have lunch with her at the mall. Now this
    was Gail's idea, and as far as I'm concerned, as I told you, you two
    are grounded for the next three months. But I'm going to let you
    go because Gail wanted it. She said you've been doing well. And
    you have been doing well, so I'm going to let you go." Then they're
    going to go to the mall. And will they behave?
Brian: I don't think so.
Consultant: So meanwhile, what's going to ensure that the girls are go-
    ing to behave at the mall?
Brian: Me.

The new roles have been thoroughly and repetitively described, and the
parents have begun to incorporate them as inner programs. The consultant then uses a detailed behavioral rehearsal technique to shape and
reinforce the couple's teamwork.

Consultant: So what are you going to say to them before they go? *(to Gail)* See, he already forgot. He was going to let you go with those two, and they would pig out there, and they would have completely forgotten about everything.

Brian: A couple of little words.

Consultant: What are they? Let me hear them.

Brian: Remember your manners.

Consultant: Remember your manners.

Brian: Yeah, and "Listen to Gail." Two simple little things that shouldn't be hard to do.

Consultant: Yeah. Let me hear you say it to them.

Brian: That's how I would say it to them.

Consultant: (very meekly) "Remember your manners, girls, and listen to Gail." That's going to work?

Gail: Get tougher.

Consultant: Come on, Bri, let's go.

Brian: (more firmly) Listen to Gail when you go to the mall, and if you don't, I'll break your head.

Consultant: No.

Gail: No.

Consultant: You're not going to break their heads. You can never give a consequence like that.

Brian: Well, you'll answer to me when you come home.

Consultant: (nods his head) "I want you to pay attention to your mother, to Gail." You've got to say, "I expect you to behave like . . . "

Brian: " . . . two adults instead of . . . "

Consultant: " . . . young ladies." They're not adults.

Brian: Young adults.

Consultant: You're not even an adult. Young ladies. "I expect you to behave like young ladies, so that you have a good time with Gail. If you don't, here's what's going to happen." *(to Gail)* What's going to happen?

Gail: (to Brian) What's going to happen when they come home?

Brian: I'll put them in their room.

Consultant: (to Brian) Because if you don't . . .

Gail: (to Brian) . . . I'm going back out shopping.

Consultant: (to Gail) And?

Brian: No nooky.

Consultant: No nooky. So you're going to say . . . are you going to say that to your daughters, "Because if you don't behave, I get no nooky"? You can't say that. *(to Gail)* But we're saying it 'cause he doesn't know what to say. You're going to say that to him. You know you're going to take him aside like this and you're going to say, "Now I want you to understand something. If they misbehave on this trip, NN." *(to Brian)* So what are you going to tell the girls?

Brian: "You're going to do it. You're going to go to the mall and you're going to act that way. And if you don't, I'll handle it when you come home."

Consultant: "And you're not going to like it," you're going to tell them.

Brian: They won't like it.

Gail: "Behave!"

Consultant: (to Gail) NN.

Gail: (to Brian) NN.

Consultant: (touching Gail's hand) I know it's painful. It's a painful thing.

Brian: (to Gail) Quick way to learn.

Gail: Yeah, real quick.

Consultant: Molly *(the therapist)* told you to go out and treat yourself.

From the outset of treatment, the therapist has been mothering the stepmother by elevating her self-concept and having her nurture herself.

Gail: Right.

Consultant: That's right. Well, such a shame that he's going to miss out as you become more and more beautiful, take better care of yourself. He'll miss out. *(shrugging his shoulders and looking at Brian)* Hey, that's just how it is sometimes, you know? You know what I mean? These things happen.

Here the consultant gives a paradoxical intervention and ties it in with Brian's passive stance in life. Brian immediately becomes oppositional.

Brian: Well, we'll try and prevent it from happening. We're going to prevent it from happening. OK, we wouldn't be here, I don't think.

Gail: Right.

Consultant: We're going to prevent it?

Brian: No, I am.

Again, the consultant holds the husband to an individuated and responsible position.

Consultant: You're going to prevent it.

Gail: I'm going to watch.

The stepmother is actively in her new role.

Consultant: You're going to watch and make sure he does it right.
Gail: Uh-huh.
Consultant: Be just strict enough.
Gail: OK.
Brian: What happens if it doesn't work?
Consultant: (looks at Gail)
Gail: (with her hand on Brian's leg) NN, NN!
Brian: (to consultant) What happens if it doesn't work?
Consultant: (looks at Gail again)
Gail: Brian.
Brian: I know.
Gail: You're going to have to make it work! That's why he keeps point-
ing to me. Get it?
Brian: Uh-huh.
Gail: Good.
Consultant: (to Brian) What happens if it doesn't work?
Gail: NN. I'll have to tell this one at the bar. "What are you doing tomor-
row?" "NN!"

Consultant: My impression is that, for some reason or other, you love
each other.
Brian: A lot.
Consultant: Of course, you don't really know what love is yet. But, you
know, people who have only been together a few years don't really
understand.

Here the practitioner piques the couple's interest in optimal functioning.

Brian: The other night made me realize things about Gail that I didn't
realize.
Consultant: Yeah. What did you realize?
Brian: I appreciate her.

Brian: Gail was going to the doctor's, getting checked for ulcers.
Consultant: That's right, and you're sitting around twiddling your thumbs
while Rome burns.

In making a diagnostic comparison of this marriage to an optimal one, it is clear that the husband has been neither protective nor attentive enough toward his wife.

Brian: No, we're thinking she's sick, you know, we're not thinking about it . . .
Consultant: Emotional.
Gail: . . . coming from the girls.
Consultant: Right. You didn't think it was emotional.
Gail: No. I'm at the point when I'd like to take a real long vacation alone.

The vivification of the problems, plus the holding of her husband accountable for them and the programming to leave, has increased the wife's sense of having been used and let down by her husband. She has become more prepared to move out and away from the family in order to preserve her integrity.

Consultant: Is that right?
Gail: Yeah.
Consultant: Hey.
Gail: (to Brian) I'll send you postcards.
Consultant: I like that.
Brian: I don't.
Gail: I don't like coming home every night and having to argue with them.
Brian: Yeah.
Gail: Get into the same thing that I've been repeating for a year and a half 'cause I get sick of hearing myself say the same thing over and over again.
Consultant: Absolutely, it's boring.
Gail: Yeah. So I work overtime.
Consultant: Hey, this is fantastic. So you're not going to fight with the girls, right? You're going to give the job to him. If he doesn't shape up.
Gail: (to Brian) NN.
Consultant: NN. Right. Very good. And if he still doesn't shape up?
Gail: I'm going to take a vacation.
Consultant: Aloha. You like Hawaii, right?

The consultant immediately incorporates the wife's longing into the fear-of-loss strategy.

Gail: Yeah.

Consultant: Yeah, aloha, that's right.

Brian: Then I'm going to be stuck with these two girls.

Consultant: So they have nice-looking guys there in Hawaii?

Gail: Uh-huh.

Brian: Everything's nice in Hawaii.

Consultant: (to Brian) Well you won't know, because you'll be here with the girls. She'll be in Hawaii. *(to Gail)* Make sure you take, like, a Polaroid camera with you.

Gail: To send him pictures?

Consultant: Yeah. Of the different guys you're with.

Gail: OK.

Consultant: I don't think it'll take, maybe, one trip like that to fix him.

Brian: Well, I don't know . . .

Consultant: On a permanent basis, know what I mean?

Gail: I could be packed.

Consultant: Yeah. You could be packed. Do you have a suitcase?

Brian: You don't need any suitcase to go there.

Consultant: Do you have one?

Gail: Yeah.

Consultant: Hey, you know, when women have babies, they have a suitcase packed ready to go.

Gail: Uh-huh.

Brian: Well, this is to get rid of the babies.

Consultant: That's right.

Gail: OK, Brian.

Consultant: So Brian, what happens if it doesn't work?

Brian: It's going to work!

Brian indicates that the entire fear-of-loss maneuver will be effective in helping him to change.

Consultant: Well, how am I going to know if this works?

Gail: Molly will tell you.

Brian: Gail can be tough when she wants to be.

Consultant: Yeah, when she wants to be.

Brian: Takes a whole lot. You have to push her into a corner, just about strangle her, then . . .

Consultant: . . . then she becomes a real tough guy. I understand. You need a tough guy. Never had a father. So what's going to happen in the long run? So you straighten out the girls, right? So now you're feeling better toward him. So you're not running off with that nice Hawaiian doctor that you met, right? And then, ah. . . .

So then what happens? Eventually they really feel good about you. They treat you as a mother, right? They go off to college. You want your daughters to go to college?

The consultant, using the optimal family process model, suggests that Gail would provide Brian with the fathering he needs, and then focuses on high-level goals for the girls.

Brian: Uh-huh.
Gail: Tomorrow.
Consultant: Tomorrow? Right. But you'll get 'em off in good speed. They won't be pregnant, right?
Gail: No.
Brian: Uh-huh.
Consultant: Then what?
Gail: (to Brian) Then we're alone.
Consultant: Then you're alone to do what?
Brian: The girls prosper.
Consultant: Well, the girls are prospering. *(to Gail)* What about business? How's his business? Do you want it to be successful?

Continuing into other areas, the practitioner widens the therapeutic contract, laying the groundwork for an intramarital therapeutic coalition by which the spouses can promote each other in their independent transactions as well.

Gail: Sure.
Consultant: (to Gail) And what about you, what are you going to do when you grow up?
Gail: It's a long way off.
Consultant: Well, it is a long way off. Have you two talked about her career? What she wants to do?
Brian: Sometimes. We spoke about it last night.
Consultant: Last night. Gee whiz! This whole process has really been good. *(to Gail)* What are you going to do when you grow up, do you know?
Gail: Oh, I have a few ideas.
Consultant: Yeah, like what? Can I hear?
Gail: Eventually, I'd like to go back to school.
Consultant: College?
Gail: Uh-huh.
Consultant: Yeah. . . .

Gail: . . . and working.
Consultant: What might you be interested in?
Gail: Business administration.
Consultant: Yeah.
Gail: I haven't really thought a whole lot about it. Taking my time.
Consultant: Well, would you just dream ahead with me. Humor me for
    a minute. So you would get a master's degree in business? An
    MBA? What do you want to do with an MBA? Do you want to
    work in a corporation?

The consultant explores Gail's dreams for herself in order to open up
the area for future encouragement and programming from the therapist
and Brian.

Gail: Uh-huh.
Brian: That's what you do now, right?
Consultant: Be an exec?
Gail: (nodding her head) Sit back and watch everybody else work.
Brian: Vice-president.
Consultant: Yeah, you'd like to be vice-president?
Gail: I don't know if I'd go that far.
Consultant: Why not?
Gail: There's a lot involved in it.
Consultant: You mean responsibility? So what, you don't mind respon-
    sibility.
Brian: You like it.

Brian joins in to parent his wife.

Consultant: So you're going to be a vice-president some day? *(to thera-
    pist)* Is she vice-president material? Don't lie. Honest?

The therapist nods her head, indicating her belief in the client's potential.

Gail: I don't know what I want to be. I have to think about it.
Consultant: It'll be heartbreak to lose a woman like this, Brian.
Brian: I know, that's why I picked her.
Consultant: It's going to be heartbreak.
Brian: I'm not going to lose her.
Consultant: You're not going to lose her. Molly will have to tell me how
    things are going.
Brian: Yeah. Should be good reports, too.

Consultant: Or else!

Brian: Or else! Yeah.

Consultant: (to Gail) You think he should report to me also?

Gail: (to Brian) Give Sam a call.

Brian: I will.

Consultant: (to therapist) What do you think?

Therapist: That would be good.

Consultant: I think he has to show his dad his report card. Listen, I'm willing to check it.

The consultant closes the interview with a repeat reference to the earlier fear-of-loss maneuver and offers fatherly follow-through to Brian.

Therapist: Yeah.

Brian: (smiles and leans toward the consultant)

Consultant: (to Gail) See, he's happy. He likes that idea. *(they shake hands)*

After this interview, the family continued in treatment with the therapist. Initially, Cheryl, the older girl, balked severely at Brian's discipline, but as he and Gail persisted in their roles, she became quite cooperative. On the other hand, her younger sister was initially more open to Brian and Gail's new roles, but later on manifested some difficulties at school.

Five months later, both girls were on the scholastic honor roll. Gail and Brian were able to triangulate the girls more consistently with healthy parental role division, although they still had periods of lapsing into their old roles. They were also continuing to work toward marital and personal fulfillment.

Afterword

Arthur Stein's discoveries about the nature of family life and growth seem to be valid and useful in clinical practice. However, CFT has its limitations. Applying CFT is quite challenging to the practitioner; it is a lengthy treatment process which has not been tested through rigorous research; CFT reflects a white, middle class American value system; and finally, it tends to ignore the role of cultural, ethnic, and biological factors in psychosocial health.

First, the application of CFT poses a challenge to the therapist. The mantle of responsibility inherent in the assumption of a reparental posture is enormous. The therapist has to press beyond the limits of his or her own anxiety regarding intimacy, personal power, success, and the expansion of selfhood. Errors must be minimized. The self, which is the fundamental therapeutic tool, must be continuously examined and developed. With all the different needs that people manifest in treatment, the practitioner must develop flexibility in style, demeanor, and approach. He or she must learn to be comfortable with a full, androgynous behavioral repertoire. Thus, the practice of CFT requires a good deal of clinical artistry.

Second, the full CFT treatment is a lengthy one, because the goals in CFT are so high and the areas of family life that are dealt with are so numerous. Usually it takes at least three years to help establish a PAR growth process in a two-parent family. The cases presented in this book are successful ones that have, by and large, continued on to complete most of the CFT treatment process. Of course, not every case is successful and not every case completes the full treatment.

Because of the length of treatment, CFT may not be applicable in certain clinical situations. Moreover, given the current trend in the field toward briefer therapy, a full course of treatment in CFT may be impractical. The Institute for Comprehensive Family Therapy has been exploring ways to reduce treatment time and to develop more cost-effective methods that could still be used to bring about the most comprehensive change.

CFT has already been used effectively in briefer form in both the juvenile justice and child welfare systems, where the emphasis has been on remediating serious problems in the rearing transaction. With these cases, treatment has averaged six months to a year, with good outcome in terms of the remediation of rearing-based symptomatology. Further experimentation and research should prove useful in shortening the length of a full course of treatment with all clinical groups.

In general, controlled treatment outcome studies of CFT need to be carried out in order to further delineate its effectiveness in symptom amelioration and the promotion of health. Research sponsored by the Institute has focused on gross measures of health, such as child placement prevention and reunification of families where a child was in placement. Other studies have been of the idiographic variety. These have examined developmental milestones such as marriage, improved school performance, career success, and the like, along with client and therapist reports of increased marital and personal fulfillment as criteria for judging clinical success. More rigorous and extensive research into treatment outcome is presently in the planning stages.

In addition, it is important to further establish baseline data for family variables along the continuum of psychosocial health. The clinical studies that involved healthy families were conducted by interviewers with knowledge of the optimal family process model. Thus, they may have skewed results in the direction of the model. The validity of various aspects of the optimal family process model should be explored in a more controlled fashion.

A further concern about CFT is that the optimal family process model and reparental approach might in fact be substantially different, depending on culture and ethnicity. CFT has been used successfully with various minority groups, but the model has simply been adapted by individual clinicians to reflect the particular problems, resources, and world views of certain minority families. Continued study is necessary to establish firmer normative and clinical guidelines for nonwhite populations.

A further limitation is that the theory tends to ignore biological factors that impinge on family life. The whole area of medication and the biochemical basis for behavior has not been addressed as yet in CFT. In general, there has been a bias against the use of medication. Also, while clients tend to improve their diets, exercise more frequently, and, in general, take better care of their health as they develop in self-esteem, CFT has no structured approach to promoting holistic health. Thus, although CFT offers promise as an approach to working with clients, it must be further refined.

A FINAL NOTE ABOUT THIS BOOK

Healing is more art than science. In every session thousands of impressions flood the therapist. From these the therapist must choose to attend to one family member or transaction, or to others. Then, he or she must sort through clients' nonverbal signals, gestures and affect, as well as verbalizations and communication patterns, integrating all pertinent information into a coherent schema. Next, the therapist must select appropriate goals and then choose techniques to enable the client family to move toward these ends. Finally, the therapist must execute the interventions with expert ability and correct timing in order for healing to take place. The practitioner's conscious mind alone cannot accomplish all of these tasks. Some deeper part of the self — an intuitive, less conscious aspect — helps us to perform the work. Thus, the art of healing is difficult to teach and describe fully in words. All we can hope for is that this book helps to point the way.

References

Abroms, G. (1978). The place of values in psychotherapy. *Journal of Marriage and Family Counseling, 4,* 3–17.

Ackerman, N. (1958). *The psychodynamics of family life.* New York: Basic Books.

Ammons, P. & Stinnett, N. (1980). The vital marriage: A closer look. *Family Relations, 29,* 37–42.

Balint, M. (1979). *The basic fault.* New York: Brunner/Mazel.

Bandler, R. & Grinder, J. (1975). *The structure of magic I.* Palo Alto: Science & Behavior Books.

Bandura, A. (1971). Psychotherapy based upon modeling principles. In A. E. Bergin & S. L. Garfield (Eds.), *Handbook of psychotherapy and behavior change: An empirical analysis* (pp. 653–708). New York: John Wiley & Sons.

Basseches, M. A. (1980). Dialectical schemata: A framework for the empirical study of the development of dialectical thinking. *Human Development, 23,* 400–421.

Bateson, G. (1961). The bisocial integration of behavior in the schizophrenic family. In N. Ackerman, F. L. Beatman, & S. Sherman (Eds.), *Exploring the base for family therapy* (pp. 116–122). New York: Family Service Association of America.

Blake, W. (1946). *The portable Blake.* New York: Penguin Books.

Bopp, M. J. & Weeks, G. R. (1984). Dialectical metatheory in family therapy. *Family Process, 23,* 49–61.

Boszormenyi-Nagy, I. (1965). Intensive family therapy as process. In I. Boszormenyi-Nagy & J. L. Framo (Eds.), *Intensive family therapy* (pp. 87–142). New York: Harper & Row.

Boszormenyi-Nagy, I. (1973). *Invisible loyalties.* New York: Harper & Row.

Bowen, M. (1961). Family psychotherapy. *American Journal of Orthopsychiatry, 31,* 40–60.

Bowen, M. (1978). *Family therapy in clinical practice.* New York: Jason Aronson.

Bowlby, J. (1973). *Separation.* New York: Basic Books.

Brodey, W. M. (1967). A cybernetic approach to family therapy. In G. H. Zuk & I. Boszormenyi-Nagy (Eds.), *Family therapy and disturbed families* (pp. 74–84). Palo Alto: Science & Behavior Books.

Buber, M. (1958). *I and thou.* New York: Charles Scribner's Sons.

Buckley, W. (1967). *Sociology and modern systems theory.* Englewood Cliffs, NJ: Prentice Hall.

Capra, F. (1975). *The tao of physics.* Berkeley: Shambala Press.

Carroll, L. (1978). *The illustrated Lewis Carroll.* London: Jupiter Books.

Chodorow, N. (1978). *The reproduction of mothering, psychoanalysis and the sociology of gender.* Berkeley: University of California Press.

Cuber, J. & Harroff, P. (1965). *Sex and the significant americans.* Baltimore: Penguin Books.

Denham, J. (1928). Of prudence. In T. H. Banks (Ed.), *Poetical works of Sir John Denham* (2nd ed.). New Haven: Yale University Press.

Dicks, H. V. (1967). *Marital tensions*. New York: Basic Books.

Fairbairn, W. R. D. (1952). *An object relations theory of the personality*. New York: Basic Books.

Foley, V. (1974). *An introduction to family therapy*. New York: Grune & Stratton.

Framo, J. L. (1965). Rationale and techniques of intensive family therapy. In I. Boszormenyi-Nagy & J. L. Framo (Eds.), *Intensive family therapy* (pp. 143–212). New York: Harper & Row.

Framo, J. L. (1970). Symptoms from a family transactional viewpoint. In N. W. Ackerman (Ed.), *Family therapy in transition* (pp. 125–171). Boston: Little, Brown & Co.

Framo, J. L. (1976). Family of origin as a therapeutic resource for adults in marital and family therapy: You can and should go home again. *Family Process, 15*, 193–210.

Frank, J. D. (1974). *Persuasion and healing*. New York: Schocken Books.

Freud, S. (1975a). An outline of psychoanalysis. In J. Strachey (Ed. and Trans.), *The standard edition of the complete psychological works of Sigmund Freud*. (Vol. 23, pp. 141–208). London: Hogarth Press. (Original work published 1923)

Freud, S. (1975b). Some psychical consequences of the anatomical distinction between the sexes. In J. Strachey (Ed. and Trans.), *The standard edition of the complete psychological works of Sigmund Freud* (Vol. 19, pp. 248–258). London: Hogarth Press. (Original work published 1923)

Friedman, P. H. (1980). Integrative psychotherapy. In R. Herink (Ed.), *The psychotherapy handbook* (pp. 308–313). New York: New American Library.

Gibran, K. (1983). *The prophet*. New York: Alfred A. Knopf.

Gilot, F. & Lake, C. (1964). *Life with Picasso*. New York: McGraw-Hill.

Gregory, J. F. (1983). *The relationship between self-actualization and marital adjustment in intact families with teenage children*. Unpublished doctoral dissertation, Temple University, Philadelphia, PA.

Guntrip, H. (1969). *Schizoid phenomena, object relations and the self*. New York: International Universities Press.

Gurman, A. S. (1981). Integrative marital therapy. In S. Budman (Ed.), *Forms of brief therapy* (pp. 415–457). New York: Guilford Press.

Haley, J. (1962). Whither family therapy? *Family Process, 1*, 69–100.

Haley, J. (1963). *Strategies of psychotherapy*. New York: Grune & Stratton.

Haley, J. (1976). *Problem-solving therapy*. San Francisco: Jossey-Bass.

Haley, J. (1984). *Ordeal therapy*. San Francisco: Jossey-Bass.

Jackson, D. D. (1957). The question of family homeostasis. *Psychiatric Quarterly Supplement* (Part I), *31*, 79–90.

Jackson, D. D. & Weakland, J. H. (1961). Conjoint family therapy: Some considerations on theory, technique, and results. *Psychiatry, 24*, 30–45.

Jacobson, N. S. & Margolin, G. (1979). *Marital therapy*. New York: Brunner/Mazel.

Kaplan, H. S. (1974). *The new sex therapy*. New York: Brunner/Mazel.

Kaplan, H. S. (1979). *Disorders of sexual desire*. New York: Brunner/Mazel.

Kleiman, J. (1981). Optimal and normal family functioning. *American Journal of Family Therapy, 9*(1), 37–44.

Klein, M. (1975a). *Envy and gratitude*. New York: Dell Publishing Co.

Klein, M. (1975b). *Love, guilt, and reparation*. New York: Dell Publishing Co.

Koestler, A. (1980). *Bricks to Babel*. New York: Random House.

Laing, R. D. & Esterson, A. (1971). *Sanity, madness and the family*. New York: Basic Books.

Lebow, J. L. (1984). On the value of integrating approaches to family therapy. *Journal of Marital and Family Therapy, 10*, 127–138.

Levenkron, S. (1982). *Treating and overcoming anorexia nervosa*. New York: Charles Scribner's Sons.

Lewis, J., Beavers, R., Gossett, J., & Phillips, V. (1976). *No single thread: Psychological health in family systems*. New York: Brunner/Mazel.

Lidz, T. (1963). *The family and human adaptation*. New York: International Universities Press.

Mahler, M. (1980). On the first three subphases of the separation-individuation process. *International Journal of Psycho-Analysis, 53*, 333–338.

Mahler, M. S., Pine, F., & Bergman, A. (1975). *The psychological birth of the human infant: Symbiosis and individuation*. New York: Basic Books.

Mandell, A. J. & Salk, J. (1984). Developmental fusion of intuition and reason: A meta-biological ontogeny. In D. Offer & M. Sabshin (Eds.), *Normality and the life cycle* (pp. 302–314). New York: Basic Books.

Maslow, A. (1954). *Motivation and personality*. New York: Harper & Row.

Maslow, A. (1962). *Toward a psychology of being*. Princeton, NJ: D. Van Nostrand Co.

May, R. (1969). *Love and will*. New York: W. W. Norton.

Minuchin, S. (1974). *Families and family therapy*. Cambridge, MA: Harvard University Press.

Napier, A. & Whitaker, C. (1978). *The family crucible*. New York: Harper & Row.

Olson, D. H. (1983). Circumplex model of families. In D. H. Olson, H. I. McCubbin & associates (Eds.), *Families: What makes them work* (pp. 47–80). Beverly Hills: Sage Publications.

Olson, D., Sprenkle, D., & Russell, C. (1979). Circumplex model of marital and family systems. *Family Process, 18*, 3–28.

Peck, M. S. (1978). *The road less traveled*. New York: Simon & Schuster.

Pinsof, W. M. (1983). Integrative problem-centered therapy. *Journal of Marital and Family Therapy, 9*, 19–35.

Richards, M. C. (1964). *Centering in pottery, poetry and the person*. Middleton, CT: Wesleyan University Press.

Rilke, R. M. (1975). *On love and other difficulties*. New York: W. W. Norton.

Rosen, J. N. (1975). *Direct analysis*. Doylestown, PA: The Doylestown Foundation.

Sager, C. (1976). *Marriage contracts and couple therapy*. New York: Brunner/Mazel.

Satir, V. (1964). *Conjoint family therapy*. Palo Alto: Science and Behavior Books.

Scheflen, A. E. (1974). *How behavior means*. Garden City, NY: Anchor Books.

Searles, H. F. (1965). *Collected papers on schizophrenia and related subjects*. New York: International Universities Press.

Selvini-Palazzoli, M., Boscolo, L., Cecchin, G., & Prata, G. (1978). *Paradox and counterparadox*. New York: Jason Aronson.

Sonne, J. C. (1967). Entropy and family therapy. In G. H. Zuk & I. Boszormenyi-Nagy (Eds.), *Family therapy and disturbed families* (pp. 85–95). Palo Alto: Science and Behavior Books.

Stanton, M. D. (1981). An integrated structural/strategic approach to family therapy. *Journal of Marital and Family Therapy, 7*, 427–439.

Stanton, M. D. & Todd, T. C. (1982). *The family therapy of drug abuse and addiction*. New York: Guilford Press.

Stein, A. (1980). Comprehensive family therapy. In R. Herink (Ed.), *The psychotherapy handbook* (pp. 204–207). New York: New American Library.

Stern, D. N. (1971). A micro-analysis of mother-infant interaction. *Journal of the American Academy of Child Psychiatry, 10*, 501–517.

Stuart, R. B. (1980). *Helping couples change*. New York: Guilford Press.

Sullivan, H. S. (1953). *The interpersonal theory of psychiatry*. New York: W. W. Norton.

Teilhard de Chardin, P. (1973). *The prayer of the universe*. New York: Perennial Library.

Tolstoy, L. (1960). *Anna Karenina*. New York: Bantam Books.

Truax, C. B. & Carkhuff, R. R. (1967). *Toward effective counseling and psychotherapy: Training and practice*. Chicago: Aldine.

U.S. Department of Commerce, Bureau of the Census (1980). *Current population reports*. Washington, DC: U.S. Government Printing Office.

Wachtel, P. L. (1977). *Psychoanalysis and behavior therapy: Toward an integration*. New York: Basic Books.

Watzlawick, P. (1978). *The language of change*. New York: Basic Books.

Weintraub, J. D. (1982). *A psychological investigation of the structural characteristics of healthy stepfamilies.* Unpublished doctoral dissertation, Fielding University, Santa Barbara, CA.

Wertheim, E. (1975). The science and typology of family systems II: Further theoretical and practical considerations. *Family Process, 14,* 285–308.

Westley, W. A. & Epstein, N. B. (1970). *The silent majority.* San Francisco: Jossey-Bass.

Whitman, W. (1891). *Leaves of grass.* New York: Random House.

Winnicott, D. W. (1965). *The maturational processes and the facilitating environment.* New York: International Universities Press.

Index

Abandonment anxiety, 13, 15–16, 34, 53, 68
  assessment of, 88
  case examples, 110, 134, 179, 182, 205
  discipline experienced as, 78
  fear-of-loss strategy and, 166–167, 185–186
  marital transaction and, 148
Abroms, G., 22
Achievement, 7, 41
Ackerman, N., xv, 22–23
Acting-out behavior, xv–xvii, 100
Actualization, 2, 25–26, 28, 32, 35, 62
Adolescents, 24, 130, *see also* Children
  independent transactions and, 42
  severe psychopathology and, 131
Adults, single, 188–213
Altruism, 28, 43–44, 62
Ammons, P., 24
Anchoring, 72–73
Anger, 54–56, 162
  as a disciplinary tool, 79–80
Anger-releasing techniques, 81–82
Annihilation fears, 53–55
Anorexia nervosa, 127, 141
Anxiety, 25, 209
  incorrect therapeutic stance and, 84
  rapprochement and, 10
  separation, 16
Assessment, 86–89
  case example, 120–121
Attachment needs, 4
Autonomy, 12, 16, *see also* Separation-individuation in marriage, 27

Balint, M., 54
Bandler, R., 64

Bandura, A., 21
Bartering, 163
Basseches, M. A., xix
Bateson, G., 23
Beavers, R., 24
Bedwetting, 136
Behavioral techniques, xviii
Bergman, A., 9
Body language, *see* Nonverbal cues
Bonding, 64–65
  case examples, 96, 98, 109, 116, 205
  initial interview and, 85–86
Bopp, M. J., xix
Boscolo, L., xvii
Boszormenyi-Nagy, I., xviii, 14, 23
Boundaries, 5, 23–24
  stepfamilies and, 220–221
  young married couple and, 150
Bowen, M., 4–5, 14, 22
Bowlby, J., 16
Brody, W. M., 23
Buber, M., 170
Buckley, W., 23

Career progression, 192–194
Carkhuff, R. R., 21, 49
Cecchin, G., xvii
Child abuse, 13, 131–132, 145
Childrearing transaction, 6–7, 17
  enmeshed-disengaged parental configuration, 129–130, 133–136
  mother/child relationship, 9–10
  optimal, 34–42, 132
  parental disagreement concerning, 125
  in single-parent and stepfamilies, 44–45, 214–216
  treatment of, 124–132

Childrearing transaction, treatment of
  assessment for, 87
  case examples, 94–95, 101–103, 112, 118, 121
  initial tasks in, 128–130
  progressive strategy in, 57
  reparental contracting, 126–128
  with single-parent and stepfamilies, 214–216, 229–230, 233, 235, 239–241
Children, *see also* Adolescents; Discipline
  identity and role formation, 8–9
  independent transactions and, 42
  scapegoated, 13, 15
  optimal triangulation of the daughter, 39–41
  optimal triangulation of the son, 37–38
  self-actualization, 35
  severe psychopathology and, 131
  sexual identification and, 10–11
  in single-parent families, 218
  in stepfamilies, 219–220
Chodorow, N., 10
Coalitions, 6–7, 12–13, 143, 145
  in the blended family, 45
  case example, 95–96
  therapeutic, 169–173, 185
Comprehensive family therapy, xix, *see also* Childrearing transaction; Marital transaction; Treatment
Constructive fighting, 161–162, 179
Contracts, 57, 74–75, 80, 92
  case examples, 120, 206, 212, 224, 231
  reparental, 126–128
  single-parent family and, 218–219
Control issues, 3, 5
Countertransference, 50, 81, *see also* Transference
Cross-sex identification, 15
Cuber, J., 24
Cybernetics, 1, 23

Dating, 194–196, 200–202, 210–213
Decentering technique, 215
Defense mechanisms, 127
Denial, 131
Dependency needs, 28, 51, 174
  discipline and, 77
Depression, 16, 84
Developmental needs, 72
Diagnostic tools, 89
Dicks, H. V., xviii, 11–12, 14
Direct suggestion, 67
Discipline, 17, 43, 77–80, 84
  case examples, 96, 101, 113, 121, 135, 143
  limit setting, 9, 35

out-of-control child and, 129–130
  parental disagreement concerning, 125–126
  same-sex parent and, 129
  stepfamily case example and, 228–231
Divorce, 157–158, *see also* Marital transaction
Dreams, 89, 210
Drug abuse, xviii

Ego
  bisphasic growth, 31
  discipline and, 77
  foundation of the, 9–10, 16
    regressive strategy and, 53–54
  immature, xv
Ego strength, 61, 81
Engulfment anxiety, 15–16, 53–54
  assessment of, 88
  case examples, 134, 141
  marital transaction and, 148, 164–165
Enmeshment, xvi, 6–7, 12, 15, 57, 129–130
  case examples, 96–97, 133–136, 178
  young adults and, 190, 197
Entropy, 19
Epstein, N. B., 24
Esterson, A., 69
Existential change, xix

Fairbairn, W. R. D., 9, 14
Family, *see also* Childrearing transaction; Marital transaction; Independent transactions
  attendance at initial interview, 85–86
  behavioral transactions and, 3–8
  governed by homeostasis and morphogenesis, 2–3
  healthy dynamics within the, 23–25
  holon, xix, 1–2
  life cycle, 2, 41, 149–151, 184, 187
  mapping of the, 90–91, 95, 103, 122, 142–144, 204
  movement in the, 18–19
  optimal functioning in the, *see* Optimal family process
  single-parent, 44–45, 61, 214–219
  society and, 8
  stepfamilies, 44–45, 219–221
    case example, 222–247
  treatment goals and, 50
Family of origin
  future marital roles and, 4–5
  individuation from the, 189–192
  replication of pathological transactions and, 14
  self-system and, 9

Family therapy, xvi–xvii, *see also* Child-rearing transaction; Marital transaction
Fear-of-loss maneuver, 166–169
    case examples, 139–140, 185, 234, 236–238, 243–244
    unproductive client monologues and, 80
Feedback, 8, 23
Foley, V., 22
Foundation of the ego, 9–10, 16
    regressive strategy and, 53–54
Framo, J. L., xviii, 14, 18, 23
Frank, J. D., 21, 49
Freud, S., 10, 48
Friedman, P. H., xvii
Frustration tolerance, 43, 121

Gilot, F., 69
Gossett, J., 24
Grinder, J., 64
Growth-oriented therapy, xvii
Guilt, 79, 126, 131, 221
Guntrip, H., 9, 49
Gurman, A. S., xvii
Gwynedd Family Psychotherapy Center, xi–xii

Haley, J., xvii, 4, 21, 57, 77, 80
Harroff, P., 24
Holon, *see* Family
Homeostasis, 2–3, 24, *see also* Morphogenesis
    marital transactions and, 4–5
    parental disagreements and, 125–126
    progressive abreactive regression and, 26
    rearing transactions and, 6
    spousal role division and, 148–149
    transference and, 48
Homoaffiliative alliances, 6, 13
Homoaffiliative needs, 11, 16, 67
    case example, 141
Hypnosis, 69–70, 72, 134, 191

Identified patient, 149
"If" icon technique, 66
Impulse disorder, xv
Incest, 13, 131, 205
Independent transactions, 7, 41–42
Individuation, *see* Separation-individuation
Inspiration, 71
Institute for Comprehensive Family Therapy, xi–xii, 32, 250
Intake phone call, 85
Interventions, *see* Techniques and interventions

Intimacy, 27, 30–32, 134, 148, 183
Intramarital therapeutic coalition, 169–173, 185
Introjection, 9, 200

Jackson, D. D., 14, 23
Jacobson, N. S., xviii

Kaplan, H. S., xviii, 161
Kleiman, J., 24
Klein, M., 16, 55
Koestler, A., xix, 47

Laing, R. D., 69
Lake, C., 69
Lebow, J. L., xviii
Levenkron, S., 48, 52
Lewis, J., 24
Lidz, T., 22–23
Life cycle, 2, 41, 184, 187
    marital transaction and, 149–151
Limit setting, 9, 35
Loss, 4, 16, 25, 95, *see also* Fear-of-loss maneuver

Mahler, M., 9, 26
Mandell, A. J., 3
Mapping, 90–91, 95, 103, 122, 142–144, 204
Margolin, G., xviii
Marital transaction
    as critical to family life, 8
    dialectic and, 28–29, 147–149
    healthy family functioning and, 24–25
    healthy self-interest and, 27–29
    intramarital therapeutic coalition and, 169–173, 185
    marital teamwork in, 56–57
    mature love in the, 44
    noncustodial parents and, 217–219, 221
    optimal, 25–34
    optimization of parental teamwork and, 132
    positive and negative morphogenesis in the, 18–19
    power relationships in the, 3–6
    progressive abreactive regression in, 25–34
    psychopathology and, 14–18
    treatment of, 147–173
        assessment for, 87
        beginning, 151–152
        case examples, 93–94, 98–100, 102–105, 107, 111–112, 176–187
        conjoint and concurrent sessions in, 152–154

Marital transaction, treatment of
　constructive fighting as a goal in,
　　161–162
　couple time as a goal in, 159
　life-cycle issues in the, 149–151
　power equalization as a goal in, 160
　preservation of marriage as a goal in,
　　157–158
　progression of, 60–62
　reframing in, 92
　role reversal technique in, 75–76
　sexual life enrichment as a goal in,
　　160–161
　stepfamily case examples, 226–228,
　　232
　unfinished business as a target in,
　　159–160
Maslow, A., 25, 31, 35
May, R., 28
Medical model, xvii, 21
Metaphor, 74, 87, 107, 110
　case examples, 116, 119, 137–138, 205
　marital transaction and, 151–152
　reparental, 126–127
Minuchin, S., xvii, 5, 23, 57
Model of optimal family process, 25–45,
　see also Optimal family process
　model
Modeling, see Role model
Morphogenesis, 2–3, 18–19, see also
　Homeostasis
　case example, 108–109
　programming and, 69
　progressive abreactive regression
　　and, 26–27
　transference and, 48

Napier, A., 18
Negative transference, 54–56, 81–82, 154
Nonverbal cues, 64–68, 70–71, 125,
　151–152
Nurturance, 17, 43, 68–69, 83
　case examples, 97, 101, 112, 117, 121
　discipline and, 77–78
　opposite-sex parent and, 129
　stepparents and, 221

Object relations, xviii, 53, 148
Oedipal fantasies, 36, 40, 69, 89,
　106, 220
　triangulation and, 12
Oedipal loss, 13
Olson, D. H., 2, 21, 23
Optimal family process model, 25–45
　assessment and, 90
　clinical use of, 45–46

in single-parent and stepfamilies,
　44–45, 220–221
　treatment goals and, 21–22
Ordeal therapy, 77

Paradoxical interventions, 57, 74, 81–83,
　127–128, 136, 140
　case examples, 146, 177, 179
Parents, noncustodial, 217–219, 221
Peck, M. S., 48–49
Phillips, V., 24
Physical abuse, 131–132, 145, 158–159
Pine, F., 9
Pinsof, W. M., xvii
Power, 160, 164
　childrearing and, 6
　marital transaction and, 3–6
Prata, G., xvii
Presenting problem, 59–60, 85–86, 91–92
　enmeshed-disengaged parental con-
　　figuration, 129–130, 133–136
Program of three, 194–196, 210
Programming, 69–73, 84
　career goals and, 194
　case examples, 95, 99, 105–106, 114,
　　116–119
Progression of treatment, 59–62
Progressive abreactive regression, 18–20,
　25–34, 42, 44, 47
　assessment and, 89
　marital transaction and, 163, 171
Progressive strategy, 50, 56–59
　programming and, 73
Projection, 4, 8–9, 147
Psychopathology, 14, 131
Psychosomatic complaints, 185–186
Punishment, 77, 79

Rapprochement, 10, 16, 35, 51
　case examples, 59, 112
　marital transaction and, 28, 30–31
　progressive/regressive movement
　　and, 26
　therapist's role and, 49
Rearing transaction, see Childrearing
　transaction
Reciprocal identification, 28
Reframing, 71, 92, 165, 184
　case examples, 98, 111, 143, 209
Regression, 4, 65–68, 209
　case example, 118
　initial interview and, 87
Regressive strategy, 50–56, 58–59
　programming and, 73
Relabeling, 71, 73, 165
Releasers, 42, 63

Reparental contract, 126-128
Reparental strategy, xix, 47-59
Resistance, xviii, 74-75
  assessment when there is, 88-89
  initial interview and, 86
  joining with the, 127-128
  marital therapy and, 155-157
Reward and punishment, 77, 79
Rilke, R. M., 27
Role allocation, 128-129
Role division, 148, 150
Role model, xvi, 11
  case examples, 96, 116-117, 119, 121
  parents function as, 35-37
  therapist's stance as a, 65, 78,
    165-166, 174-175
Role playing, 135, 165-166
  case examples, 179, 181, 183
  single adults and, 191
Role prescription, 75-76
Role reversal, 6, 75-76, 163-165,
  173-174, 184-185
  anger-releasing techniques and, 81-82
Rosen, J. N., 48
Runaways, 131
Russell, C., 21

Sager, C., xviii, 4
Salk, J., 3
Satir, V., xvi, 22
Scapegoat, 12-13, 15, 57
  case examples, 100, 121
Scheflen, A. E., 69
Schizoid, 10, 16, 135
Searles, H. F., 54
Self-actualization, 2, 25-26, 28, 32, 62
  of children, 35
Self-disclosure, 111
Self-esteem, xvi, 26-28, 182
Self-image, 69, 140
Self-interest, 27-29
Self-system, 8-14, 42-44
  assessment of the, 88-89
  spousal, 147-149
Selvini Palazzoli, M., xvii, 23
Semans method, 161
Sensate focus exercises, 161
Sensory-based terminology, 64
Separation anxiety, 16
Separation-individuation, 9, 12,
  22-23, 82
  single adults and, 189-192, 197-199
  from the therapist, 61-62
  young married couple and, 4, 150
Sex therapy, xviii, 160-161
Sexual abuse, 131-132

Sexual dysfunction, 16
Sexual identification, 10-11, 14, 32-33,
  36, 43
  assessment of, 88
  case examples, 93, 98, 106, 110,
    134-135, 181, 224-225, 227
  marital transaction and, 148-149
  pathogenic, 15-16
  progressive strategy and, 58
  regressive strategy and, 52-53
  single adult and, 192, 205, 208
Sexual life, 5, 160-161, 182-183
  single adult and, 194-195
Sexual promiscuity, 42
Sibling relationships, 7, 52
Single adults, 188-213
Single-parent families, 44-45, 61
  treatment of, 214-219
Social relationships, 194-196, 200-202,
  210-213
Sonne, J. C., 23
Splitting, 55, 154
Sprenkle, D., 21
Stanton, M. D., xviii, 73
Stein, A., ix, xvii, 3, 18, 22, 51, 58-59,
  62, 151, 194, 215, 249
Stepfamilies, 44-45, 219-221
  case example, 222-247
Stern, D. N., 65
Stinnett, N., 24
Structural techniques, xviii
Stuart, D. N., xvi, 57
Sullivan, H. S., 14
Symbiosis, 9-10, 97, 170
Symptom amplification, 166
Symptom prediction, 107, 166
Symptom prescription, 82, 166
Systems theory, xvi-xix

Task giving, 74-75
Techniques and interventions
  anger-releasing, 81-82
  bonding, 64-65, 85-86
  as diagnostic tools, 89
  discipline, *see* Discipline
  used in marriage therapy, 162-169
  nurturance, *see* Nurturance
  paradox, 57, 74, 81-83, 127-128,
    136, 140
    case examples, 146, 177, 179
  programming, 69-73, 84, 194
    case examples, 95, 99, 105-106,
      114, 116-119
  regression, 4, 65-68, 87, 118, 209
  reparental contract, 126-128
  symptom prescription, 82, 166

Techniques and interventions
  (*continued*)
  transactional, 73–80, 91–92
Termination, 22–23, 62, 173, 187
Therapeutic alliance, 63, 65, 171–172
Therapist, 249, 251
  client separation from the, 61–62
  courtship of the client, 68–69
  destructive dependency on the, 50–51
  as inspirational, 71
  reparental stance and, 49–50, 63,
    65, 162
  triangulation with the marital couple,
    154–155
  values and goals, 50
Todd, T. C., xviii
Trance, 118
Transactional regression, 66
Transactional techniques, 73–80
Transactional vivification, 74
Transference, xviii, 48–49
  assessment and, 88
  case example, 207–208
  competitive, 52
  countertransference, 50, 81
  discipline and, 78–79
  fear-of-loss strategy and, 167
  negative, 54–56, 81–82, 154
  programming and, 73
  progressive strategy and, 57
  regression techniques and, 66
Treatment, *see also* Childrearing
    transaction; Marital transaction

length of, 249–250
limitations of, 249–250
progression of, 59–62
research concerning, 250
techniques, *see* Techniques and
    interventions
termination of, 22–23, 62, 173, 187
goals of, xvii–xviii, 21–23, 50, 157–162
  life-cycle issues and, 149
  optimal family process and, 45–46
Triangulation, 11–14, 15, 32–33, 44
  case examples, 95, 121
  of the daughter in optimal model,
    39–41
  marital transaction and, 149
  of the son in optimal model, 37–38
  with the therapist, 154–155
  young adults and, 190
Triangulation level, 11–14
  progressive strategy and, 57–58
  regressive strategy and, 51–52
Truax, C. B., 21, 49

Verbal cues, 64–65, 67, 70–71, 151–152

Wachtel, P. L., xvii
Watzlawick, P., 71
Weakland, J. H., 23
Weeks, G. R., xix
Wertheim, E., 23
Westley, W. A., 24
Whitaker, C., 18
Winnicott, D. W., 9